CHRIST BEFORE JESUS

EVIDENCE FOR THE SECOND-CENTURY ORIGINS OF JESUS

MATTHEW BRITT & JAARON WINGO

To Lynne and Ellie. Thank you for making me the
happiest husband and father.
Matthew Britt

Per la cara mia. Sono capace dell'impossibile per te, il mio cielo.
Jaaron Wingo

Note From the Authors

First of all, from the bottom of our hearts, thank you for taking the time to read this book. Please know that none of the words written in this book come from a place of anger or hate towards any religion or organization, nor do they come from a dislike of any individual, religious or otherwise. We are simply presenting our findings, and we welcome feedback and explanations of exactly where we may have made mistakes with the data. We care about the truth, and we hope you do too - regardless of if it is uncomfortable or unfamiliar.

Secondly, if you're super strapped for time, but want to know what the strongest parts of our argument are, we have a "TL;DR" section at the end of the book with summaries of each chapter. Feel free to jump ahead, because at times, this book can be hard to read. Not just because it goes against what you may believe, but because all the details we have to present may be a bit overwhelming at times. There's not really any easy way around that.

The stories of Jesus have been around for a very, very long time. As you can imagine, over the last 1,900+ years, there have been plenty of opportunities for the people who believe in Jesus to "clean up" the history of the Christian church. What we're doing is uncovering some of those clean up attempts for you. In order to do that, there's a lot of names, dates, and information we've got to throw at you.

In no way are we saying any of our readers are stupid or implying you *can't* understand something. We just know people learn in different ways. If at any point you need some extra clarification for any topic or person we mention in this book, we have videos and resources available on our YouTube and TikTok accounts (@christbeforejesus), as well as our website: christbeforejesus.com. We'll be coming out with more resources over time, and if there's still something you need help with, reach out to us at christbeforejesus@gmail.com. We even have livestreams on Tiktok where you can ask questions, connect with us, and get some clarification on our points and arguments.

"Why do you have questions in your book?"

That's a great question! Whenever someone says, "I don't think Jesus existed," there are always responses to that. We compiled 50+ of those responses, in the form of questions, so you can easily jump to one of those sections if you like. Of course, you can follow along from the start as well, but don't let us hold you back if you already know about a topic. If you'd like to skip ahead to another chapter/question, or to our timeline in Chapter 9, you can do that too!

As a reminder, feel free to reach out if you have questions or feedback, and check us out online for video explanations and more information.

Thank you again!

TABLE OF CONTENTS

Introduction

Twelve individuals make themselves comfortable in their black leather chairs. A few of them make note of the pewter nailhead trim, the red tint of the cherry wood arms, or the black swiveling gas lift columns. Once positioned to their liking, they think of their task; what brings them to this courtroom; why they have been selected to serve a civil duty. An important, yet sometimes daunting chore. They will all have a vote in a final decision for the defendant sitting across the room from them. At the conclusion of this trial, if all goes according to plan, the court will determine if said defendant is one of two things: guilty or not guilty.

A *guilty* verdict means the prosecution has done their job. They have presented enough evidence to convict the defendant beyond reasonable doubt. The jury will hear this evidence and consider whether it proves sufficiently that the defendant is, in fact, guilty.

However, contrary to popular belief, a *not guilty* verdict does not imply the defendant is innocent. It simply means the prosecution, who the burden of proof rests upon, did not present enough proof that the defendant is guilty.

It is here where many atheists, theists, historians, and Bible scholars begin the trial. The case? If Jesus of Nazareth is guilty of existing. Many find what they consider to be evidence beyond reasonable doubt, loudly declaring with their voices and their actions what they believe is the obvious verdict: "Jesus is guilty of existing!"

But still, there are some who don't find the evidence to be convincing. To them, Jesus is, for the moment, not guilty. The prosecution hasn't presented the proof. They're just not totally sure yet. They're not saying he's innocent - a court doesn't seek to find that specific conclusion. They just haven't seen strong enough evidence.

But we have. For the contrary.

You see, the mainstream position is that Jesus probably existed. Most historians feel it is safe to assume the natural Jesus (without the miracles or deification) likely existed. We disagree with this assumption.

In this book, we will explain the evidence for why Jesus of Nazareth didn't exist at all. You, the reader, are a jury member sitting in your aforementioned black leather, cherry wood swiveling chair with pewter nailhead trim. The case is now, "Whether Jesus of Nazareth is guilty of not existing." The burden of proof is on us, and we intend to prosecute to the fullest extent. We will now lay out our journey from the mainstream position regarding the historicity of Jesus to the position of our exhibited theory.

CHAPTER 1

The Mainstream

Our journey begins with the mainstream opinion that Jesus was likely a real historical person. Prior to taking a deep dive into the beginning of Christianity, we were both well-entrenched in that mainstream position. However, this is no longer the case. As you will read, we will be presenting evidence for our theory regarding the existence of Jesus and the formation of Christianity. Before moving forward, allow us to present our theory:

Evidence shows that Jesus, as presented by the gospels and New Testament books, never existed. Despite Christianity's claim of Jesus living during the first three decades of the first century CE, the character was actually a second-century construction.

Christianity, being defined as the belief in Jesus as both the Jewish god Yahweh and a historical human who was crucified and resurrected, did not emerge until the second century. It evolved from earlier Jewish and Greco-Roman cults, and developed the narratives for its books from previous works. The stories of a first-century Jesus movement, his disciples, and Paul are all part of a "creation myth" from the second century when the religion began to come together.

While small portions of the New Testament books may have been written late in the first century, evidence shows that these writings were not explicitly Christian, and in some cases, co-opted from other religious communities. The remaining majority of the New Testament books were written well into the second century, with the canonical Gospels, for example, not being written until the 140s at the earliest.

Our take on the second-century composition of the New Testament might be one of the first of its kind, but the idea that Jesus never existed isn't new. The name for such a belief is "mythicism", and, as you can imagine, the mythicist arguments we present to people are regularly responded to with numerous questions. The first questions we get asked about mythicism are usually variations of the ones mentioned in this chapter.

"Don't most historians and Bible scholars believe Jesus existed?"

Most historians take a natural, or neutral, stance when it comes to Jesus. Due to the number of people of antiquity who claimed Jesus lived (namely, the Christians), the default position historians and scholars tend to take is that he existed. This is in no way an acceptance of supernatural claims or the miraculous works alleged by the New Testament writers. The mainstream consensus is that Jesus, the natural man from Nazareth, existed during the first century CE and likely preached his message to his followers. As an itinerant rabbi of sorts, Jesus is viewed in this way by atheists and theists alike. To distinguish the two groups (people who think he lived and people who don't), we will use the terms "historicists" and "mythicists."

Christians often use the mainstream consensus presented by historicists as a springboard for further claims of divine nature. Despite obvious fundamental differences from theists, most atheists don't mind the consensus either, as it provides a fairly reasonable explanation as to the person on which the fantastic stories from early Christianity were built.

We, the authors of this book, acknowledge that we are going against the scholarly consensus. Hopefully, we'll be able to provide enough evidence to change their minds as well. After all, the mainstream consensus is where we ourselves started.

As an atheist from age 21, I had always gone with the mainstream consensus regarding the historicity of Jesus. Jesus probably existed, and I had no problem with that. Of course, I didn't believe any of the supernatural claims of the Gospels, but a natural man from Nazareth named Jesus seemed incredibly plausible.

I was intrigued by the idea that something had to have happened in the early-to-mid-first century that served as a catalyst for the earliest writings. Looking into the earliest days of Christianity was my first step towards mythicism.

Jaaron Wingo

Because of the large amounts of early church figures writing about Jesus (regardless of if the writings made it into the Biblical canon or not), historicists generally agree that there must have been someone behind it all. But what exactly did early Christianity look like? What was going on in the Roman Empire during the first century CE that made such an impact on these people?

3

"Why are you going against what other atheist writers/scholars/groups, like Bart Ehrman or The Jesus Seminar, have to say about Jesus' existence?"

At first, we wanted to take the side of the vast majority of scholars. That would be the easiest thing to do. When reading more into the earliest period of Christianity, we found most people saying just about the same thing. The question of "why" definitely came up. Is there a particular reason why most scholars agree on the natural Jesus? Surely there must be something that they have seen, read, or have access to that would set the record straight.

When reading online and watching videos, I started seeing familiar faces within Biblical scholarship. On the historicist side of the atheist community, you find people like Bart Ehrman, who has been very successful as a writer and speaker, and has been a guest on internationally broadcasted television shows numerous times. He is very quick to dismiss mythicism and repeatedly claims that Jesus had to have existed.

Then there are atheists like Matt Dillahunty, a great debater, moderator and host/co-host of multiple very informative atheist call-in talk shows online. He takes a more relaxed approach to Jesus and claims to not have much of a problem with Jesus existing, but clearly draws a line at the supernatural. Even still, he has also spoken of mythicism with a tinge of disdain.

The overwhelming rejection I saw of mythicist claims from other atheists made me wonder why those mythicists even bothered arguing against the mainstream consensus at all.

Jaaron Wingo

There are many popular atheist writers who share their thoughts on Jesus' existence. The ones who agree with the mainstream opinion use the same arguments that theists use. It's all old hat. The biggest problem we have with this is conceding potentially false points can and will lead to further falsehoods.

As we stated, Christians tend to use the mainstream consensus as a major building block for claims of the supernatural. When the mainstream opinion is worn like a badge of honor by the most popular of "atheist" scholars, you can find their books, debates and interviews quoted in countless religious articles and fundamentalist arguments.

Now, we definitely aren't saying that the only reason we claim Jesus never existed is so religious people can't have a foothold. We're just explaining why the matter of historicity is no minor issue.

The Jesus Seminar, a group of 150 individuals composed of both scholars and laymen, met together periodically starting in 1985 until 2006 to discuss the historicity of Jesus. The group included theists and atheists alike, some of which are active in the realm of theology, philosophy, and religious studies today. After meeting to present and discuss information regarding different stories of Jesus found in both the canonical and non-canonical gospels, epistles, and other historical references available at the time, they routinely took votes of the group to establish a consensus.

While this seems fair initially, the voting system has been strongly criticized by both the religious and non-religious. As one should obviously expect, personal biases and presuppositions came out strongly in the votes, making it hard to really establish a "fair" consensus. Along with the fact that science doesn't work that way (by way of voting), it's not hard to see why the Jesus Seminar, while well-intentioned, doesn't meet the standard anyone should be looking for when investigating the historicity of Jesus. Lastly, additional evidence and points of view continue to present themselves as time goes on, so relying on evidence no later than 2006 isn't scientific nor final whatsoever.

"Could Jesus just be an amalgamation of multiple itinerant rabbis of the time?"

One of the ideas put forth by historicists is the idea that Jesus could have been multiple first-century teachers rolled into one. As you will read later, this is a fairly accurate idea. The only issue with how it is usually presented is it typically implies the natural version of the gospel story happened in part to *someone*. It claims the life in Nazareth may have belonged to one teacher, while the Sermon on the Mount could have been preached by another.

We are absolutely granting some credence to this concept, but before you stop reading here and grant the historicists a victory, you might be (as we say in the South) counting your chickens before they hatch. There is definitely proof of different stories coming together to form the gospel narratives, but transferring the natural story of Jesus from one first-century character to multiple isn't showing the complete picture. Specifically where the ideas of Jesus came from is important, and that's what we were trying to figure out.

While some will try to cast mythicism as a polemical position that people take only because they are opposed to Christianity, this isn't how we approach it. There are two possibilities: Jesus Christ was a historical person who was deified, or he was a deity who was historicized. If we were to ask this about another deity or figure found in another culture's mythology, such as the Greek god Zeus, the Egyptian god Osiris, or another god that is claimed to have been on or visited Earth, this would not be treated with the same disdain.

It's only the entrenchment of Christian tradition in our understanding of history that makes asking the same question about Jesus so controversial. In this book, we aren't attempting to dispel anyone's belief in a deity so much as asking and hopefully answering the question of which way the Jesus story originated: from a deity to a person or from a person to a deity.

Matthew Britt

What can we learn from the Gospels? After years of holding the mainstream position, we wanted to see what the natural story of Jesus even looked like. What exactly does the proclaimed "Savior of the World" look like from a historical standpoint? We opened our Bibles, and what appears after you remove the supernatural is as follows:

1. Born in Bethlehem

2. Raised in Nazareth

3. Started his ministry in Galilee

4. Put to death in Jerusalem

Chapter 1 | *The Mainstream*

CHAPTER 2

The Gospels

While on the surface the aforementioned reduction of the Gospel narrative seems natural and reasonable, we found that an astonishing amount of the natural life appears to be either lifted from prior stories of deities or not even possible at all. In this chapter, we'll share the ways that the Gospel narrative and the picture it paints of Jesus' natural life bounces from anachronistic to plagiarism to outright dishonesty.

"Why aren't the Gospels themselves reliable sources?"

One might assume that since the New Testament starts with the Gospels, they were written first. This is, somewhat surprisingly, incorrect. While the lifetime of Jesus is said to have been between roughly 6 BCE to around 30 CE, the earliest gospel written (Mark) is dated by mainstream scholars to roughly 70 CE. The Gospels of Matthew and Luke were supposedly written not too long afterwards, with John rounding it out somewhere between 90 and 100 CE.[1] These are the rough dates given by the vast majority of scholarship, with a handful of evangelical Christians trying to place them all within a decade or so of Jesus' supposed death.

This is one of the first problems we noticed about the Gospels. You have a miracle worker who routinely healed people, fed thousands, cast out demons, and literally raised a man from the dead, but apparently no one thought to write these things down for another 40 years. Eventually writing a biography of just some random preacher is one thing, but waiting an entire generation to write about the actual son of God seems like a travesty.

But again, we're looking for the natural Jesus. Can the Gospels be reliable when presenting such a character? Let's examine the points of the natural framework we have.

Bethlehem Birth

The story of the Bethlehem birth is an odd one, as the reasons for why Joseph and Mary were there vary from outlandish to reasonable. Luke has them coming from Nazareth to Bethlehem due to a census. Not only was there no census at this time, according to the story Joseph packs up and heads for Bethlehem because his great-great-great-great-great-great-great-great-great-great-great-great-grandfather is from there. That's not at all what a census requires you to do. That defeats the entire purpose of a census. Plus, no wonder there was no room in the house - you've got to share it with everyone from your immediate family to your 13th cousins!

Top it off with the fact that Quirinius, mentioned in Luke 2, didn't reign until 6 CE, making the mentioning of Herod the Great in Luke 1 make no sense, as Herod ended his reign no later than 1 BCE. As luck would have it, Lysanias, mentioned in Luke 3, was the tetrarch of Abilene solely in the middle of the first century BCE. The author of Luke doesn't have his birth story dated correctly at all. He's clearly taking guesses, and none of this should be taken as historical fact.[2]

Matthew doesn't have the census. In that gospel, the family is in Bethlehem from the beginning. This seems like a much more reasonable take, but it loses credibility when "wise men from the East" follow a star to Bethlehem, then King Herod throws a temper tantrum and kills all the male children under the age of 3.

Setting aside the obvious supernatural problem of "that's not how stars work," Herod's Massacre of the Innocents was never recorded once by any historian - not even Josephus, who gladly shared all the transgressions and misdeeds of Herod he could. The killing of John the Baptist is mentioned, but not the murder of an entire area's male babies and toddlers?

This issue is one of a much deeper nature. The star, the virgin birth, the angels singing to shepherds, Joseph and the wise men getting divine dreams - even the natural parts of the Gospels' stories of Jesus are completely saturated with supernatural claims. Why? Is it impossible to tell the story of Jesus without making supernatural claims? Where are these stories coming from?

Some sources for Jesus' stories are likely lost to time, but in this instance, Herod plays the role of Pharaoh in this remake of Exodus' "Prince of Egypt." According to the Torah, Pharaoh did the same thing to the Israelites while they were slaves in Egypt in order to squash a potential slave rebellion. But nonetheless, Moses was born and eventually was called to start his leadership after he left Egypt. What does the author of Matthew do for Jesus while Herod carries out murder? He has Joseph and Mary go to Egypt only to leave Egypt later so Jesus can start his leadership.

The Gospels are filled to the brim with call backs and rehashings of old stories. While Christians are quick to claim these references to the Torah as fulfilled prophecies, one has to wonder when the line gets crossed into "someone is making this up as they go" territory.

How hard is it to create a character when you already have the blueprint for what you need them to do? Stretch the story as much as possible to get as many references as you can. Does your audience like Moses? Have your character come out of Egypt. Does your audience like the books of Isaiah? Make your character a "suffering servant."

But, as the Christians claim, that is the point. The Jewish scriptures and prophecies may have just been filled! However, as we'll discuss soon, there's more than just Jewish stories getting plagiarized here.

Hometown of Nazareth

This is a strange one. Like Bethlehem, the canonical gospels tell multiple stories of how Jesus got into Nazareth. Luke says Joseph was from Nazareth originally. Matthew has Joseph moving to Nazareth for the first time sometime between 4 BCE and 6 CE during the reign of Herod Archelaus. Yet again, not a great start to claims of historicity.

But it gets worse. Far, far worse.

To put it simply, Nazareth wasn't a place in the first century CE. It just wasn't. The mental gymnastics needed to create such a place go far over the line of "what is most likely to happen" that any reasonable historian should have.

People have pointed to examples of some pottery or some coins, but nothing more than what amounts to proof of human activity near the area. No garbage dumps, no buildings dating to the early first century, and no contemporary lists, documents, or maps containing the name of the city. Are there people living in towns nearby? Of course. There's even evidence of a cemetery not far away from where people claim Nazareth was. But there's nothing to prove Nazareth was there in the beginning of the first century. We would even say there's evidence *against* the idea.

Nazareth isn't mentioned outside the circle of Christianity until the fourth century CE.[3,4] It's not even mentioned by Christians until the second century CE. Some people have tried to claim that it was a small, relatively unknown hamlet of only a few families, but the Bible calls it a city, it has a synagogue, and enough men to mob Jesus. People even make comments throughout the Gospels to the effect of "Isn't this the man from Nazareth?" and "What good can come from Nazareth?" Those rude questions only make sense if someone is familiar with the city.

Matthew 2:23 claims that the hometown of Nazareth is prophesied by "the prophets" because Jesus was to be "a Nazarene," but there's no mention of Nazareth or a Nazarene anywhere in the Old Testament.

This is where it's important to step outside of the canonical gospels for a moment. There are roughly 40 gospels that were written by the fourth century, including our four canonical gospels, the Gospel of Thomas, Gospel of Mary, and many others often attributed to followers of Jesus. Most of them clearly date themselves out of the realm of realistic historical value. However, there are a few that are thought to be written prior to the 140s, when Marcion of Sinope, an early Christian theologian, presented what is considered the first New Testament collection. None of those gospels mention Nazareth. Marcion's gospel, called "Evangelion," was a precursor to the Gospel of Luke. It didn't have a story of Jesus' birth or juvenile years at all. It started with Jesus descending from Heaven into Capernaum as an adult.[5]

The first of the canonical gospels to be written is Mark. This is a view held by the majority of modern Biblical scholars. The understanding is that the other gospels used Mark as a reference. The author of Matthew practically plagiarized from Mark at times, copying many phrases and verses verbatim. At other times, verses are borrowed and written just slightly differently. One such verse is found in Matthew 3:13, which is talking about Jesus coming from Galilee to the Jordan River to be baptized by John the Baptist:

Then Jesus came from Galilee to the Jordan to be baptized by John.

Mark 1:9 has the same statement, but with Nazareth added:

At that time Jesus came from Nazareth in Galilee and was baptized by John in the Jordan.

We know Mark had been edited at some point, evidenced by multiple endings (see the footnotes for Mark 16:8 in the NIV). If the author of Matthew took the line of Jesus coming to John the Baptist from Mark, he would have most likely been taking it from an early version of Mark - one that didn't have Nazareth in the verse.

This isn't the only time Nazareth is mentioned in Mark, but that's because of a dishonest translation. The Greek phrase translated to "Jesus of Nazareth" in the Gospel of Mark is actually "Jesus the Nazarene" - which, as stated earlier, the author of Matthew goes into an explanation for. Presumably due to a misunderstanding of what the author of Mark meant, the author of Matthew placed Jesus into a town called Nazareth, but that place didn't exist in the first century CE.

The author of Matthew may have been trying to connect the birth of Jesus to part of Judges 13:5, which says:

[T]he boy is to be a Nazirite, dedicated to God from the womb. He will take the lead in delivering Israel ...

The author of Matthew says the Nazareth upbringing comes from "the prophets," but there are no prophets in the Old Testament that mention the place. Chapter 19 in the book of Joshua lists dozens of new towns and villages in that area, but not a single one is Nazareth.

We know of a small first-century town that was a 45-minute walk away from where Nazareth is now located named Sepphoris, but it isn't mentioned in the Bible at all. Despite only being a few acres large, it is clearly documented in history books and maps. The famed historian Josephus was a commander in Galilee during the middle of the first century, and he mentions tons of different villages and towns (including Sepphoris), but again, no Nazareth until the 140s.

So what does Nazarene mean if it doesn't mean "from Nazareth"? The name itself might come from *nzr*, a Hebrew prefix meaning "truth." It appears to be a particular sect of Christianity - as shown in Acts 24:5, which uses a similar term, Nazoraeans, as a group that Paul doesn't exactly deny being a part of:

We have found this man to be a troublemaker, stirring up riots among the Jews all over the world. He is a ringleader of the Nazarene sect.

Note that the translation above (along with the vast majority of English translations) uses the word Nazarene any time either Nazarene (*Nazarene*) or Nazoraean (*Nazoraios*) is actually used in the original text. In this case in Acts, the plural for Nazoraean was used. We, along with a handful of ancient text and Bible translators, are using the different English counterparts to show the subtle, yet potentially significant difference in the Greek words.

That's where even more mystery enters the scene. While the term Nazarene is already puzzling in its origin, the term Nazoraean comes up even more frequently. Oddly enough, the word that directly translates to Nazarene is the only version found in the Gospel of Mark, while Matthew and John both exclusively use Nazoraean. As an extra twist, the Gospel of Luke actually uses both!

It would seem that a Nazoraean would be a person from Nazareth, but Acts makes it seem like the Nazoraeans were a sect of Judaism. Epiphanius, a Christian bishop writing in 370 CE, seems to echo this in *Panarion*:

> *I mean the Nazoraeans, whom I am discussing here. They were Jewish, were attached to the Law, and had circumcision.*

Epiphanius also said that the term Nazoraeans could refer to a sect of Christians who came after the Ebionites. He then goes on to explain the Ebionites and says they were impacted "by the teachings of Elchasai."

Elchasai was the teacher of a story about a Jewish son of God eerily similar to Jesus, but with a sister who joined him on his multiple trips to Earth from Heaven. Though we only have small excerpts of *The Book of Elchasai* (thought to have been written during the reign of Trajan from 98 to 117 CE), there is no evidence that this son of God character was named Jesus.

The problem this presents is quite damning for historicists. According to Epiphanius, the Nazoraeans (which he says later in *Panarion* is, in fact, the group Paul was accused of belonging to in Acts) came *after* the Ebionites. Which not only means Paul would have never had that particular verbal exchange, but also means the Gospel of Luke and Acts were written in the second century.

We'll have more about the evolution of terms and the progression of early Christianity in Chapter 6, but an important takeaway is that in *Panarion*, while Epiphanius was sometimes confused about where the name of many of the Jewish and Christian sects came from, he is very adamant that the Christian Nazoraeans did not come from the

Nasaraeans (*Nasaraioi*). Despite obvious similarities in the names, he is aware of the fact that the Nasaraeans existed before the supposed life of Jesus. The resemblance is highly suspicious to us, but more about that later.

After the Bar Kokhba Revolt, a devastating Jewish rebellion against the much more powerful Roman military from 132 to 136 CE, many Jewish families resettled into the areas surrounding Jerusalem. There's a chance that Nazareth, which could have been started around that time, was founded by the Jewish Nazoraeans. At any rate, people were living in this town after 136. The author of Matthew may have just used that town as Jesus' home.[6]

Galilean Beginnings

As mentioned above, the Gospels took ideas from many sources. Some are very familiar to Christians, such as the Jewish prophets. Others require a closer look to recognize, but the evidence for them is incredibly clear.

There are seemingly countless claims of Jesus sharing all sorts of different attributes with previous gods/myths. A quick online search presents you with video after video of borderline conspiratorial claims. Somewhere around early 2011, I was shown a video that listed just about every similarity conceivable between the story of Jesus and Mithras, Horus, Krishna and other similar miracle working gods. However, I noticed that a good number of the similarities were based on non-gospel concepts like the birth of Jesus on December 25th and meeting on Sundays. It also made tons of references to "God's sun" (an obvious comparison to the phrase "God's son") without recognizing that "sun" and "son" are only homonyms in English (or Proto-Germanic at best). Those languages were not even spoken until roughly 400 years after the start of Christianity.

The idea that Christianity stole ideas from other cults isn't lost on me, but when the evidence gets scarce, or the claim involves an entire government keeping the lid on the operation for centuries, it crosses over into conspiracy theory territory - a place I try my best to avoid.

Jaaron Wingo

Many mythicists have made claims regarding the similarities between Jesus and other prior gods, but we found it incredibly difficult to find the source for many of the claims. Whether it be because the mythicist made an honest mistake, the information we have about an ancient deity became outdated, or they outright lied to bolster their point, there are times that their claims need to be effectively tossed out. But some of the claims seem to be barking up the right tree.

This is one of those times. A few mythicists have come to a particular conclusion - albeit in different ways: the writings of Josephus had an impact on the Gospels.

Before we get into the evidence for this claim (and those of you familiar with this claim need to know this especially), we need to tell you this claim is not a particularly recent one. It has been presented, published, and printed in books and on pamphlets for decades. However, most of the times any mythicist makes these claims, there is an element of governmental conspiracy that is packaged with it.

For instance, some of the mythicists presenting this "Josephus theory" believe that Josephus himself was hired by the Romans to write the Gospels in a last-ditch effort to turn militant Jews away from their faith. His willingness to be involved in the conspiracy varies depending on the mythicist. Other presenters claim Josephus is the pen name for a Roman aristocrat. None of these specific Josephus theories have any historical merit, so we object to their use in this case due to lack of evidence.

Nonetheless, as we delved into this theory, we found a certain level of validity to the claims. The Gospels do have a shockingly clear connection with Josephus' *Wars of the Jews*. With consistency, the Gospel of Mark has Jesus in scenarios that are pulled from *Wars*. The most interesting fact of these similarities is how they are written into the story in order. It's not as if a particular similarity found in *Wars* happens in the middle of Mark, while the next similarity has the reader going back to the beginning of the gospel to find it. As more gospels were written, there was more expansion on the Josephus similarities. It's as if the authors were aware of where the previous authors were pulling the story from. This is where the idea of Jesus' Galilean beginnings seems to have been sourced.

Wars of the Jews talks of the First Jewish-Roman War, in which Josephus was a Jewish rebel commander in Galilee. Vespasian, the Roman general who would soon be Emperor and heralded as a deity, launched an invasion in Galilee in 67 CE. His son, Titus, was brought with him. Eventually, Titus finished the campaign started by his father. He made his way down to Jerusalem and laid siege to the city in 70 CE.

The ancient Jews considered 40 years to be a generation.[7] It seems the gospel writers attempted to place Jesus' start of his ministry 40 years before Titus starting his military campaign in Galilee. Then, three years later, just like the fall of Jerusalem three years after Vespasian's campaign started, Jesus' ministry ended in Jerusalem.

In *Wars*, Titus, the son of a god, is killing men in the Sea of Galilee as they are getting into ships and while they are out in the water. The Romans were effectively fishing for men in the lake, pulling the Jews out of the water. The Gospel of Mark has Jesus, the son of God, calling his disciples to be fishers of men at the Sea of Galilee. This story of Jesus, along with others, is a link to *Wars*. While the link may seem precarious, void of any connection with Josephus the phrase "fishers of men" is an uncharacteristic pun from Jesus, and the phrase never gets used again outside of this particular story.

Let's examine another scene at the start of Jesus' ministry. If you were to look around for reasons as to why scholars think Jesus existed, one of the claims you might find is that he was baptized by John the Baptist. While yes, this does appear in many of the gospels, and John the Baptist is discussed by Josephus, their justification is more of a psychological argument than a historical one. The idea is that Jesus being baptized by John would make Jesus look subservient to someone else. Also, because John baptized people for the remission of sins, scholars claim that including the baptism scene would make Jesus seem like he sinned, when he was believed by the Christians as being perfect and sinless. Including such an embarrassing moment, they claim, must make the story true.

There are a number of problems with this reasoning, but we're going to focus on the most glaring ones. Nowhere in the first, second, or third centuries do we see proof of anyone having an issue with Jesus being baptized (or with his numerous servile gospel scenes). We don't even have any proof that anyone outside of Christianity in the second century even knew about the baptism. Furthermore, how else would Jesus interact with John the Baptist? If the goal of adding John to the story was to win over the followers of the now dead Baptizer, the author of the Gospel of Mark would have been obligated to include a scene of the *very* thing John was known for. Later gospels would build up the relationship between Jesus and John the Baptist, but the first gospel needed a historical preacher, found one, and threw him in.

As for sinlessness, you might be able to assume Jesus' perfection from the Gospel of Mark's lack of a childhood story. Other than that, it's never explicitly stated. Pilate makes comments in the gospels about finding no fault with Jesus, but that is solely for the case before him, and not a statement about how Jesus never even told a fib as a child. Likewise, Jewish leaders finding no good excuse to punish Jesus wouldn't be an argument for lifelong perfection either, as they wouldn't know everything he did behind closed doors. The Gospel of Luke mentions Jesus being obedient to his mother after getting lost in Jerusalem for three days, but that can be explained away as him being obedient by actually following them home (as opposed to purposely staying behind the first time).

We're not trying to argue the supernatural claim that Jesus was sinless, we're just pointing out that the idea that he was sinless wasn't an established or explicit claim of the initial gospel writers. The only reason scholars make the argument based on the sinlessness of Jesus is they assume most of the theology and ideas of Jesus found in the New Testament were around by the time the gospels were written.

However, the more explicit references to the lifelong perfection of Jesus were first seen in the Epistles (more on them and how they were written *after* the Gospel of Mark in Chapters 4 and 8). This, along with the fact that the embarrassment of Jesus' baptism wouldn't have been a concern of the early Christians, and the lack of evidence of the baptism even being known by non-Christians (much less mocked), means the argument that the baptism scene is evidence for the historicity of Jesus is moot.

Crucified With Christ

The parallels with Josephus don't stop once the entrance to Jerusalem begins. While there is already enough to say that Jesus' arrival to Jerusalem is synonymous with Titus reaching Jerusalem at the end of the campaign, the most eye-opening references are found at the crucifixion scene.

Jesus is crucified with two other men. The Gospel of Mark doesn't have the conversation between them and Jesus, but they (presumably) died on their crosses. Jesus dies, and then Joseph of Arimathea gets permission from Pilate to take down Jesus' body. The body is taken down, and as we all know, Jesus comes back to life.

A couple things to quickly note: Joseph seems to come out of nowhere. He's not mentioned in the gospel prior to just about the ending of the story. We also have no idea where Arimathea is, and people have been trying to guess what city or area it was for centuries. If both Joseph and Arimathea were made up, where would the ideas have come from?

In *The Life of Flavius Josephus*, his biography written between 95 and 99 CE, Josephus recounts seeing three friends crucified. He asks Titus for permission to take down the bodies, and although two of them die, one of them survived. To top it off, Josephus' Jewish name was Joseph, and his father's name was Matthias. While Joseph bar Matthias witnessed a crucifixion and got involved, Joseph of Arimathea witnessed a crucifixion and got involved in Mark. A common concept of the day was to creatively place your name near the end of your work,[8] so the obvious tie-in of Josephus makes some mythicists think he personally had a hand in the work.

We want to reiterate that we don't subscribe to the theories of Roman political conspiracy to explain the connection with Josephus. Due to Greek being used instead of Hebrew, the dating of the New Testament books/beliefs, and the existence of Christians prior to the gospels, the conspiracy theories are virtually impossible (especially with the obvious lack of knowledge and cordiality between the Roman leadership and the Christians for centuries after the death of Josephus). That being said, Josephus being potentially name dropped as Joseph of Arimathea in the Gospels, and then potentially name dropped again in

Acts 1:23 with the names Joseph and Matthias, seems way too large of a coincidence to overlook. Perhaps the author of the Gospel of Mark simply wanted to add this quasi-cameo into the story because he saw Josephus as a "coauthor" of sorts, or possibly because he wasn't trying to write literal history and was name-dropping Josephus to point to the "real" author. It seems the Gospels of Matthew, Luke, and John picked up on the Josephus connection, and expanded on it in their own books (and Acts, written by the author of the Gospel of Luke).

To make this idea even more compelling, the surname of a Joseph listed in Acts 1:23 is Justus, which is the name of a first-century rival of Josephus (and whose life we now only know of from *The Life of Flavius Josephus*). Justus, along with another man named Judas mentioned in Acts (who is a likely candidate for the origin of the Judas Iscariot character), was accused by Josephus as being responsible for the rebellion that started the First Jewish War. It's only fitting that not only was Judas Iscariot replaced as a disciple, but Justus wasn't chosen to be one either. It would make sense to place Justus in the middle of another Josephus reference to allow for the other educated readers to pick up on the vilification of a man who would have been knowingly found in Josephus' works.

So with Josephus in one hand and some myth-soaked creativity in the other, you've got the natural life of Jesus. When you add the supernatural events back into the story, they paint a picture of broadscale plagiarism. A holy man or oracle using spit to cure ailments? Serapis. The healing pool of Bethesda? Asclepius. Water converted into wine at a party? Dionysus. The ascension? Romulus. Walking on water? Orion. Simon denies Jesus after his death in Jerusalem? A general in Josephus' *Wars* named Simon puts on different clothes and denies involvement after Jerusalem is destroyed. Jesus helps the disciples catch exactly 153 fish? Pythagoras.

The Gospel authors were coming up with their superhero's story, and just like if we were to create a superhero from scratch right now, there would be tropes and abilities that we'd need to take from previous comic books. That would be especially so if we were trying to market our stories to the fans of other heroes. Very little of the story of Jesus is original, and if you take out the supernatural parts, the natural story is flimsy, contradicting, and consisting of rip offs of previous books and tales.

We also don't want to overlook the extensive use of the Old Testament in the creation of Mark and the other New Testament content, either. It's just that this is commonly accepted, even if not to the extent that many realize.

Some, such as Thomas L. Brodie, the Dominican priest and mythicist scholar, see the narrative of Jesus and other New Testament figures as part of a fictional interpretive work of Old Testament stories, such as the Elijah-Elisha narrative. There is also extensive work on how deities, such as Osiris, the Egyptian god that dies and gets resurrected, start out entirely mythical but get historicized, just as Plutarch tries to do with Osiris.

These documents and stories largely pre-date the dating of Jesus, though, and therefore don't give us anything to work with in terms of determining the historicity of Jesus. The clear links to Josephus, however, are evidence to a date after those writings were completed late in the first century CE.

Matthew Britt

"Weren't the Gospels written shortly after the death of Jesus?"

When looking into early Christianity, we were initially under the impression that the mainstream dating of the authorship of the Gospels was more or less correct. However, it is simply a major issue that none of the authors would have been eyewitnesses, and none of the authors wrote within four decades of the supposed life of Jesus. Since most historicists (especially the atheists) seem to not take issue with these problems, for the longest time we swept the problems under the rug as well.

Nevertheless, as we stated in Chapter 1, we don't place the writing of the Gospels in the first century. We're sure plenty of our readers have been dying to read our evidence for this. It's time we explained ourselves.

We don't see the names attached to the canonical gospels until roughly 180 CE in the works of Irenaeus. The gospels were written anonymously, and we know there were edits made along the way. They were written in Greek while all the main characters spoke Aramaic, and no one even mentions them at all during the first century (we'll have more on that later).

The second century theologian Marcion presented his "New Testament" in the 140s, and suddenly there was a boom in gospel mentions, gospel critiques, and even gospels! In his New Testament, Marcion included a gospel that he called Evangelion. It is, in some circles, called "Proto-Luke," as it appears to be a smaller, more basic version of what would eventually be called the Gospel of Luke. Most scholars like to claim that Luke came first and Evangelion was created by Marcion stripping away parts of Luke. This claim is primarily due to two reasons: many religious people want to place the gospels as close to Jesus as possible in an effort to maintain his historicity, and Tertullian, an early Christian author, made this claim around the turn of the third century. Keeping the Gospel of Luke on the earlier side of Evangelion would be very beneficial for Christianity, but we found some good reasons as to why that was not the case:

A Short Story

The length of Marcion's Evangelion is a small, but important reason as to why the gospel likely came before Luke. Frankly, there's not much of a reason to remove pieces from Luke. It includes Nazareth, and it has plenty of pasted passages from Mark. If Marcion wanted to remove certain parts, it's not clear what he wanted to remove or why. The main gist of the story is there. It's not like Marcion set out to remove huge chunks a la Thomas Jefferson's "no miracle" Bible. There are even some references to the Old Testament found in Evangelion which would have contradicted Marcion's theology. If he set out to rewrite Luke, he likely would have left those parts out. We'll explain how they got in there in Chapter 9.

Mark is the shortest gospel, and shorter generally means it's not going to have a lot of the finer details. There is a term used to describe the branch of theology that dives into the particulars about Jesus, his life, and his divinity: christology. Mark is considered to be the first gospel written at least partially because it has a "lower christology." In other words, because it doesn't have as many details about the divinity of Jesus as the other gospels, it is assumed that the earliest version of Mark, dubbed "Proto-Mark," was used as a sort of launching pad for the later writings and teachings.

This is the situation created by the shorter Evangelion. Luke builds onto it - proof that the inverse isn't true.

No Miraculous Births

Two of the biggest parts of the Gospel of Luke that Evangelion lacks are the surprise pregnancies of not one, but two famous mothers. Just about all of Luke's first chapter is devoted to the story of John the Baptist's birth and the angelic proclamation of it. The chapter only ties in Mary as a secondary character, which is a bit striking, but she comes roaring back in Luke 2, as Jesus is born of a virgin in a manger in Bethlehem while his parents live out the time-bending quasi-census vacation that never was.

I'm not going to lie. I don't really understand Luke's first chapter at all. Short of being an absolutely shameless marketing ploy to the followers of John the Baptist (who at some point started calling themselves the Mandaeans), it really doesn't make any sense. John serves virtually no purpose in the entire story of Jesus, and the one interaction they have is honestly not important at all. Jesus getting baptized isn't a prerequisite for dying for humanity's sins at all, and Jesus never instructs anyone else to be baptized in water, nor does he baptize anyone else. He just lets John do it. The whole thing is just an attempt to create a familiar connection with John the Baptist, so the Christians could convert some of his followers after his death. Luke goes one step further than the other three canonical gospels and literally makes him a cousin of Jesus, something that doesn't seem to align with the baptizer's demeanor in the other gospels.

Jaaron Wingo

Because it's considerably shorter, Evangelion's lack of certain stories is generally excusable, but it's what is shared in their place that helps make the argument for Evangelion's priority. Marcion doesn't just skip over the birth story, he has a fully grown Jesus descend from Heaven into Capernaum.

Convincing your Christian readers that Jesus wasn't born of a virgin and Jesus wasn't the cousin of one of the most famous preachers of all time seems like an incredibly daunting task for Marcion to decide to take up. Jesus just showing up to Capernaum one day doesn't sound too exciting, but it serves as evidence that Marcion wrote first. We're also not done with Capernaum quite yet...

The Capernaum Caper

One of the final nails in the coffin of this debate is right in front of us. In the fourth chapter of the Gospel of Luke, Jesus is praised by a group of people listening to him read scriptures. He responds dismissively, and in doing so, mentions that the people want him to show signs like he "did in Capernaum."

The only problem is, he hasn't been there yet.

Luke has Jesus going to Capernaum and performing miracles, but this is done after Jesus says his dismissive line. Evangelion has Jesus in Capernaum from the beginning, doing signs and healing people. Then Jesus gives the dismissive line later.

On top of all this, at the very beginning of his gospel, Marcion explains that Capernaum is "in Galilee" because this is Evangelion's first geographical location for Jesus. In Luke 4:31, Jesus goes to Capernaum for the first time in the canonical gospel. This verse is ripped directly from Evangelion, and as such, includes an unnecessary explanation that Capernaum is in Galilee, even though Luke explicitly states Jesus was already in the Galilee region since verse 14.

This is proof that the author of Luke used Marcion's Evangelion as a blueprint, added the virgin birth in lieu of Jesus' descent from Heaven, but then forgot to place all references to the prior gospel's narrative in chronological order.

Evangelion was the basis for the Gospel of Luke.

Because of this, we know that Luke was written post 140 CE. How much later? Likely around 160. This is because the new later date for the writing of Luke places it right during the lifetime and career of a man named Theophilus of Antioch.

Theophilus was a prominent Christian figure in Antioch (a city in modern-day Turkey). According to his writings, he was originally a pagan, but he claimed that he became a Christian by studying texts. He was the bishop of Antioch from 169 until 182. This means he would have needed information about Christianity some time before this. The Gospel of Luke is addressed to a man named Theophilus, and no scholar has been able to conjure up a strong argument for a person from the first century with the same name. The dates of the Gospel of Luke, according to our theory, line up perfectly with Theophilus, and therefore answer a question that has been asked for nearly 1,800 years. We'll share more about Theophilus in Chapter 5.

But remember, the Gospel of Mark was the very first gospel written. As we talked about earlier, Mark relied heavily on Josephus' *Wars of the Jews*, so while that gospel was written earlier than 140, it had to be some time after 75. *The Life of Flavius Josephus*, the autobiography of Josephus which includes the reference to the three men he saw crucified, was written between 94 and 99 CE, so that places the composition of Mark in the first half of the second century.

As for the Gospels of Matthew and John, they were written after 140 as well. Matthew was written shortly after Evangelion (most likely as a response to Marcion), and John was written even later as a kind of summary of the prior gospels.

Big Trouble Little Apocalypse

We will discuss Matthew and John in further detail in Chapter 8, but one of the key pieces of evidence for Matthew being written after Evangelion is the inclusion of a section that is sometimes called "Little Apocalypse." In short, it is a passage that has Jesus predicting/discussing the destruction of Jerusalem and the scattering of the Jewish people that followed. Found in Matthew 24 and 25 (as well as Mark 13 and Luke 21), the passage is very commonly used to try to date the gospel. The majority of scholars claim that the destruction of Jerusalem in the story is specifically referring to the First Jewish-Roman War, which we've already touched on.

However, there's another particular time the passage could be referring to: the Bar Kokhba Revolt. This would place the writing of Matthew sometime after 136 CE. But Little Apocalypse isn't just found in the Gospel of Matthew. It's also found in the Gospel of Luke, as well as the Gospel of Mark. This doesn't mean Mark was written after 136 as well, because our theory posits that Little Apocalypse was not in the earliest version of the gospel, and was added later. Again, we will go into the evidence for this in much further detail in Chapter 8.

If it wasn't in the original version of the Gospel of Mark, but it's found in the Gospels of Matthew and Luke, who wrote it first? The answer, as you may have guessed by now, is Marcion.

Roughly 70% of the Gospel of Matthew is found in Luke as well, with just over 34% of those passages being shared only between Matthew and Luke (the remainder being found in Mark as well as those two gospels). The Gospel of Luke, as we now know, lifted from Evangelion - and not just a little. The vast majority of Luke was taken from Marcion's book. Little Apocalypse is simply a passage from Evangelion, and was therefore used in Matthew and Luke, then added to Mark retroactively. This places the creation of Matthew post 140 CE, with our estimate being somewhere in the 150s.

A Tale of Two Theories

While the majority of scholars believe the Gospel of Matthew was written after Mark but before Luke, there are some who subscribe to the concept of "Matthean Posteriority." They claim that Matthew was written as the last book in the "Synoptic Gospels" (the name for the Gospels of Matthew, Mark and Luke due to their extremely clear similarities and excessive use of the early version of Mark). The arguments for Matthean Posteriority are actually quite convincing. The only real problem is why the arguments are *also* so good for Luke being the third Synoptic Gospel.

Among others, one of the best arguments for the Gospel of Matthew being written after Luke is the author of Matthew's tendency to combine multiple passages from Mark and Luke into one story.

For example, in Mark 6:34, it says:

*When Jesus landed and saw a large crowd, **he had compassion on them, because they were like sheep without a shepherd**. So he began teaching them many things.*

And in Luke 10:2 it says:

*He told them, "**The harvest is plentiful, but the workers are few. Ask the Lord of the harvest, therefore, to send out workers into his harvest field.***

Neither of the above passages is connected to any version of the other. However, in Matthew 9:35-38, we find elements from both of these passages fused together in one story:

*Jesus went through all the towns and villages, teaching in their synagogues, proclaiming the good news of the kingdom and healing every disease and sickness. When he saw the crowds, **he had compassion on them, because they were harassed and helpless, like sheep without a shepherd**. Then he said to his disciples, "**The harvest is plentiful but the workers are few. Ask the Lord of the harvest, therefore, to send out workers into his harvest field.***

Other than the example shown above, the author of Matthew combines passages from Mark and Luke five other times in his gospel.

This action is not done in Luke at all, so this shows that the author of Matthew wrote his gospel with a copy of Mark and a copy of Luke in his hand.

Except, it wasn't Luke, per se.

This is where our theory helps explain why both groups of scholars are, in a sense, correct. Since the Gospel of Luke takes heavily from Evangelion, the Gospel of Matthew came *after* Luke's main source, but *before* the canonical gospel. Because of our understanding of where the authors of Matthew and Luke got their source, multiple arguments for either book coming after the other lay perfectly within our theory.

The Anonymous Q

Many scholars believe there was another text that the Gospels of Matthew and Luke were pulling from. This is because roughly 58% of the Gospel of Luke is not found in Mark. Likewise, 44% of Matthew is absent from Mark. According to these scholars, there would need to be some explanation for where so much of this new content came from.

A hypothetical document, named Q (short for *quelle*, which means "source" in German), was in the hands of the authors of Matthew and Luke, along with their copies of Mark. Because this Q document has never been found, it is considered to be lost to time. As you may have pieced together already, by shifting the composition dates for the gospels into the second century, we can deduce that the extra source for the authors of Matthew and Luke was simply Evangelion.

Only 20% of Matthew is unique to that gospel. While that is a decent sized chunk of the text, the rest of the book is sourced from Mark and Evangelion. As we'll see later, the author of the Gospel of Luke added Luke 1-4 and Luke 24 (among other small edits between those chapters). If the vast majority of the rest of Luke is also in Mark,

Matthew, and Evangelion, then the estimated amount of text unique to Luke is about the same as Matthew. The point we are trying to make here is that it seems reasonable that the authors' own "creativity" accounts for about 20% of the books - even if that "creativity" is actually just pulling from older myths.

The author of Matthew pulled from Evangelion and Mark, and Luke is an edited version of Evangelion, with bits of Matthew and Mark sprinkled in.

The Gospel Jesus Loved

The Gospel of John is considered to be the last of the canonical gospels written. We subscribe to this idea as well, with, of course, the exception that it would need to be written in the mid-to-late second century.

Multiple times in John, the author mentions elements found in the prior Gospel of Luke, without giving good explanations as to what they are. For instance, in John 11:1, the story of Jesus raising a man named Lazarus from the dead begins with:

Now a man named Lazarus was sick. He was from Bethany, the village of Mary and her sister Martha.

Mary and Martha are characters that are only previously found in the Gospel of Luke. They do not appear in Matthew or Mark. But here in John, the author assumes the reader is already familiar with them. Otherwise, their introduction would have been in the story involving the women that immediately follows, not as a reference point or defining detail of the village of Bethany.

The author of John also takes moments to explain who some characters are, in some instances, even giving away the ending. In John

6:68-71, Jesus calls out Judas, the disciple who betrayed Jesus in the gospel story:

Simon Peter answered him, "Lord, to whom shall we go? You have the words of eternal life. We have come to believe and to know that you are the Holy One of God."

Then Jesus replied, "Have I not chosen you, the Twelve? Yet one of you is a devil!" (He meant Judas, the son of Simon Iscariot, who, though one of the Twelve, was later to betray him.)

The last sentence definitely needs a spoiler alert. Why would anyone present the gospel this way? Why would anyone read this and not be very confused? Because the author is well aware that the reader knows the gospels. They've already been released.

The author (or maybe even *authors*) of the Gospel of John was not shy with these explanations, as he used them for Mary, the Jewish high priest Caiaphas, and "the disciple Jesus loved." Nor was the author shy about the fact that it wasn't really John writing it. Multiple times, the gospel talks about John the Disciple being the apparent source of the stories. However, John (if he did in fact exist) would have been long dead by this point, and the author would be at least one or two generations removed from any possible disciple's lifetime.

This is all evidence of a composition date that follows the Gospels of Mark, Matthew, and Luke. There is also no mention of the Gospel of John until roughly 170 CE, which further serves as evidence to a mid-to-late composition date (we estimate roughly 165).

The Gospel of John is the most brazen of the canonical gospels. Jesus is shown as a much stronger character who doesn't downplay his divinity at all. He is depicted with a much bolder personality, and even during his death scene, he is making commands to his mother and one of his disciples.

34

Tucked away in John's fifth chapter, Jesus heals a man on the Sabbath at the Pool of Bethesda while in Jerusalem for a Jewish festival. The man, who had been disabled for decades, complained that he was unable to get into the pool "when the water was troubled." Jesus heals the man, and when Jewish leaders see the man carrying his mat and walking away, they get furious with Jesus for healing people on the Sabbath.

At first I thought it was just another routine miracle story culminating with a clash between Jesus and the Jewish leaders, but I had overlooked an important detail: the pool. The Pool of Bethesda was discovered by archaeologists, and is part of a larger "Asclepion". Asclepia were temples used for the worship of Asclepius, the Greek healer god who had been worshiped since before the fifth century BCE. His cult was massive and spread throughout all the Empire, and injured/sick people flocked to the asclepia to receive a miracle.

But Jesus never stated that the healing powers of Asclepius were fake. Could this be because the Christians were trying to recruit members of the Asclepius cult? Even more importantly, what was a large Asclepion doing in Jerusalem in the early first century? The presence of the nearby Jewish leaders on the Sabbath during a Jewish festival seems suspicious as well. And what's with a Jewish man trying to use a pool in a temple for Asclepius? This seems like a fabricated story with a more Hellenized, post-70 CE Jerusalem as the backdrop - not Jerusalem in the early first century.

Jaaron Wingo

"What about the other roughly 40 gospels?"

While trying to find anything that would disprove our developing hypothesis, we quickly came across a point made by both historicists and some mythicists: roughly 40 gospels were written, so it's possible they share information that would pose a hurdle too large to overcome. However, the mythicist position and theory we have come to find sees this "issue" as no issue at all.

There are 4 canonical gospels (Matthew, Mark, Luke, and John), and over 30 more that were written sometime during the first few centuries. These gospels generally include either less information about Jesus than their canonical counterparts, or so much information the story turns comically fantastical. The "Infancy" gospels, loaded with stories of Jesus during his childhood, have some of the most fantastical of all the tales, with Jesus making birds out of clay, performing low-scale miracles, and occasionally committing literal murder, such as in the Infancy Gospel of Thomas.

Most of these gospels, part of a group of non-canonical books dubbed "the Apocrypha," are generally dated to the late second century at earliest, so the testimony given is well past its sell-by date. The more extraordinary claims found within them require even more extraordinary evidence, of which there is none.

Many historicists have claimed these gospels as further proof of Jesus. Most do not advocate for the historicity of the wilder stories found in the Apocrypha, but use the stories that the Apocryphal books have in common with the canonical gospels as evidence for the shared stories.

But just like the childhood game of telephone, every new book can and will introduce new variations to the initial story. Just because other books maintain the core of the first gospel, that in no way means the story is true. Following that logic, literally any repeated part of the story must be true - not just the existence of Jesus!

Quite simply, numerous people copying and pasting from one book's story of a supernatural Jesus doesn't prove the existence of a natural Jesus anymore than Harry Potter fanfiction proves the natural existence of "the boy who lived."

The argumentum ad populum also falls flat when you realize that the Christians are unambiguously the victors of the Western world. To the victors go the spoils, and once Christianity became the official religion of the Roman Empire, they wasted no time destroying the temples of other religions,[9] deeming numerous Christian opinions heretical, rebranding events and practices from non-Christian cultures, and spreading Christian propaganda by claiming any of the religions they just stole from were actually satanic in nature.[10]

We discuss this at length in Chapter 6, but the main takeaway is that just because the prevailing religion has numerous copies, fragments, and shreds of documents telling what could best be described as "roughly the same story," that doesn't make the initial documents true.

If it wasn't for Christianity (or, more accurately, the victorious sect of Christianity after centuries of infighting) becoming the state religion and initiating a scorched earth campaign against every other thought, we wouldn't have those fragments.

"What about John the Baptist, Jesus' cousin and contemporary?"

One way historicists explain Jesus is through his supposed familiar connections. In the Gospel of Luke, John the Baptist is portrayed as a cousin of Jesus. He is even given an extensive birth story soaked in supernatural elements. His parents are both mentioned by name, and his aunt Mary (of the Virgin sort) comes to visit him while both he and his cousin Jesus are in utero. This blood relationship only clearly occurs in that one gospel, with the other gospels mentioning John to a much smaller degree.

Even if John the Baptist was his cousin, every gospel has him playing a rather doubtful character, asking Jesus if he is indeed who everyone hopes he will be: the Messiah. It seems very unlikely that someone who grew up alongside Jesus would have doubts as to who he was. If the miraculous parts of the gospels (and especially the Infancy gospels starring a young, impulsive Jesus) are true, John would have already witnessed or grew up around constant miraculous activity.

To put it bluntly, the odds of John the Baptist being the cousin of Jesus are slim to none. We know John the Baptist existed (there is natural evidence for him in the writings of Josephus) and we know that he was killed by Herod, and we even have a pretty good idea as to why he may have been put to death. But, no thanks to the tumultuous confidence John's character seems to have in his own potential cousin, we don't have any solid evidence of a blood relation to Jesus.

This is where we really started to see a pattern. We wondered for quite some time just why John was even mentioned at all. The abnormal story of John's birth seems out of place for a character with so little to add to the remainder of the narrative. Jesus gets baptized by John, but Jesus never tells anyone to be baptized in water or performs any baptisms of his own. John's death is sometimes later in the story, depending on which gospel you're reading, and in some cases practically swept out of the way within the first few chapters.

Christians promote the idea John was simply a preparer of the way, and therefore bowed out of the story quickly (albeit not in the most ceremonious of ways), but we eventually understood what he was doing in the story: bridging a gap.

Continuously throughout the Gospels, well-known figures from antiquity are mentioned or alluded to. John was a real person, baptizing people in the desert one after another, and had amassed quite the following prior to his untimely imprisonment and death. His followers, the Mandaeans, surely wandered around for a bit after losing their leader. The Christians added John the Baptist to their story, and the rest is pseudo-history. The first chapter of the Gospel of Luke seems to be lifted from some sort of gospel of John the Baptist, based on narratives from the Mandaeans. They believed their leader had mystical origins as well. Naturally, tying him in with Jesus' story was a perfect cohesion of the adherents, and the familiar relationship was created.

This type of campaigning is clearly seen throughout just about every aspect of the Gospels. Whether it be for the followers of Apollo, Dionysus, or Mithras, the Christians wanted to grow, so they added connections to bridge those gaps.

Interestingly enough, John's supernatural birth story doesn't have any Old Testament connections, and the big to do about the naming of John seems odd. That's because the author of Luke was working with a real person. There really wasn't too much wiggle room with the prophetic callbacks. John the Baptist wasn't related to Jesus, and there's no proof they even knew each other whatsoever.

"Didn't Jesus appear to people after his death?"

We're tempted to directly answer this question with a "no." We even considered avoiding this question entirely, because Jesus appearing to someone after his death is a textbook example of a supernatural claim. However, Jesus' sudden post death appearances are allegedly a recurring phenomenon even today within certain Christian circles, so we will address this further.

What's In Your Head

The post-death scenes from the gospels do not tell the same stories. The canonical gospels don't even share the same opinion of how many people the women who found the empty tomb shared their news with. The author of Matthew has the women telling all the disciples (presumably the remaining eleven since Judas Iscariot was now dead), the author of Luke explicitly says they told eleven disciples, the author of John says they told two disciples, and the author of the early version of Mark says they told no one.

While an argument could be made that the statement of the women telling eleven disciples *technically* also means they told two disciples, telling "no one" literally cannot mean any disciples were told. That's a massive contradiction and therefore discernibly different stories.

A frequent response to the logical problem above is that the women must have told someone eventually, otherwise the story couldn't have been spread. However, throughout the gospels, there are numerous examples of private conversations and inner thoughts that are mentioned. For example, unless someone relayed to the author of the Gospel of Matthew the private conversations of Herod found in Matthew 2:4-8, it would seem as if the gospel was written as a work of fiction.

This leads us to a very significant point: there is evidence to suggest that some early Christians did not believe in an actual historical Jesus, even after the stories of Jesus were circulating. A similar point is argued by historian Richard Carrier. He has presented the suggestion that Paul, who most of the New Testament books are traditionally attributed to, believed in a sort of celestial Jesus - rather than a Jesus who lived, died, and was resurrected here on Earth. Our theory has room for Carrier's position. The church leader Irenaeus, writing in roughly 180 CE, wrote in his book *Panarion*:

But Marcion, mutilating that according to Luke, is proved to be a blasphemer of the only existing God, from those [passages] which he still retains. Those, again, who separate Jesus from Christ, alleging that Christ

remained impassible, but that it was Jesus who suffered, preferring the Gospel
by Mark, if they read it with a love of truth, may have their errors rectified.

Other than the false accusation that Marcion stole from the Gospel of Luke, what is being discussed in that quote is "Docetism": the belief some early Christians had that Jesus and Christ were two different concepts. The subscribers to Marcion's version of Docetism believed Christ was a deity, and therefore couldn't have a human body. To the Marcionites, Jesus was some kind of earthly illusion of a human form.

We're not claiming Docetism was the position held by all the earliest Christians. Much like Marcion himself, all forms of Docetism were eventually branded as heretical. What we're left with, though, is the quote from Irenaeus. Of course, you must remember that by the time he was writing *Panarion*, lengthy additions had been made to the Gospel of Mark. But just why was Proto-Mark such a fan favorite among the Christians who didn't believe Jesus was historical?

Well, as we pointed out earlier, Proto-Mark doesn't really present Jesus as the Jewish man from Galilee that the other gospels portray him as. It ends with an empty tomb. There's no ascension. There's no post-death appearances. There's nothing. The women see the tomb is empty and they tell no one. The story just ends. It plays out like a drama or divine comedy. In fact, it feels so much like a piece of Greek theater that some researchers believe it was written to be a play - either for new converts to a mystery cult or for purely comedic purposes.

But does this have anything to do with whether Jesus appeared to people after his death? Indeed it does. If the earliest form of Mark was so vague in historicity that it gave a voice to people who literally thought Christ couldn't have a human body, the idea of post-death appearances must not have had a profound impact until later. We don't have a written story of a character seeing the resurrected Jesus until the 140s at earliest. Then, more and more post-death scenes get added. The Gospel of John has an entire chapter devoted to such scenes - including a scene where the disciple Thomas gets his doubts of Jesus' physical body refuted.

The point is, Jesus gets more and more physical as the gospel story develops over the decades. Along with his humanity, his post-death screen time starts at zero and increases with each new book.

Chapter Notes

1. Ehrman, Bart D. *The New Testament*: *A Historical Introduction to the Early Christian Writings*. Oxford University Press, 2000.

Throughout the book, we refer to the mainstream dates quite a bit, so it's important to keep them in mind. Yes, we're arguing for much later dates of composition, but even the mainstream dates are suspiciously later than the stories in the Gospels.

The mainstream dates rely not only on a generation or more oral tradition but even hypothetical, made-up documents such as the Q source (which, of course, also is considered to have relied on oral tradition as well). Oral tradition is notoriously unreliable, particularly regarding dates and details, and is how we hear so many people claim things like, "My great-grandmother was a Cherokee princess," even when the person turns out to have no Cherokee ancestry at all. The further we move away from the supposed date of the original events, this game of Telephone gets even further from the truth, which is one reason mainstream scholarship is so reluctant to consider later dates for the books of the New Testament.

2. Novak, Ralph Martin. *Christianity and the Roman Empire : Background Texts*. Trinity Press International, 2001. p. 292

The opinion of nearly all modern Bible scholars is that the author of the Gospel of Luke just flat out got it wrong. It's clear that the attempt was to provide a historical basis for the birth of the Jesus character, but this is a great example of how Luke was nothing more than a work of fiction. Why this glaring problem a mere three chapters into the book doesn't destroy the argument for the gospel's authenticity is beyond us.

3. Horsley, Richard A. *Archaeology, History, and Society in Galilee*. 1996. p. 110

4. Carruth, Shawn, et al. Q 4:1-13,16. 1996. p. 415

We both grew up in rural Texas. Small towns with only 200 people or fewer were all around us. We're familiar with unincorporated communities. We're also familiar with sprawling grasslands where no Texan settlement has ever been established. Even still, you can find coins, silverware, and even clothing while digging or simply walking in these areas. That's not proof of a town, that's just proof of civilization. After all, we're not claiming all of Judaea or the Roman Empire didn't exist.

5. Beduhn, Jason. *The First New Testament : Marcion's Scriptural Canon*. Salem, Oregon, Polebridge Press, 2013.

6. Salm, René. *The Myth of Nazareth: The Invented Town of Jesus*. American Atheist Press, 2008.

When we were in our early twenties, we sat down and had conversations with Mormon missionaries. We asked them questions about the fantastical stories in the Book of Mormon. These stories had millions of people living in North America, with multiple wars and battles with people dying left and right. Elephants, steel bows, and thousands of horse-drawn chariots were used in large cities filled with houses, towering forts, and stone walls. We asked the missionaries, "Do you have any proof of that?"

They said, "Yep. Horse teeth."

They were referring to a false claim that horse teeth were found in North America dating back to the time of the Mayan civilization. While this was obviously never proven, as the first domesticated horses in North America were very clearly introduced with the Europeans, the Mormon apologetics websites went wild over the initial discovery. Even if it had been proven, it wouldn't have done anything to prove the Elephants, steel, or missing fortresses. Likewise, the dating of already insignificant ancient items found in Nazareth tends to get edited to later as more data comes in.

7. "Forty, the Number - JewishEncyclopedia.com." www.jewishencyclopedia.com, www.jewishencyclopedia.com/articles/6248-forty-the-number. Accessed 12 Dec. 2023.

For a fairly explicit biblical reference, 40 years was considered to be long enough for a change in a generation in Numbers 32:13:

The Lord's anger burned against Israel and he made them wander in the wilderness forty years, until the whole generation of those who had done evil in his sight was gone.

8. Rosenmeyer, Patricia A. *Ancient Epistolary Fictions* : *The Letter in Greek Literature.* Cambridge ; New York, Cambridge University Press, 2008.

9. Rowe, Alan. *A Contribution to the Archaeology of the Western Desert.* 1957.

10. Justin Martyr, and Michael Slusser. *Dialogue with Trypho.* Washington, D.C, Catholic University Of America Press, 2003. ch. 69

Interestingly enough, Justin Martyr mentioned the Greek god Asclepius as a healer god in this cited chapter. He was well aware of the similarities with Jesus, but rather than understanding Jesus' abilities were clearly taken from the ~600-year-old myth of Asclepius, Justin blamed Satan for "imitating" the Old Testament prophecies of a foretold healer. The logic of this argument isn't very sound, but apparently God let the Asclepius cult wander in delusion for 400 years before showing up himself and setting the record straight. And nevermind the countless healer gods prior to the writing of the Old Testament books.

Further Reading:

1. Flavius Josephus. *The Wars of the Jews or History of the Destruction of Jerusalem - the Original Classic Edition*. Tebbo, 1 June 2012.

2. Edelstein, Emma J, and Ludwig Edelstein. *Asclepius : Collection and Interpretation of the Testimonies*. Baltimore, Md., Johns Hopkins University Press, 1998.

3. Luttikhuizen, Gerard P. *The Revelation of Elchasai*. Mohr Siebeck, 1985.

Chapter 2 | *Further Reading:*

CHAPTER 3

The Ancient Historians

Next, our journey led us to an obvious point: up against the historians of antiquity. While the New Testament authors and early church figures were clearly biased towards the religion, historians offered what is usually considered to be the closest we can get to the raw story. We're sure many of our readers have already been internally screaming for sometime now for us to acknowledge the chroniclers of the first few centuries. In this chapter, we will do just that.

"Didn't Josephus write about Jesus?"

The most famous of all the historical references to Jesus is found within the writing of the Jewish Roman historian Flavius Josephus. Dubbed the "Testimonium Flavianum," the passage is written below in context:

But Pilate undertook to bring a current of water to Jerusalem; and did it with the sacred money: and derived the origin of the stream from the distance of two hundred furlongs. However, the Jews were not pleased with what had been done about this water: and many ten thousands of the people got together, and made a clamor against him; and insisted that he should leave off that design. Some of them also used reproaches, and abused the man; as crowds of such people usually do. So he habited a great number of his soldiers in their habit; who carried daggers under their garments; and sent them to a place where they might surround them. So he bid the Jews himself go away. But they boldly casting reproaches upon him, he gave the soldiers that signal which had been beforehand agreed on. Who laid upon them much greater blows than Pilate had commanded them; and equally punished those that were tumultuous, and those that were not. Nor did they spare them in the least. And since the people were unarmed, and were caught by men prepared for what they were about, they were a great number of them slain by this means: and others of them ran away wounded. And thus an end was put to this sedition.

Now there was about this time Jesus, a wise man; if it be lawful to call him a man. For he was a doer of wonderful works; a teacher of such men as receive the truth with pleasure. He drew over to him both many of the Jews, and many of the Gentiles. He was [the] Christ. And when Pilate, at the suggestion of the principal men among us, had condemned him to the cross; those that loved him at the first did not forsake him. For he appeared to them alive again, the third day: as the divine prophets had foretold these and ten thousand other wonderful things concerning him. And the tribe of Christians, so named from him, are not extinct at this day.

About the same time also another sad calamity put the Jews into disorder: and certain shameful practices happened about the temple of Isis that was at Rome. I will now first take notice of the wicked attempt about the temple of Isis; and will then give an account of the Jewish affairs.

Debate rages regarding how much of the Testimonium is fabricated, with the vast majority of experts saying the only addition is the "He was [the] Christ" line. Josephus, who to our knowledge never professed to be a Christian, wouldn't have deemed Jesus the Christ. A portion of these experts say the line as a whole was added later, while another portion say the original line was "He was *called* the Christ."

Then you have the experts who believe the entire Testimonium is an interpolation - a later addition made to look like Josephus knew of the Christians and their Jesus. Their argument, in part, hinges on the issue with the context. As you can see above, the paragraph preceding the Testimonium is recalling a terrible event that happens to the Jewish people. Right after the Testimonium, it picks up where the previous paragraph left off with "another sad calamity." This implies that the original writing didn't have the paragraph about Christianity at all.

Another thing to realize is when and where the earliest copies of Josephus' texts that we have were collected. Lost to time for hundreds of years, the earliest Greek manuscript we have of *Antiquities of the Jews* is dated to the eleventh century. A theologian named Gabriel Severus had the manuscript in his collection, and he gave it to a library founded by the Catholic church shortly before his death in 1616.

Leaving such a monumental history book in the hands of theologians could lead to interpolations. But don't take our word for it. Consider how Eusebius, an admittedly biased early Christian writer who has since been proven to be a liar, remarked in his book *Demonstratio Evangelica* in 311 CE, "let us make use of Josephus the Jew" (you'll see Eusebius mentioned dozens of times in this book). After he made that comment in *Demonstratio Evangelica*, he then went on to present the Testimonium.

This was the first time anyone had brought up that paragraph in Josephus. It was roughly 215 years after Josephus had supposedly written it. Obviously, it would have proven beneficial for the Christian authors to repeat earlier, as they had their fair share of critics starting in the mid-to-late second century. It's not like the authors prior to Eusebius quoted everything in the paragraph *but* the "he was the Christ" line. There's no mention of the entire Testimonium before *Demonstratio Evangelica*. The fact that a known presenter of fake history would be the first person to mention such a valuable passage 215 years later makes Eusebius' reference to the Testimonium doubtful at best.

In fact, the one part of the Testimonium that historicists and mythicists seem to agree on is that Josephus wouldn't have said "he was the Christ," but Eusebius has that particular line in his quote of Josephus. That's a huge problem. This is the first time in history we ever see the Testimonium being discussed, and at least part of it is an obvious fabrication. Why on Earth would anyone assume Eusebius didn't just create the paragraph and "make use of Josephus" by claiming the Testimonium was real?

The style and some of the words/phrases used in the Testimonium are also very Eusebian themselves. As expert Ken Olson puts it:

The Testimonium follows Eusebius' line of argument in the Demonstratio Evangelica so closely that it is not only very unlikely that it could have been written by Josephus, but it is unlikely it could have been written by any other Christian, or even by Eusebius for another work. There is nothing in the language or content of the Testimonium, as it appears in the Demonstratio Evangelica, that suggests it is anything other than a completely Eusebian composition.

As proof of this claim, Olson states:

The term [paradoxon ergon poietes] is markedly Eusebian. Poietes never occurs in Josephus in the sense of 'maker' rather than 'poet,' and the only time Josephus combines forms of paradoxos and poieo it is in the sense of 'acting contrary to custom' rather than 'making miracles.' Combining forms of paradoxos and poieo in the sense of 'miracle-making' is exceedingly common in Eusebius, but he seems to reserve the three words paradoxos, poieo, and ergon, used together, to describe Jesus. (D.E. 114-115, 123, 125, H.E. 1.2.23)[1]

This doesn't look good for Eusebius and the Testimonium. The evidence points to a fabrication, and we postulate the whole paragraph was faked.

Josephus does not talk about Christians anywhere else. This is odd, as he makes note of different sects of Jews and other pagan cults. This is doubly important, as he seems to have information for Christianity that would only come from a Christian themselves. He says Jesus was crucified by Pilate and appeared to others on the third day. From a purely traditional and religious standpoint, that seems like a normal statement to make. However, Rome would most likely not have information for all the crucifixions done in Judaea decades prior (especially after the multiple fires in Rome). They also wouldn't have information about Jesus appearing to people on the third day after his death.

In fact, the Christians wouldn't even have this information either. As we showed earlier in Chapter 2, the Gospels of Matthew and Luke were written in the middle of the second century after Marcion produced his New Testament. This means that the first gospels with the stories of Jesus appearing to multiple people on the third day weren't written until that point. As we learned in Chapter 2, even *if* the gospel narrative found in Mark was shared at the time of Josephus, it ends with the women at the tomb being told Jesus had risen and then telling no one. Josephus wouldn't have even been alive to hear the version of the story mentioned in the Testimonium!

We've already established that the Gospel of Mark relied on the works of Josephus for many of its narratives, but for the sake of avoiding circular logic, let's set that aside for the moment. If Josephus, born in 37 CE, had received the information given in the Testimonium from the Christians, he would have likely needed a fairly in-depth conversation with them. Therefore, the lack of any other references to the Christians seems highly suspicious. Throughout the rest of his works, he references different sects of Jews, but never Christians. It seems odd that a Jew with intimate knowledge of a group that claims to know who the Messiah was wouldn't mention said group except in one dubious paragraph.

The absence of his comments on the Christians is even stranger, when you consider what we'll discuss in the next section: the idea of Nero persecuting the Christians in the 60s. Josephus would have been roughly 27 years old when Nero supposedly blamed the Christians for the Great Fire in Rome in 64 CE. The next oldest historian who talks about the Christians is Tacitus, who was only 8 at the time of the fire. While Josephus never talks about the Great Fire due to his explicit desire to avoid the topic of Nero altogether,[2] he had ample opportunity to mention the Christians as enemies of the state or competitors within the Jewish sects. He would have been the best historian to do so, yet, outside of the Testimonium now in question, he never did.

The Testimonium also has nothing but good things to say about both Jesus and the Christians. This wouldn't have possibly been written by someone who was at that time living in a room in Caesar's house. If Jesus was real, then the stories from Suetonius and Tacitus (more on them in a moment) would also likely be true, meaning the Roman government would have already been at violent odds with the Christians. Josephus wouldn't have spoken so highly about this cult (after putting down others) if he wasn't a Christian and also wanted to keep his head attached to his shoulders.

Finally, the smoking gun for the experts who deny the entire paragraph's authenticity is the fact that early Christian writers Justin Martyr, Theophilus Antiochenus, Melito of Sardis, Minucius Felix, Irenaeus, Clement of Alexandria, Julius Africanus, Pseudo-Justin, Tertullian, Hippolytus, Origen, Methodius, and Lactantius do not use the Testimonium in their writings. They were all familiar with the works of Josephus, and also faced non-believers all the time. They would have very easily been able to use the quote to show that even the non-believers of the first century knew who Jesus was. It would have been absolutely perfect, but they didn't mention it at all. The earliest copies of Josephus must not have had the Testimonium.

In summary, we know the entire paragraph is a later addition because:

1. The text flows better from one "sad calamity" to the next once the Testimonium paragraph is removed.

2. The man who first quotes the Testimonium in the fourth century also seems to have written the Testimonium himself based on the specific words used.

3. The knowledge of Christianity shown in the passage is anachronistic at best, due to the fact that the gospels containing said information weren't written until later and the extended ending of Mark didn't get added until the second century.

4. The passage displays an intimate knowledge of Christians without Josephus ever mentioning them before or after, even though he lists multiple sects of Judaism and Gentile cults.

5. The passage speaks highly of Christians when he wouldn't/ shouldn't have.

6. Despite numerous times the Testimonium would have been beneficial to quote, no Christian leader mentions it until the fourth century.

7. The passage speaks about the "tribe" of Christians while Pliny the Younger (a lawyer in Rome, Senator, and Governor of Bithynia and Pontus who wrote letters to the also ignorant-to-Christianity Emperor Trajan in 111 CE) had no idea who the Christians were.

The Testimonium is not the only potential Jesus reference in *Antiquities* that historicists point out, however. The next one is dealing with a Jesus who is the brother of the high priest, James. Because of the historicists' repeated suggestion that this specific James is the brother of Jesus from the Bible, we will discuss him further in Chapter 4.

"Didn't Tacitus write about Jesus?"

Josephus wasn't the only famed historian that historicists point to for proof of Jesus. Tacitus is also considered to be one of Ancient Rome's best historians due to his connection with Roman officials and (more importantly) the Roman archives. In his book *Annals*, written in 116 CE, he has a paragraph devoted to the Christian cult. In researching his mention of Christians, we didn't find too many claims of interpolation at first, so we dug deeper into our research under the assumption that his passage on Jesus was authentic.

Suddenly, we saw a peculiar issue with his report - an issue that will continue to pop up as our journey continues. One that has been noticed, but dismissed, for just about 2000 years. We have coined this issue "The Synonym Problem." Please allow us to explain.

The Synonym Problem: An Introduction

We'll talk in depth about this fact later in the book, but the term "Christ" doesn't always mean "Jesus." Christ is not a name; it is a title. It was used many times for a variety of different people from different religions. Even if the term was used by Christians in the earliest stages of Christianity, that doesn't mean they have any idea who Jesus is. Again, more on this later.

In a nutshell, Tacitus doesn't say Jesus. He says "Christ." He either spoke with Christians or with Pliny (more on him in a moment), and they told him about the religion.[3] That's the issue here.

Tacitus, while talking about the crucifixion story, wouldn't have called Jesus by the name Christ. It doesn't make sense. That would basically be him saying the Romans killed the Messiah. He clearly didn't fact check it or cross-reference it with any records. The record absolutely wouldn't have said, "We killed the Messiah late last Friday." Tacitus is just writing down what the Christians are saying.

Rome had gone through the Great Fire by this point, so there's an additional question there of why the records in Rome would even have such a small situation in Judaea listed and kept it safe for so long.

But what is important to note here is if Jesus didn't exist (because the character hadn't been named and written down yet), they wouldn't have used the name. Just the title. This happens again in multiple historian accounts. Historians will talk about this particular cult's existence and explain their belief in Christ - specifically not Jesus. If they had a name, they'd use it.

One might wonder if this could mean the story is true, even if the historical Christ's real name wasn't Jesus, or if the Christians that got interrogated just didn't know his name. While we admit that at this point we felt like that could be possible, afterwards it became increasingly obvious it wasn't. Of course, the stories have to start somewhere, and awareness of the Christians was just beginning here in the second century. Some Christians even believed the name Jesus was just a title, given to the character after his death for mankind. We don't subscribe to that theory per se, but it's important to note that people today are starting to see Christ was around before Jesus ever was.

Tacitus, like many Romans in authority positions, showed no respect for cults that had just started, and giving this much information about Christianity was doing little more than pointing out how this new cult was full of superstition. This was not an expose of a thriving new religion or a marketing ploy to increase membership; this was a diatribe against another mystic movement and the Empire should laugh at them.

Not to beat a dead horse, but Tacitus also got Pilate's political title wrong. That would have been clear if he was reading the Roman record. It seems the Christians didn't have their story developed quite yet. The ideas were swirling, but this was Christ before Jesus.

"Didn't Pliny write about Jesus?"

As we briefly explained earlier, the Synonym Problem keeps rearing its head throughout all of apologetics. This instance is no exception. Pliny the Younger talks about Christians in his letter to Emperor Trajan in late 111 CE. He writes at length regarding his run-ins with the Christians, and how he doesn't know what to do with them.

Setting aside the obvious and terrible violence towards beliefs outside the state religion, the first issue is Pliny's lack of a Jesus.

Without a Jesus, we can still have Christianity - we just don't have a gospel just yet.

So just how long has Christianity (in its pre-gospel form) been around while he was writing? Chances are, not long. Pliny was an accomplished Roman lawyer, praetor, prefect and eventually imperial governor. He was one of, and brushed shoulders with, the most powerful people in Rome during his lifetime (spanning from 61 to 113). His confusion as to who the Christians were and what to do with them is incredibly damning. If there was a mass execution of Christians due to the fire in Rome, why Pliny has never heard of Christians is beyond us. If Christianity was spread throughout the Empire as much as traditional dating/understanding of the letters of the New Testament would imply, he would have known about it.

But he doesn't. Neither does Trajan. They both come up with a plan of how to deal with the new cult, but the evidence is clear: they haven't dealt with them, nor have they even heard anything about them.

Something to note is where Pliny is writing. He's writing while he is the imperial Governor of Bithynia and Pontus (in modern-day Turkey). This is where we figure the first gospels were likely written. A man who is crucial to the foundation of Christianity as we know it would, at the time of Pliny's letter, be emerging on the scene from this very same region.

"Didn't Lucian of Samosata write about Jesus?"

Lucian of Samosata was a Greek writer of satire who wrote a number of critiques on different cults, religions, and superstitions that existed during his lifetime (from 125 CE to some time after 180 CE). Shortly after 165, he wrote The Passing of Peregrinus, a story about a philosopher from modern-day Turkey who lived a life of popularity thanks to the financial backing of the Christians before upsetting them and being kicked out of the community. As such, the story mentions Christians in four paragraphs. This quote is sometimes used by historicists today as evidence for Jesus. The quote is found below:

The Christians, you know, worship a man to this day—the distinguished personage who introduced their novel rites, and was crucified on that account... You see, these misguided creatures start with the general conviction that they are immortal for all time, which explains the contempt of death and voluntary self-devotion which are so common among them; and then it was impressed on them by their original lawgiver that they are all brothers, from the moment that they are converted, and deny the gods of Greece, and worship the crucified sage, and live after his laws. All this they take quite on faith, with the result that they despise all worldly goods alike, regarding them merely as common property.

Obviously, the fact that he was writing in the mid-to-late second century is a dead giveaway that his quote isn't good evidence. It's incredibly clear from the text that he is referencing the beliefs of a cult that are common knowledge at this point in time. Because Lucian was no stranger to writing about different cults or superstitions, the mere mention of the beliefs is in no way a confirmation of their historicity.

Lucian writing about the Christians at that point in time and in that area of the Roman Empire he was writing is in no way helpful to the historicists' cause. What is interesting, however, is *who* he is talking about.

The Peregrinus Grift

Peregrinus Proteus, the main character of this short story, hailed from Parium, a city in modern-day Turkey. According to some modern reconstructions of his life story, Proteus (as he either preferred to be called or changed his name to) was born in 95 CE. Accused of the murder of his own father around the age of 25-30, he ran away from home and found financial support from the Christians in Palestine. The Christian community, filled with extremely gullible people, saw him as a great philosopher on par with Socrates and gave him positions of authority for some time. As Lucian says, Proteus also interpreted, wrote, and edited religious books for the Christians. Near the end of Lucian's tale, it mentions that Proteus also wrote many letters addressed to famous cities.

Eventually, his grift of the Christians came to an end when they supposedly saw him eating food they frowned upon and they banished him from the community.

There are three independent sources for Proteus, with only Lucian telling the story of his swindling of the "simple folk." As far as we can tell, there's nothing pointing to the date of 95 CE for his birth. It's merely an estimate. Only two parts of his story are corroborated with dated history. The first is his run-in with Herodes Atticus, a consul in Rome beginning in 143 who lived from 101 to 177. During the Olympic festival of 157, Proteus spoke ill of Herodes' newly installed aqueduct. The second is his death in 165, when he held a public funeral procession for himself, and then burned himself to death on a pyre at the Olympic festival in 165. With just two things in 157 and 165 to go off of, it is nearly impossible to date the rest of his travels and life events.

Seeing as the crowd at the 157 festival chased after him and hurled stones at him in protest of his anti-aqueduct speech, he must have not been too terribly old in order to run away, as Lucian claims he did. We estimate Proteus' death to be around 60 years of age, shifting what has (quite arbitrarily) been constructed as his life's timeline. Some historians have posited his imprisonment, which was for reasons unknown and sometime after meeting the Christians, had to do with the Bar Kokhba Revolt. There is no evidence that his connection with the Christians was during this time, so in lieu of proof of his time in Palestine being during the revolt, it follows that he was with the Christians during the 140s.

In our theory, the 140-150 timeframe is the decade when all of Christianity starts to really take off. New books are written, letters are faked, and history is invented. Some books such as Proto-Mark and some of Paul's "authentic" letters are already around, but they start to get their edits, additions, and retractions during this period.

With all that being said, while Lucian may have mentioned the Christians, in no way was he writing a well-researched record of people who may or may not have existed 150 years prior. Proteus, however, gives us better insight into one of Christianity's earliest periods, with plenty of secondhand embarrassment for the "poor wretches." To top it off, Peregrinus Proteus' brush with the Christian community may be much more revealing than previously thought.

There are some researchers, dating back to 1892, who suspect Proteus' handprint is still seen in early church history, even indirectly impacting the New Testament. Ignatius, an early Christian writer whose death is traditionally dated to 108 CE, has quite a few similarities with Proteus. The dating of his death was first proposed by the oft-perfidious Eusebius, writing in roughly 300. Scholars now place the supposed death of Ignatius around 140.

According to church tradition, Ignatius was arrested by government officials and taken from Antioch, where he was a bishop (located in modern-day Turkey), to Rome for his execution. While his transport from Antioch to Rome in lieu of a swift and local punishment is already strange and still perplexes scholars today, what's even stranger is the farewell tour his captors allow for him to make. He apparently stops in multiple cities along the way, is allowed to give speeches and write to congregations, and in some cases, is able to meet one-on-one with other Christians. We couldn't find any other instance where a prisoner was given the freedom to communicate with his comrades in this manner. Meanwhile, Proteus, according to Lucian, would have gone through a very similar path on his way back to his home in Parium, which he arrived at after being imprisoned. Not to mention, Lucian said that Proteus wrote many letters to famous cities during his life. Could Ignatius have actually been Proteus? The Christians may have wanted to use his work but remove his name and specific story from the documents.

As the icing on the cake, the name Ignatius appears to be a nickname, as he would have been from Antioch with a Greek name and Ignatius is a Latin name - Latin for "fiery one." Could that be a reference to the eventual death of Proteus? The theory was first proposed in 1892 by Daniel Völter, a Dutch-German writer who died in 1942, but the theory never seemed to take hold in academia. It's also possible the theory was swept to the side during the growing political tensions between the Western and Eastern world of that time.

The Völter scenario is an interesting example of the unfortunate overlap of religious belief, historical study, and reality. In this instance, the politics of the world's largest nations caused a potentially important hypothesis to fall into the cracks. Time and time again, I've come across historical articles and archaeological discoveries viewed exclusively through the lens of religion. Though the stories in the Bible, Quran, and Torah are laced with supernatural claims, the experts who present something contradicting the traditional religious view have to treat the arguments as valid as any other. While I'm not arguing against listening to all points of view, if something isn't even close to accurate, science needs to move on without it. Sometimes that makes people feel uncomfortable, but the truth is important.

Jaaron Wingo

Peregrinus Proteus, whether his story as told by Lucian be real or fake, seems to at the very least show the gullibility of the Christians: casting doubt on anything and everything they wrote and believed in. We cannot say for certain if his involvement is still preserved in the writings of "Ignatius," but one could absolutely make an argument for it. Lucian and Proteus are yet again proof of our theory, showing Christianity to be a second-century religion.

"Didn't Suetonius write about Jesus?"

Suetonius, coming in either second or third for the most popular ancient historian quoted by historicists, has just two sentences written in his *Lives of the Twelve Caesars* (published 121 CE) that get quoted. The most commonly quoted statement (with context) is as follows:

During his reign many abuses were severely punished and put down, and no fewer new laws were made: a limit was set to expenditures; the public banquets were confined to a distribution of food; the sale of any kind of cooked viands in the taverns was forbidden, with the exception of pulse and vegetables, whereas before every sort of dainty was exposed for sale. Punishment was inflicted on the Christians, a class of men given to a new and mischievous superstition. He put an end to the diversions of the chariot drivers, who from immunity of long standing claimed the right of ranging at large and amusing themselves by cheating and robbing the people. The pantomimic actors and their partisans were banished from the city.

Again, as we've pointed out before while explaining the "Synonym Problem," the mentioning of Christ and of Christians doesn't mean that Jesus is the worshiped character behind it all. Before we go into detail regarding Suetonius, let's revisit the aforementioned Synonym Problem in depth.

The Synonym Problem: Evolution of (a) Man

Christianity existed prior to the story of Jesus ever hitting paper or entering the minds of the early church leaders. We know this because multiple Ancient Roman authors talk about Christians - and even share their beliefs - without ever saying the name Jesus. We don't see the name Jesus mentioned in a non-interpolated secular document until at least the third century!

Most historicists find this hard to understand. How can you have Christianity without Jesus? It's simple. The early Christians didn't have a gospel narrative. Jesus' teachings weren't necessarily the first of their kind. The writings of the great Greek philosophers Plato, Socrates, and Aristotle were hundreds of years old by this point. The Jews had multiple "messiahs" who came and went, each with their own leadership style. Some were militant revolutionaries, and some were preaching rabbis. There were even a couple named Jesus. Some are recorded in the intertestamental (the centuries between the Old and the New Testaments) books of the Maccabees.

John the Baptist had followers. The Gospels mention this as a way to get his followers to accept the teachings of a different cult. His followers surely believed him to be the Messiah as well, or, at the very least, they viewed him as some supernatural reincarnation of a previous Jewish prophet. You don't get followers like that without them putting you on an incredibly high pedestal. That pedestal was so high even the Christians had to recognize and respect it, hoping the entire time that they could sway his followers into their camp.

Another messiah was the Teacher of Righteousness. Predating Jesus by at least 100 years, he was a religious leader from Judaea, who was said to fulfill prophecies of Isaiah. His followers believed that after his death he had been exalted to the throne of God. Interestingly enough, similar to the story of Jesus, his followers believed that he would come back in 40 years. Presumably because of the vastly superior logic of his followers, once he didn't return, his following faded away. His teachings survive in fragments and mentions of him in other texts, but there is reason to believe that his teachings made it into the gospels either through osmosis or through more blatant, direct rip-offs.

The term Christ means "Messiah," or "anointed." The word Christ would have been used for realistically any leader, depending on if people felt the leader was appointed by God. King David, for instance, would have been a Christ.

Taking the word Christian to mean "anointed ones," any cult that practiced anointing of its members could have been called Christians as well. According to a quote from a much later scribe, Emperor Hadrian, in a letter to a friend in Alexandria, Egypt around 135 CE, wrote:

The Egyptians, whom you are pleased to commend to me, I know thoroughly from a close observation, to be a light, fickle, and inconstant people, changing with every turn of fortune. The Christians among them are worshippers of Serapis, and those calling themselves bishops of Christ scruple not to act as the votaries of that God. The truth is, there is no one, whether Ruler of a synagogue, or Samaritan, or Presbyter of the Christians, or mathematician, or astrologer, or magician, that does not do homage to Serapis.

Interestingly enough, a little over two decades prior, the Ancient Roman historian Tacitus claimed in *Histories* (110 CE) that the worship of Serapis in Alexandria was due to the god being brought down to Egypt from Sinope. Remember, Sinope (in modern-day Turkey) is where Marcion, the theologian who introduced the first New Testament collection in 144, was from. In this explanation, he states that Vespasian, the Roman Emperor from 69 to 79 CE who spared the life of Josephus, was in Alexandria during the year 70. Tacitus tells of a "miracle" Vespasian performed that seems oddly similar to some in the gospels:

In the course of the months which Vespasian spent at Alexandria, waiting for the regular season of summer winds when the sea could be relied upon, many miracles occurred. These seemed to be indications that Vespasian enjoyed heaven's blessing and that the gods showed a certain leaning towards him. Among the lower classes at Alexandria was a blind man whom everybody knew as such. One day this fellow threw himself at Vespasian's feet, imploring him with groans to heal his blindness. He had been told to make this request by Serapis, the favourite god of a nation much addicted to strange beliefs. He asked that it might please the emperor to anoint his cheeks and eyeballs with the water of his mouth. A second petitioner, who suffered from a withered hand, pleaded his case too, also on the advice of Serapis: would Caesar tread upon him with the imperial foot? At first Vespasian laughed at them and refused. When the two insisted, he hesitated. At one moment he was alarmed by the thought that he would be accused of vanity if he failed. At the next, the urgent appeals of the two victims and the flatteries of his entourage made him sanguine of success. Finally he asked the doctors for an opinion whether blindness and atrophy of this sort were curable by human means. The doctors were eloquent on the various possibilities. The blind man's vision was not completely destroyed, and if certain impediments were removed his sight would return. The other victim's limb had been dislocated, but could be put right by correct treatment. Perhaps this was the will of the gods, they added; perhaps the emperor had been chosen to perform a miracle. Anyhow, if a cure were effected, the credit would go to the ruler; if it failed, the poor wretches would have to bear the ridicule. So Vespasian felt that his destiny gave him the key to every door and that nothing now defied belief. With a smiling expression and surrounded by an expectant crowd of bystanders, he did what was asked. Instantly the cripple recovered the use of his hand and the light of day dawned again upon his blind companion. Both these incidents are still vouched for by eye-witnesses, though there is now nothing to be gained by lying.

It truly is a breath of fresh air to read about a miracle explained in natural ways and chalked up to good ol' pageantry and trust in the advice of medical experts - even if it is a story about a lying politician. This is not the first time a "miracle" is done in the name of Serapis. Another scene had a politician cured by a priestess of Serapis placing mud made from dirt and spit onto an injured leg. The Gospels take stories like these and add them into the narrative.

Obviously, this book is not about denouncing the supernatural things Jesus is said to have done, but explaining where these ideas come from is paramount to explaining away even the most natural bits of the story. Besides, there is no evidence of an early Christian leader who believed in the natural Jesus without the supernatural. To them, it was all the same. Their ability to reason was flawed from the get go. Reconstructing a natural Jesus is a fairly recent idea, compared to the thousands of years he has been worshiped as a god. Not to mention, explaining *when* the sources for the Gospels came about is imperative to our theory.

We have one final note on the Synonym Problem. It's possible the term "Christian" could have simply meant something along the lines of "messianic extremists." Our reasoning for this possibility stems from the idea that Nero could have used the term "Christian" to mean militant Jews who were causing issues in Rome. That would give an alternate explanation to the problem of "how was Nero able to recognize the difference between Christians and Jews after the Great Fire in Rome in 64 CE, even given the mainstream dating of the New Testament?"

The only issue we have with this "extremist" theory is that, yet again, Pliny and Trajan would have heard the term and both should have known who the Christians were in 111.

We propose a variation on the theory could potentially be the reason for Nero's hatred. It's possible that the fire in Rome was caused by (or at least blamed on) a sect of extremist Jews (like the very violent Jewish group at the time named the Sicarii), and when Tacitus spoke to Christians regarding the beginning of their new cult, he drew a conclusion that they may have been the extremist sect who was responsible. It's even possible that later Christians took credit for it, and added it to their history as a badge of honor, venerating the martyrs. Revisionist history was absolutely rampant during the creation of the Torah, the New Testament, and Christian history, so some form of this could definitely be true. Unfortunately, we may never know. All we know is that Christianity seemed to evolve out of different cults around the Empire sometime around the early second century, merging into one thanks to Proto-Mark (the first Gospel written) and its subsequent adaptations.

Remember, all of this assumes that there are no interpolations.

An E for an I

Let's return to Suetonius again. The second potential mention of Christians is found in an even more obscure way. Here is the statement:

Since the Jews constantly made disturbances at the instigation of Chrestus, [Emperor Claudius] expelled them from Rome.

Here we have another case of the Synonym Problem in action. Just because it mentions Jews and someone named Chrestus, that doesn't mean it's a mention of Christians. In fact, there are only a few ways this line can even be taken.

Most modern scholars now assume Chrestus was an unknown instigator in Rome at that time (49 CE). The evidence for this assumption is very strong. Suetonius probably wouldn't have made the spelling error (Chrestus instead of Christus) if he knew that these people were Christians - who he *potentially* mentions with the correct spelling in his other statement we already touched on. He also mentions Jews here, while he doesn't mention Jews at all in his other statement. If he believed the Christians were just a sect of Judaism or an offshoot who simply followed another Jew named Chrestus, it seems odd that Jews weren't mentioned in the other statement.

We'll have more on this in a moment, but there's a good chance the original text from Suetonius said Chrestians instead of Christians, which, at least at the time, meant something different. Finally, due to the utter ignorance of Christianity's existence displayed by Pliny and Emperor Trajan in 111, any mention of the Roman government's knowledge of Christianity (in Rome, of all places) during the first century is simply anachronistic.

As you'll read later in Chapter 5, the name Chrest (Chrestos, not Chrestus) was sometimes used instead of Christ, but Chrest was also found within Jewish apocalyptic literature as well. It's also possible that these followers of a Chrest may have been a cult that would later merge with others to evolve into Christianity as we know it in the second century. All this to say that the Chrestus mentioned here is not the Christ you're looking for.

"Didn't Mara bar Serapion mention Jesus in a letter?"

The Syriac letter of Mara bar Serapion is dated anywhere from 73 CE to the third century. The passage in his letter is as follows:

What advantage did the Athenians gain from putting Socrates to death? Famine and plague came upon them as a judgment for their crime. What advantage did the men of Samos gain from burning Pythagoras? In a moment their land was covered with sand. What advantage did the Jews gain from executing their wise king? It was just after that their Kingdom was abolished. God justly avenged these three wise men: the Athenians died of hunger; the Samians were overwhelmed by the sea; the Jews, ruined and driven from their land, live in complete dispersion. But Socrates did not die for good; he lived on in the teaching of Plato. Pythagoras did not die for good; he lived on in the statue of Hera. Nor did the wise king die for good; He lived on in the teaching which he had given.

The date range of this letter is very broad, and we cannot just select the earliest date. Realistically, without any other information, we should put it in the middle of the date range, around 135-175 depending on when in the third century the latest date possible could be. This more limited range works well with what some scholars, such as Etienne Nodet, who dated the text to around 165, have suggested. The content itself repeats the story that the Jews, rather than the Romans, killed Jesus, meaning we are already seeing the development of a later gospel narrative which also pushes the letter to a later date.

In terms of the "complete dispersion" discussed, this is likely a reference to either the First Jewish War or the Bar Kokhba Revolt, and if it's in reference to the latter, then that would be 135 at the earliest. The statement that their "Kingdom was abolished" sounds like a reference to Hadrian's dissolution of Judaea and creation of Roman Palestine at the end of the Bar Kokhba Revolt, too. As such, the letter dates too late to be a direct witness to Jesus, even if that is who it is talking about. It seems to talk about his death, but the details are more similar to what one would find in the second century.

"Didn't the Jewish Talmud mention Jesus?"

The references to Jesus in the Talmud are slightly less straightforward than the other references. Because Jesus derives from Yeshu, a variant of the Jewish name Joshua, there are a number of "Jesus" figures, or at least figures with a similar name or variant of the name, in the Talmud that date back all the way into the first century BCE. We have Jesus ben Pantera, Jesus Ha-Notzri, Jesus the sorcerer, Jesus who was summoned by Onkelos, a Jesus the son who burns food in public, Jesus student of Joshua ben Perachiah, and Jesus ben Stada, among other figures with variations of the name Yeshu and Joshua. Not only is this an issue with finding the historical Jesus of Christianity in the Talmud, it's made more difficult by the fact that Christians edited and censored the Talmud multiple times since the 500s.

Even if there were a reference to the Christian Jesus in the Talmud, it would've been written hundreds of years after his life, meaning it's even less reliable than our other historical sources. The content that is usually cited as a reference to Jesus, even if it was about him, contradicts what we get from Christian sources. For example, if Jesus ben Pantera is the Jesus in question, then Jesus' father was actually a Roman soldier. If this is an attack on Jesus' virgin birth, then we know the story is being written not only after the virgin birth story was added into later gospels, but also as a biased attack, meaning there is less emphasis on documenting the historical events that unfolded. Another reference says the Jesus in question had 5 disciples, and only one of those names, Matthai, is anything like the names of the disciples we hear about with the Christian Jesus. In another, Jesus is the spirit summoned during an Ebenezer Scrooge-like experience by Onkelos. The variations go on.

In short, none of the accounts were written around the time to be significant witnesses of true events, the stories vary greatly from what we expect and have quite a bit of supernatural dealings in them, and the texts were edited afterwards by Christians very heavily. The Talmud is not a witness to a historical Jesus of Christianity.

We'd like to take a moment to restate the obvious here. Outside of the religion, the name Jesus had not once been honestly written in relation to Christianity, and we have covered 150 years since his supposed death. We are well aware that the Christian religion existed, but the character was simply not invented until the early second century. If a miracle worker started his supernatural ministry during the early first century, he left an unnaturally small impact on anyone around him - which contradicts the stories. If a teacher named Jesus from Galilee preached during the early first century and amassed a following, he must have been an absolutely dreadful public speaker with a miniscule group of students, because no one even remembers his name despite remembering others. Quite frankly, if Jesus had existed in any capacity, and the Christians knew his name during the 110s, why didn't anyone tell Tacitus his real name? If they did and he just didn't add it, why didn't anyone tell Suetonius? Furthermore, why didn't Pliny get a name after literally torturing the Christians for information about their beliefs? The answer is incredibly simple: the character was still in development. Christ existed before Jesus.

The Inundation of Interpolation

Despite our assumptions of authenticity, the references in Tacitus, Suetonius, and Pliny have all been questioned at one point or another. In particular, the reference found in Tacitus has had a strong case made against it, such as in Richard Carrier's 2014 paper "The Prospect of a Christian Interpolation in Tacitus, Annals 15.44." The case is similar to that of the "James, who was a brother of Jesus, that is called the Christ" found in Josephus. While the passage as a whole is likely authentic, the insertion of Christ is added by a later Christian scribe. Just about all our manuscripts of these documents come from medieval churches, as they were often the only ones with the means and skills to make such copies at the time.

If Tacitus contains an interpolation or if a later scribe changed Chrestus, as attested to in Suetonius, to Christus, which is found in Tacitus (which we have evidence was done elsewhere), this would make everything much clearer. Both Tacitus and Suetonius would then likely be talking about a Jewish man named Chrestus, a common slave name, who started a revolt in Rome. The followers of Chrestus would have likely been called Chrestians, just as later followers of Christ would be called Christians, and the earliest manuscript we have of *Annals* clearly shows that scribes erased the "e" and put an "i" in Chrestians.

This would make a lot more sense of both the passages found in Tacitus and Suetonius, as well as help explain the spelling variations found in them. It also explains why Pliny and Trajan know little to nothing of the Christians in the early second century. These educated figures weren't uninformed or confused by spelling errors in their written documents, but knew that the Chrestus who led a revolt in Rome under Nero had nothing to do with these followers of a Christ from modern-day Turkey.

Chapter Notes

1. Olson, K. A. "Eusebius and the "Testimonium Flavianum."" *The Catholic Biblical Quarterly*, vol. 61, no. 2, 1999, pp. 305–322, www.jstor.org/stable/43723559. Accessed 13 Dec. 2023.

Eusebius had no idea how much of an impact his words would have on human history. His writings on the formation years of Christianity are often the first time stories are shared, and in some cases, the only time. If only his words weren't marred by self-admitted bias and dishonest reporting.

2. Flavius Josephus, and William Whiston. *The Works of Josephus : Complete and Unabridged*. Peabody, Mass., Hendrickson, 1988. pp. 534-535

This passage is proof that Josephus knew better than to draw the ire of the Roman government. Either his rather favorable comments regarding Christians were forged, or the stories of Nero's anti-Christian persecution were fake. Historicists can't have it both ways. It is, however, possible for both to be incorrect.

3. Hansen, Chris M. "The problem of annals 15.44: On the Plinian origin of Tacitus's information on Christians." *Journal of Early Christian History*, vol. 13, no. 1, 2 Jan. 2023, pp. 62–80

Further Reading:

1. Flavius Josephus, and William Whiston. *The Works of Josephus: Complete and Unabridged*. Peabody, Mass., Hendrickson, 1988.

   We only mention a handful of parallels with Josephus throughout this book, but we recommend reading more from Josephus' *Wars of The Jews* and *Antiquities of the Jews*. Not only would you see more parallels, but it would help give further context for the events of that era.

2. Tacitus. *Annals*. Penguin UK, 29 Nov. 2012.

3. Pliny the Younger, and P G Walsh. *Complete Letters*. Oxford, Oxford University Press, 2009.

4. Lucian. *The Works of Lucian of Samosata*. Phoemixx Classics Ebooks, 24 Dec. 2021.

5. Gaius Suetonius Tranquillus, et al. *The Twelve Caesars*. London, Penguin Books, 2007.

CHAPTER 4

The Epistles

Our next stop along the journey had us back in our Bibles. By this point, we realized there was no evidence of Jesus from the Gospels or the ancient historians, but surely there must be something from the earliest stages of Christianity. The arguments we heard from some apologists (people who try to explain and defend the Bible) seemed to make sense on the surface: "If the historians of the day had truly known about Jesus, they would have been Christians. Therefore, the writings from the earliest Christians should be seen as equal to the writings from their non-Christian counterparts."

While there are obvious problems with bias at play here, it pointed us in the direction of what is considered to be the earliest Christian documents. What did the Epistles (letters) from the early church figures such as Paul, Peter, and John have to say? Since the majority of them are traditionally considered to be written prior to the Gospels, surely they have better historical information. What follows in this chapter is what we found and more questions we have been asked from people defending the Epistles.

"Why is Paul not to be believed?"

According to tradition, the Apostle Paul is personally responsible for 13 or 14 of the 27 books in the New Testament. These books are written as letters to churches in different cities, as well as personal letters to specific people. Today, only seven of those books are considered by scholars to be "Pauline." Some, such as 19th-century German scholar Ferdinand Christian Baur, believed only four: Romans, 1 Corinthians, 2 Corinthians, and Galatians. The criteria vary for why the remaining books are not considered to be from him.

Hebrews, an anonymous text sometimes attributed to Paul, is no longer considered to be Pauline. Scholarship has long accepted that this letter might've been written to look like Paul but is not actually his, nor does it claim to be. The Pastoral Epistles, 1 Timothy, 2 Timothy, and Titus are almost universally agreed upon to have been written much later after Paul's lifetime. The vocabulary, topics, church structure, and numerous other things point to them being later writings. They also aren't included in our earliest canon lists, another sign they were created later.

Ephesians and Colossians are also broadly agreed to be inauthentic letters, as the vocabulary and sentence structure does not match the letters considered to be authentic. These letters are usually dated to several decades after Paul's life. Likewise, 2 Thessalonians is often considered to be written by a later author other than Paul for its differences in theology and style. We present our positions on each letter later in the book, though we do confirm in Chapter 8 that these letters are inauthentic.

Although he is not placed into the Gospels as one of the famed "12 disciples of Jesus," Paul's supposedly authentic writings are dated by scholars to be the earliest of all New Testament texts. Because of this, he is hailed by historicists as one of the most important people in the study of Jesus' historicity.

There are some who place his writings close to about 50-60 CE, while others place his writings as within a decade of Jesus' supposed death in roughly 30. One of the biggest factors for the earliest dating is the religiosity of the scholar: the most conservative Christians tend to place Paul as early as they can to the "source material." However, as you will soon see, the way scholars have dated Paul is extremely flawed, relies on circular reasoning, and dismisses anachronisms on its way to prop up a heavily edited text.

The Right Place - The Wrong Time

The Pauline books do not explicitly state when they were written. To get an idea of when they were composed, we have to look for any historically verifiable concepts they contain. For the highest level of accuracy, these concepts also need to be discussed by other people or groups not associated with Christianity, in an effort to minimize bias as much as possible. Outside of theological content and Christian references, there are only two, perhaps three, indications of when these letters might have been written that don't require a presumption of a date.

First, there is the Council of Jerusalem, which is assumed to be discussed in Galatians. Second, there is the reference to Illyricum in Romans 15:19. Finally, 2 Corinthians 11:32 mentions a King Aretas having authority over Damascus. Some will attempt to say the Erastus Stone is proof of Paul's dates, but this is easily dismissed by the fact that the Erastus Stone is dated using Paul, and as we discuss later, there is reason to believe that the stone was not placed and carved around the time of the traditional dating of Paul's life.

The Council of Jerusalem in 49 or 50 CE is only attested to in Acts (which we will see later is a late second-century text), and the assumption is that Paul's discussion in Galatians 2 is about this same council. There is no external evidence this council ever took place. It isn't mentioned by any of the other authors of the New Testament (including figures that were supposedly there), and the accounts in Acts and Galatians don't seem to match up. As such, this is not a reliable event we can use to date the texts. The circular reasoning for dating the event based only on internal evidence does not hold up.

Some might try to tie in figures such as Peter (or even Jesus), who are referenced multiple times in Paul's letters. Aside from the Council of Jerusalem and the other two historical markers we have, there's nothing tying in these figures to the traditional dates either. One might try to reference their appearance in the gospels, which contain more specific historical references to the first century CE, but mainstream scholars put these accounts after Paul, and we date the gospels to the second century. The later gospels contain greatly expanded stories, which built off of the letters of Paul as a source. If they were a source for the gospel stories, then the gospels stories can't then be turned around and used to validate the Pauline content.

Next, we have the reference to Illyricum in Romans. Illyricum was a Roman province along the eastern coast of the Adriatic Sea across from Italy. The region had the name at least going back to the 200s BCE when the Romans fought the Illyrian Wars up until the early first century CE when the then Roman province was dissolved. It was then split into two differently named provinces after a rebellion by the locals (similar to how Emperor Hadrian later renamed Judaea to Syria Palestina after the Bar Kokhba Revolt). While we don't know exactly when Illyricum was divided into Dalmatia and Pannonia, it's clearly within the first decade of the turn of the millennium. We get references to the first Governor of Dalmatia in 9 or 10 CE in the writings of Velleius Paterculus, an author who wrote until his death in 31 CE.

Lists of subsequent governors also indicate an independent province by this time, with a military commander of Dalmatia being placed as early as 9 CE, right after a large-scale rebellion caused the province of Illyricum to be split. The problem, however, is that Paul is supposed to be writing this letter around 58-59 CE, well after Illyricum was divided. As such, this is evidence against Paul's letters having been written around the mainstream dates. The provincial name Illyricum hadn't been in use for over half a century.

Finally, we get reference to Paul's experience when "in Damascus the governor under Aretas the king" tried to apprehend him. This is often used by Christians who point to Aretas IV, reigning Nabatean king from 9 BCE to 40 CE, as validating Paul's mainstream dates. However, both the written historical record and archaeological record show that Aretas IV never had control over Damascus.

Aretas III, ancestor of Aretas IV, did have control of Damascus during his reign. Aretas III reigned from 84 BCE to around 59 BCE, and held Damascus for most of his reign. There was a three-year period between 72 BCE to 69 BCE when King Tigranes II of Armenia occupied it however, and then Aretas III effectively lost it to the Romans around 63 BCE. The story provided in Paul's own letters - not only in 2 Corinthians but also in Galatians, where Paul goes into Arabia but then returns to Damascus - matches Aretas III much better and doesn't require jumping through any hoops. It only requires reconsidering the original dating of Paul himself, which, as established, is only put in the first century CE due to tradition and references to Jesus.

Using just these few data points that are usually used to date Paul to the traditional dates for his life, we find that a BCE date for the author is actually more likely. In fact, a BCE date for Paul can be both internally consistent and match a significant amount of content and themes in Paul's letters. While we know the letters went through multiple rounds of revisions by authors after his death, many of these themes, just like the references to Illyricum and Aretas III, still linger. The only alternative would be a much later author, perhaps in the second century, being so far removed from Paul's supposed lifetime that they make such grave errors that the "facts" about his life put him a century too early.

These two references give us a starting point to narrow down when Paul actually lived if he was truly a historical figure. We know from Galatians 1 and 2 Corinthians 11 that Paul was possibly active during the reign of Aretas III and it seems more specifically that this is a reference to when Aretas III lost control of Damascus around 72 BCE. While Paul was obviously old enough to be in trouble with the authorities, this is the start of his story in terms of what we have access to. We know that he also has traveled to Illyricum by the time he writes in Romans, and Illyricum was probably dissolved around 9 or 10 CE after the Great Illyrian Revolt. As such, the original letters can't be dated any later than that. We now have a range based on the Pauline texts themselves for the dating of Paul, solely using internal evidence.

This really is all there is to date Paul. There's circular reasoning regarding the Council of Jerusalem and related figures, the Illyricum reference, and the Aretas reference. Of these three, two of them actually date him to a different time than tradition puts him. For someone to get it this wrong, they would almost have to be trying. It's just not possible for Paul to be writing in the middle of the first century CE and saying these things. If someone were forging this content later, though, these two historical misses are oddly close enough in time to work with each other, which seems unlikely to have been an accident. This is why we posit that while the theological content of the works were written much later, likely in the second century, there was possibly some kind of core content dating back to the first century BCE that got adapted into what we now know as Paul's letters - particularly 1 Corinthians, one segment of 2 Corinthians, and possibly Galatians and Romans. The only alternative is that all the content dates to the second century and the only historical references we get somehow miss the traditional dating for Paul but line up well a century before it.

Matthew Britt

A Soldier for "Christ"

What we will do now is attempt to reconstruct what kind of content the core of Paul's letters contains and what kind of person might have written them. Keep in mind while reading this section that the traditional dates for Paul don't seem to match the textual evidence and that the two alternatives are a possible figure in the first century BCE or a second-century figure fabricating Paul's life and somehow inaccurately placing the only two externally verifiable historical references in the first century BCE. This is just one alternative that demonstrates, using the same level of evidence (if not more) that Paul easily fits in another era.

What else can we learn from Paul's writings, using Aretas III and Illyricum as chronological landmarks? There seem to be two possibilities: either Paul was working on behalf of Tigranes II against Aretas III as a mercenary or operative around the years 72-69 BCE or Paul was active in Judaea's Hasmonean Civil War which took place from 67 to 63 BCE in which Aretas III was a major player. It is possible that Paul was a Pharisee, as it was one of the two major political groups in the region at the time, alongside the Sadducees. While we will see later that Philippians was likely written by another author than the main letters we find BCE Paul in, it makes the claim that he was a Pharisee from Israel and specifically the tribe of Benjamin. Supposing a core of BCE Paul in the core Pauline letters, this could either be another fragment that got recycled or a sign of the author or editor of Philippians reusing themes found in other letters.

The presentation of the Pharisees and Sadducees in the gospels is oversimplified. These groups were actually political affiliations with armed wings dating back to the 150s BCE with the formation of the Hasmonean dynasty in Judaea. Pharisees tended to be more popular with the masses and had a less literal interpretation of most religious traditions, whereas the Sadducees were more aligned with the aristocratic elite and had more literal interpretations of Judaism. By the time of our story around the 70s-60s BCE, the two factions were engaged in what would eventually become a civil war, with the majority of the Pharisees aligning with Judaean king Hyrcanus II, an ally of Aretas III.

According to Josephus, at the outset of the Hasmonean Civil War, the brother of Hyrcanus II, Aristobulus, usurped the throne and at a decisive battle at Jericho, many of Hyrcanus' troops switched sides. Hyrcanus retreated into the realm of Aretas III, who, after some convincing, joined sides with Hyrcanus and launched an attack into Judaea.

Aretas III would come up against the Romans near the end of the war when they headed south after defeating the Armenians, demanding that Aretas return to his own lands. Talks were held in Nabatean Damascus around 63 BCE at the insistence of Roman leader Pompey, but these talks ultimately failed and the war ended later that year, with Aretas III becoming a Roman vassal and Judaea becoming a protectorate of Rome. Hyrcanus was installed as High Priest while his lead adviser, Antipater I, father of Herod the Great, handled most of the decision-making. After several attempted rebellions, Aristobulus (and likely his family) was eventually captured and sent to Rome as a prisoner until Julius Caesar released him in 49 BCE shortly before he was poisoned by Pompey's agents.

If Paul had been involved in this, and particularly if he had originally started on the side of Hyrcanus and later changed sides, Aretas III would have reason to pursue Paul, specifically around the time of the discussions being held in Damascus if Paul were there trying to influence them in any sort of way. While this aspect is speculative, it explains how and why Paul would've been in Arabia and Damascus, why he eventually went to Jerusalem afterwards (likely toward the end of the war), and why Aretas III would have reason to pursue him.

But how does this Hasmonean Civil War combatant image of Paul fit with anything we find in the Pauline letters? It actually fits relatively well and does a good job explaining Paul's references to warfare, weaponry, and calling a handful of people "fellow soldier" throughout the letters. Instead of having to interpret these things entirely as metaphor and foreign to Paul's personality portrayed in Acts and Christian tradition, we can now understand them in a way with more explanatory power. With this perspective, we can piece together Paul's life and the setting of his original letters.

After the Hasmonean Civil War, Paul likely joined a Jewish Roman auxiliary. Returning to Paul's story in Galatians, he returns to Jerusalem after 14 years. If he joined the auxiliary around 62 BCE, joining under Pompey, this would place the date at 48 BCE. This is the date of the Battle of Pharsalus in the Roman Civil War between Julius Caesar and Pompey, with Pompey losing. As with many battles, foreign auxiliaries were given the offer of clemency in exchange for a loyalty oath to Caesar and fighting for him instead.

Jewish auxiliaries played important roles in a number of battles over the following decade or so, such as in 47 BCE when they rescued Caesar in Egypt under the leadership of Antipater I. This act resulted in Caesar granting Antipater Roman citizenship and later making him the first Roman procurator of Judaea. In the following years, his son Herod would flee to Rome around 40 BCE when Hyrcanus II was once again overthrown, with Herod appealing to Rome to restore Hyrcanus to power.

Herod and a number of Jewish forces later fought in the sea battle near Actium on the side of Mark Antony in the year 31 BCE, in which many ended up shipwrecked. Given that Paul claims to have been shipwrecked three times, a seemingly large number for a regular passage, it seems reasonable that as an auxiliary, he had taken part in this and perhaps other sea battles. The following year, Herod changed sides to support Octavian, Julius Caesar's adopted son, who later became known as Caesar Augustus, when Mark Antony lost and auxiliaries were once again granted clemency in exchange for a loyalty oath.

Speaking of Herod, this BCE dating of Paul also helps explain another reference we see in Romans where Paul greets the "Household of Aristobulus" and "Herodion, my kinsman." Within the mainstream dates of Paul, neither of these are significant or have any ties to known people. In fact, the Herodian reference almost seems counterintuitive if Paul was writing in the first century CE, given Herod's portrayal in Christian texts. But both the family of Aristobulus, brother of Hyrcanus II, and Herod the Great (prior to being known as "the Great") were in Rome around 40 BCE. The affix of "-ion" at the end of a name in Greek is just a diminutive, meaning "small" or "young," just as Marcion is "little Mark."

As for some of the recipients of Paul's letters, Judaean and Galatian auxiliaries fought together in a number of battles during this time, such as the Battle of Pharsalus in 48 BCE, Philippi in 42 BCE, Marc Antony's invasion of Parthia in 37 BCE, and the Battle of Actium in 31 BCE. Like some of the forces in the Hasmonean Civil War, the Galatian troops would switch sides to the winner at the last minute, which they did at Philippi and Actium above. Interestingly, in the letter to the Galatians, one of Paul's criticisms of the Galatians is for being fickle.

Why Corinth though? Two letters are sent to Corinth, and it's mentioned elsewhere in Paul's other letters. The city of Corinth was destroyed in 146 BCE, but in 44 BCE it was re-established and made a military colony for 16,000 colonists by Julius Caesar. If Paul was a leader or respected soldier of this time, particularly among those who settled in military colonies, then this would make sense.

It's implied that Romans is written in Corinth, and the specific indicator is a hot topic when attempting to prove the traditional dating of Paul. In Romans 16:23, we see Paul relay a greeting from Erastus, the city's *oikonomos*. This is often translated as treasurer in the passage but also translated as chamberlain or manager. Outside of the city context, it might mean a household manager, but we see in Romans that Erastus was the city *oikonomos*.

As we mentioned earlier, there is an inscription in Corinth known as the Erastus Stone.[1] This stone is often dated to the 50s CE, but the entirety of the logic to this dating is that it can't be before 44 BCE and Paul wrote about an Erastus with a similar position, therefore it must be this figure. The reality isn't as straightforward as that, though.

The inscription on the stone is written in Latin and translates to "Erastus in return for his aedileship laid the pavement at his own expense." An *aedile* is a Roman official responsible for maintenance of public infrastructure, games, and similar things. It can be debated whether two positions, Greek *oikonomos* and Latin *aedile*, were interchangeable at the time (similar inscriptions in Philadelphia and Izmir make it seem likely), but it isn't an open-and-shut case. Paul is writing to Greek-speaking people in Rome, who likely would have been familiar with the proper Latin term or at least a closer translation, but perhaps the word was chosen for a specific reason we are unaware of two millennia later.

What often goes unrecognized, though, is there is a second inscription in Corinth with the name Erastus. It may not surprise you that the reason we don't hear about this inscription is because it goes against the argument that the Erastus Stone was carved in the first century CE, because this second inscription dates to the second century CE. Discovered in 1960 near a cemetery in Corinth, the inscription is another dedication stone, this time from an Erastus Vitellius and his brother Frontinus to a deity whose name did not survive damage and weathering to the stone. The inscription matches the style of multiple nearby second-century inscriptions and is dated to that time.

This brings us back to our two possibilities: either there was a BCE figure that Paul is based on, or all of Paul is written in the second century CE. This second Erastus inscription in Corinth would seem to be a possible piece of evidence for the second-century writing of Romans, and also throws the dating of the Erastus Stone into question. We know that the only solid evidence for any date of the Erastus Stone is that it has to be after the reestablishment of Corinth in 44 BCE. But it could have been any time between 44 BCE up through a number of centuries that the stone was placed and inscribed. But we now have evidence of a figure named Erastus who had the money and interest to have a publicly displayed piece of stonework with his name inscribed on it, and this person lived in the second century CE. We then have two options: was there a figure somewhere between 44 BCE and the end of the first century CE named Erastus who also had the money and interest in carving his name into stoneworks, or is this all the same figure?

Regardless, throughout Paul, we see minor things that, when we look at it removed from 2,000 years of Christian interpretation, tip us off to the fact that there was something else going on with him than just a preacher traveling across the Roman Empire. As another example, we'll look at one of the most popular verses among American evangelical Christians, often claimed to be about the gifts from God.

More Evidence for the Mercenary of Mercy

For those from a Christian background, you're probably familiar with 1 Corinthians 12:28. It goes as follows:

And God has placed in the church first of all apostles, second prophets, third teachers, then miracles, then gifts of healing, of helping, of guidance, and of different kinds of tongues.

While we aren't going to spend too much time in Greek, it's important to show how this sentence could be (and possibly originally was) understood. We'll come back to the first part, "And God has placed in the church," at the end. You are welcome to use Strong's Concordance or any other reputable reference tool, as we have cross-referenced these to confirm their translations. The Greek transliteration looks like this: "*Kai hoys men etheto ho theos en te ekklesia, proton apostolos, deuteron prophetas, triton didaskalos, epeita dynameis, epeita charismata iamaton, antilempseis, kyberneseis, gene glosson.*"

Let's start with the Greek word *apostolos*. This can mean one of two things: messenger/envoy or naval commander. The reason for these two vastly different meanings is because of the second half of the word *stolos*. The Greek *stello*, usually considered the root of the word, means to send, and the *apo-* prefix meaning to send from, such as an envoy or messenger. The root *stolos*, however, means a fleet or expedition, with *apostolos* in such a case meaning a naval commander. Perhaps Paul, frequently referencing himself as an *apostolos*, was a naval commander. This would make sense given he seems to talk about opposing *apostolos* frequently, and complains when people (perhaps troops) say things like 1 Corinthians 1:12's "I follow Paul," "I follow Apollos," and "I follow Cephas," rather than looking at the bigger picture of who they serve.

Prophetas is similar to what we think of as prophets, but in a contemporary Greek context wouldn't have been limited to just the Judeo-Christian god. It would've been meant for one who speaks and interprets for a god, reads divine signs, and so on. Plato, as far back as in the 300s BCE, called poets "prophets of the Muses," so it was not exclusively a Jewish or Christian thing. It was also used for the official keepers of temples and oracles in some regions, as well as for the herald at the games. Proclaimer or herald would be a more neutral translation here.

Didaskalos is "teacher," "instructor," or "trainer" - very straightforward. *Dynameis* is a bit more complex. Literally, it means power, strength, or force (think dynamic or dynamite). It has as broad or broader of a meaning as these words have in English. It could mean anything from muscle strength to natural forces to military forces. It could be used to mean divine powers, which is why it is interpreted as miracles in the Christian reading. The most common uses are the ones aforementioned.

Charismata iamaton is a two-word phrase, with *charismata* meaning having received grace, favor, or something free (as in a gift) and *iamaton* meaning healing. Similar to the Christian translation, this would be something like "those who have the gift of healing," a poetic way of saying "healers."

Kyberneseis means someone in charge of steering, piloting, and guiding, sometimes used metaphorically for government. In other words, a helmsman.

Gene glosson means translators, another straightforward one. It's also important that *ekklesia*, usually translated at church, can just mean assembly.

If we rewrite this verse with these more common, less biased translations, we get the following: "And God has placed some in the assembly, first commanders; second, heralds; third, instructors; then the [military] forces; then the healers; helmsmen; and translators." This seems like a very straightforward and reasonable organization of a traveling military force, especially for the era.

Returning to the idea of God putting some in the assembly or church in these positions, it's important to note that this does not explicitly reference Jesus or Christ, but just "god" (in the original Greek, capitalization was not a practice). Not only could this be interpreted as the Jewish or Christian god putting these people here, it could also be interpreted as a general religious or superstitious statement of the time. Alternatively, if Paul were a particularly dedicated soldier and follower of the imperial cult, he could simply be saying that Caesar has structured the army as such.

We also see content in Philippians that lends credence to this BCE interpretation of Paul. In Philippians 1:13, we read about Paul being known by the whole "palace guard" (NIV), the "palace" (KJV), or "Praetorian Guard" in the ASV. This is a translation of *praitorio*, interpreted as the Praetorian Guard or Praetorium, the Governor's palace or household. This word was also used for the command center or military headquarters of a legion. It would make more sense if Paul were a soldier working in the command headquarters or even a prisoner of war and saying this than if he were just some preacher that got arrested. Neither the Praetorian Guard, governor's palace, nor the military headquarters are going to care enough about one religious radical, but they might care about a military commander.

At the end of Philippians we get the line, "All God's people here send you greetings, especially those who belong to Caesar's household." Given the tension Christians supposedly faced between the first and second century CE as well as various Roman historians and public officials seeming to know nothing about Christians until quite a bit later, it seems unlikely that there were members of Caesar's household that were on a first-name basis with Paul, the most notorious Christian.

In 42 BCE Philippi became a military colony established by Caesar Augustus (Philippi was the site of one of his major battles), seeing expansions likely after the Battle of Actium in 31 BCE, which Herod and possibly Paul participated in, and then again in 27 BCE when Augustus became emperor. This makes perfect sense for the city to be a recipient of Paul's "authentic" letters - all of them are military colonies (Corinth, Philippi) or Roman administrative cities (Rome, Thessaloniki). Even many other cities mentioned in the letters, such as Troas, were in one of these two categories. Galatians is the only "authentic" letter to not be to a city specifically, but as mentioned above, it was possibly written to soldiers of Galatian descent.

Note that Philippians is found to be by an entirely different author in our stylometric analysis in Chapter 8. What we are doing here is demonstrating how a BCE figure could've inspired or even been the source for

Paul using the standards and logic of mainstream biblical studies. Admittedly, Philippians is at least 3 letters stitched together into one, so some pieces might have been from the same source as the core letters but we were unable to analyze texts at such a small word count to say either way.

Matthew Britt

A BCE soldier Paul also explains Paul's travels. The travels we read about in Paul's letters would be very expensive, and it's unlikely that Paul was making the money needed to travel from donations from a divided church that started just a decade or two before (and particularly in areas where he is supposedly the first one to even tell people about the religion). If he were a soldier or otherwise attached to a military unit, especially during the first century BCE when there was so much going on with the various Roman wars and civil wars, it would make it much more feasible that he's been to all these places.

So, in short, who might have been this BCE Paul? He likely would have been a Jewish auxiliary soldier who fought for various Roman forces from roughly the 60s BCE to the 30s BCE. He took part in several battles alongside people from across the Roman Empire and was also in a number of sea battles, which left him shipwrecked. From the 40s to the 30s BCE, Paul wrote a number of brief letters, mostly to Roman military colonies and communities that started up around the same time period. These communities, being diverse given they were started as a reward for soldiers from around the Roman Empire, had Jewish and various Gentile members who had trouble getting along. Paul would frequently remind them that they fought under one banner and for one lord, Caesar, and they should try to get along. Toward the end of his letter-writing career (to the extent we have the evidence for it) he planned to make a trip to Spain, one of the few places there was still an opportunity for soldiers to make money as such, but his letters never indicate if he made it there or not before his death.

Just Vague Enough To Work

How would these letters end up getting used by early Christians? All our earliest manuscripts never spell out the name Jesus or the word Christ. All of them use "nomina sacra," sacred Christian runes or abbreviations, such as IS (interpreted as Jesus), KS (interpreted as lord), and XS (interpreted as Christ or Chrest depending on the sect and time - more on this in Chapter 5). This vagueness and ambiguity would have made it easy for someone finding these letters to repurpose them. Some church leaders such as Irenaeus and Origen (in his *Homilies on Luke*) even seem to make statements implying that perhaps these names or nomina sacra were the names themselves, or at least did not map on to the name Jesus directly.

Most of Paul's letters were written to either military colonies or cities with a large Roman military presence. Many of these colonies were founded around the time we speculate BCE Paul might have been active, and his messages to these burgeoning young communities worked well for the young Christian communities that were facing similar growing pains.

It's important, of course, to point out that not every verse in Paul or Paul's "authentic" letters is from the BCE time period we are suggesting. Actually, we would argue that the majority of it is not. We don't just mean the religious content, but most of all of his letters as we have them today were so heavily edited and added on to that we will likely never be able to disentangle it all. Once it became religiously significant to a new, growing religion, the existing works got rewritten extensively to the point of being so unrecognizable that people believed that the person lived over 100 or even almost 200 years later than he actually did.

We see in our stylometric analysis in Chapter 8 that 1 Corinthians, most of Romans, and parts of 2 Corinthians and Galatians seem to share an authorship community. The content in these letters outside this authorship community points to a second-century date for the compilation of these texts, if not their writing as well. Eventually, sometime in the 130s or 140s CE, Marcion collects these letters, perhaps even playing a role in their creation himself, and publishes them around 144 as part of a Christian canon.

The content of Paul's letters is used to fill out stories about who Christian Paul was as the proto-Catholic groups relatively unfamiliar with Paul (note that extensive writers such as Justin Martyr, writing in the 150s, never mentions the name Paul or even quotes from his letters) try to Catholicize him and make him their own. Figures from the letters are used to create Acts, an extensive attempt to rectify the various sects and make Paul an apostle in line with the teachings of the Roman churches.

Some figures might've even made their way into the gospels - it's possible that figures such as James and Peter first made their appearance in Paul's letters, for example. We have no other earlier mention of either of them. The only possible reference to a gospel character that has appearances that might be earlier is quite a stretch. Though John is not mentioned, Mark is mentioned in Paul, and Acts (written around the 150s-160s) calls him John Mark. If these two figures were the same person, then perhaps we could identify someone in Christianity that predates Marcion's Paul letters, but otherwise we are left wanting.

The traditional Christian dates for Paul are untenable to a number of accounts. While an original BCE Paul has much more explanatory power for some of the particularities within the texts, there is one alternative explanation: Paul never existed at all. In such a case, the reference to Aretas and Illyricum would be accidental anachronisms due to a misinformed author attempting to pass off his character as living in a distant past, much like the gospel writers did with Jesus.

Paul Replaces Paul

Most of what we know of Paul's life and background comes from Acts. Written by the same author as the Gospel of Luke, Acts is an attempt to cover what some of the earliest Christians did during the decades following the supposed death of Jesus. Paul, left out of the Gospel story because the first one was written prior to the "discovery" of his letters, becomes the focal point of a large portion of the book.

Just as the author of Luke brought a strong effort of historicity to his Gospel with the highest number of known historical figures named in the story, Acts has name drops and cameos galore. The disciples, along with Paul, perform healings, preach in churches around the Empire, baptize people, and escape from prisons all within 28 chapters. Unfortunately, the Paul being presented in Acts doesn't line up with the Paul known throughout his letters.

Despite being heavily edited after their creation, the letters of Paul still have a core written by a main character whose doctrine differs heavily from the Paul found in Acts. The reason for this is the late second-century church leaders' desire to change the theology of a beloved character to fit their views.

I struggled throughout the research process with BCE Paul. Clearly, the letters are not dated to the traditional dates of Paul's life, and the only internal dating references seem to be pushing the content into the BCE era.

To me, though, it was odd that some of these themes continued even in letters we know are later forgeries. This would either be proof against BCE Paul or evidence of later authors picking up themes and vocabulary in order to copy the style of "original Paul." But Illyricum and Aretas III are such glaring errors that it seems unlikely that the person putting them in would not only get them wrong, but get them wrong in a way that lines up together. By the admittedly low standard of contemporary biblical studies that uses these kinds of clues as evidence of more traditional dates for Paul, I think it's fair to say that given they can also posit a BCE date for Paul puts the dates up in the air at the very least. This is why external and physical evidence is so important for the study of history.

Matthew Britt

Twilight of the Apostle

Now that we have seen that the dates for Paul are up in the air, we return to the issue of authenticity. Mainstream biblical scholarship generally considers all the rest of the New Testament to not be written by the people they are attributed to. The apostle Matthew did not write the Gospel of Matthew, the evangelist and student of Paul named Luke did not write the Gospel of Luke, and so on. Even with close to half of Paul's letters, they admit inauthenticity. Why, then, when the trend for 20 of the 27 books and the hundreds of apocryphal Christian texts is an exception, is a case of special pleading made for the remaining 7 letters of Paul? The answer is because, for most scholars, he is the last link to anyone who wrote anything that might have lived near the time of a historical Jesus.

The reality is, though, that even within the "authentic" writings of Paul, the problems are so extensive that the position of a historical first-century author behind them all is hardly tenable. All the "letters" are actually longer than many books of the time. His longest letter, that of Romans, is being sent before he arrives. Why not just wait until he gets there or send a short letter to tell them he is on the way with things to discuss? Instead, it seems he would rather spend the time and money (writing and sending letters could be an expensive project in Antiquity) to send what amounts to the size of a book at the time. Even the shortest "authentic" letter, Philippians, is around three to four times longer than the average letter of the era.

We also know that 2 Corinthians and Philippians are clearly composite letters - multiple letters compiled into a single one. It looks like Galatians is the same. Some consider both Thessalonian letters to be composite letters as well. Letters stitched together would indicate later editing and piecing together, and is unlikely to have been done by Paul himself. Similar signs of later editing and false authorship include the "signatures" added, such as in Galatians 6:1 and 1 Corinthians 16:21. When this appears in Colossians, 2 Thessalonians, and elsewhere scholars argue that it is proof of forgery, but this is rarely, if ever, applied to these letters. The similarity between these and other "authentic letters" means that it would jeopardize the entirety of Paul, and thus, the sentence is ignored. Furthermore, if he had to prove his authenticity to the readers, then this implies he was well-renowned enough during his life that there was a threat of fake letters. How, then, do we not hear about him from any other author for nearly 100 years after when he supposedly lived?

In multiple instances, the real author (or authors) slips up and reveals that "Paul" is not who he claims to be. In Galatians 2:6, he uses the past tense to talk about Peter and the other apostles as if they are gone, but Paul is supposed to be writing when they were almost all still alive. Elsewhere similar phrases like "when I was with you" also hint that the story is being projected into the past. The author(s) also uses phrases like "Greeks and barbarians," a dichotomy only used by Gentile Greeks, not by Jews, which Paul was supposed to have been. The real author, a non-Jewish Greek, slipped up and fell out of character for a moment. Another example is how parts of 1 Thessalonians and Romans both seem to show knowledge of the destruction of Jerusalem in 70, or perhaps even the failure of the Bar Kokhba Revolt in 136. Neither of these events happened within the lifetime of Paul. The list goes on.

Even the name Paul, meaning "the small one" or "the humble one," seems to be an ironic choice by the creator of the fictional apostle. Paul is anything but humble, and we can see him brag throughout every letter. Even his openings to his letter brag even more than figures such as Cicero and many Roman emperors would. We get things such as "Paul, a servant of Christ Jesus, called to be an apostle and set apart for the gospel of God..." whereas others would simply say "Cicero greets" or "Trajan to..." This seems to be another indication of a later author applying these titles to Paul. And Paul, of course, is anything but "small" - he claims to have received the gospel directly from Christ himself and is supposedly responsible for founding most of the major churches across modern-day Turkey and Greece.

Furthermore, second-century issues permeate all of Paul's letters, particularly the supposedly authentic ones. Gnosticism, which the majority of scholars and even writers of the time consider to be a second-century trend, is found throughout Paul's letters. It is both argued for and against, sometimes in the same letter. Issues like food restrictions, circumcision, the place of Jewish Law, and other topics found in Paul likewise make sense in the context of the second century - not just because these issues were relevant after the destruction of Judaea in 136 but also because these were the exact points of disagreement later church leaders say the Roman church had with Marcion.

Even the third-century church leader Tertullian, in his Book 5 of *Against Marcion*, puts forward a case for Paul having been made up by Marcion. In fact, his only reason for not fully believing that is because he has the second-century book of Acts and his own "correct" version of Paul's letters (which turn out to be versions expanded and edited by other more orthodox church authors). This also isn't mentioning the extensive interpolations and later additions found throughout the supposedly authentic letters in the versions we have today. It seems that the only reason Paul's writings were accepted by the church is because they got away with editing them heavily enough to hide the Marcionite core of them.

Then there are the suspicious parallels between Marcion's life story and that of Paul. Both are born in modern-day Turkey to Greek-speaking families and educated well enough to write. Both spend their adult lives traveling and establishing churches with more or less identical theology despite being nearly a century apart. Both get into disputes with the more Jewish-leaning branches of the religion. Both also collect money for the poorer churches from the wealthier ones in modern-day Turkey - Paul for Jerusalem and Marcion for Rome. Both seem to be either rejected or not well received when doing so, and both of their stories more or less end after they travel to Rome. Paul supposedly dies there and Marcion, after being excommunicated from the Roman church in 144, disappears into history. All we have is a passing reference in Tertullian saying he returned to Rome and admitted he was wrong, but this seems to be a falsified story attempting to show the correctness of Tertullian's own side. It seems unrealistic that Marcion, who was clearly a busy person, would spend the time and money to attempt to recreate Paul's experience without even the guarantee of rejection to fulfill his parallel journey. However, it doesn't seem as far-fetched that Marcion had his story projected back in time onto Paul, especially considering he is the first person to compile and present the letters that we know of. In such a case, Paul was modeled after Marcion, not the other way around.

Of course, textual interpretation is one of the least reliable forms of evidence and nearly every perspective has been argued using it when it comes to the Bible. Fortunately, as we will see in Chapter 8, we have data science on our side. There are only four letters even potentially written by the same author: 1 Corinthians, 2 Corinthians, Romans, and Galatians, and each of these also appear to have entire sections written by other people. Paul, it seems, was not a first-century individual but a second-century group effort by a Marcionite school that produced some of the first Christian literature. The first-century figure of Paul, as with so many other characters found in the Bible, existed only on paper.

"Why aren't Peter or John's letters trustworthy?"

Before we can discuss the authenticity of the letters of Peter and John, we must look into who they were, and, more importantly, who they weren't. Pardon the sidestep in our explanation, but we take a similar approach to the question of the historical Moses. While the ancient Jews as a whole weren't enslaved at the time the book of Exodus claims they were, it's possible a Semitic group of people who *did* live among the Egyptians left the country and became part of the Jewish people. It's possible that the group had a leader named Moses and their stories just got absorbed with all the other formation myths of the ancient Jews. It's obvious that the character of Moses was highly revered, but there's no evidence he ever existed.

The same goes for the majority of the disciples. Peter and John seem to be standouts, with early church writers claiming other prior leaders were students of John, and Peter being woven into the fictional stories of Paul thanks to Epistle edits and the multiple "Acts" books. There are possible connections with a Simon (according to the gospels Peter was a nickname Jesus gave to his disciple Simon) and a John found within Josephus' *Wars of the Jews.* According to Josephus, they were commanders of the Jewish rebels, and the commander named Simon changed his appearance after the fall of Jerusalem in an attempt to claim not to be involved with the military.

We've mentioned the Gospels lifting people and stories from Josephus' works quite a bit so far in this book, and for good reason: the lifting is so widespread it borders on downright plagiarism. But getting away with it wasn't as hard as one might imagine. According to experts, only an estimated 1 - 3% of Judaea at the time could read or write, and very few people could have written a long biographical work connecting prophecies and introducing doctrine.[2,3] Though we consider the author of Acts to be writing nothing more than historical fiction, in Acts 4:13, he claims Peter and John to both be "unlearned and ignorant," or as the original Greek says, "illiterate" (agrammatoi).

Not only is this problematic for the potential authors of the New Testament, but the readers as well. The Gospels weren't written with the expectation that everyone would be able to read them. The authors knew the only people who read them would pick up on borrowed elements and tropes. If the author of Mark wrote Josephus' story of Simon into his gospel, the author of Matthew may have noticed where the story came from and didn't really care that it was originally from Josephus' book. Ultimately, the illiterate folk to whom they were spreading the story wouldn't know about what a Jewish commander supposedly did some 80 years prior, so why does it matter? It was a seemingly perfect lie, and, to be fair, it has worked thus far.

So were Peter and John historical people? It's rather unlikely, but it depends on how much of church tradition you apply. As very early leaders somewhere along the evolution of Christianity, they may have existed. If you try to make them fit into the "disciples of Jesus in 30 CE turned authors of New Testament books turned teachers of second-century church leaders" concept, they fall apart. Stretching their lives so far doesn't seem to add up, due to the potential claims of illiteracy of Peter and the aging mental capacities for John. However, it appears a church leader named John (or someone eventually labeled erroneously as John the disciple) *may* have existed somewhere in the early to mid-second century. We'll discuss the evolution of Christianity in more detail in Chapter 6, and we'll explain the problems with the Catholic Epistles (from James, Peter, John and Jude) extensively in Chapter 8.

"Why is James, the brother of Jesus, not to be believed?"

James, the so-called brother of Jesus, is where things get interesting. He is used as the "gotcha" moment - the single greatest argument for a historical Jesus that scholars have. When questioned about Jesus or Paul, they point to James.

The idea of James being the brother of Jesus is quite the game changer, as without him in the mix, we have no texts that would have been written by someone who personally knew Jesus.

Unfortunately for historicists, there's very little documentation that ties James to Jesus. The Epistle near the end of the New Testament that bears his name is undoubtedly a second-century forgery (as we'll discuss in Chapter 8), but the remaining connections to Jesus are tenuous at best. In fact, his relationship with Jesus is debated among different groups of Christians today.

For instance, many Catholics believe that Mary was a virgin for her entire life, and therefore don't want James to be a full-blood brother of Jesus. Instead, they opt to believe he was a step brother or a cousin. The idea that he was Jesus' brother stems from a mention in Galatians 1:18-20:

Then after three years, I went up to Jerusalem to get acquainted with Cephas and stayed with him fifteen days. I saw none of the other apostles—only James, the Lord's brother. I assure you before God that what I am writing you is no lie.

Putting aside the apparent suspicion of randomly clarifying that you're not lying to your reader, we can further examine this verse by referring to a couple of other sources. The Gospel of Mark mentions a James as a brother of Jesus in Mark 6:3 (along with a Simon, Jude, and Joses), but Jesus turns down his family in favor of his followers in Mark 3:31-35:

Then Jesus' mother and brothers arrived. Standing outside, they sent someone in to call him. A crowd was sitting around him, and they told him, "Your mother and brothers are outside looking for you."

"Who are my mother and my brothers?" he asked.

Then he looked at those seated in a circle around him and said, "Here are my mother and my brothers! Whoever does God's will is my brother and sister and mother."

This story is repeated in multiple later gospels as well. Earlier in that chapter, in verse 21, most translations of the Bible say Jesus' family called him crazy, but the Greek is a little ambiguous as to who actually said that. Some translations use "associates" or "friends." Either way, there is no indication that his family members were believers, and the gospel authors didn't make any allusions to his brother James (or Jude, for that matter) being later Christians.

In the Gospel of John, it says, "For even his own brothers did not believe in him." This shows us that not even the later gospel authors were aware of the James/Jesus connection. In multiple instances, the author of John explained who certain characters in his gospel were and what they went on to do after Jesus' life. Unsurprisingly, the author of John never mentions that James would eventually come around to the idea of Christianity.

All of these facts point to the idea that if there was a James who was influential in the beginning stages of Christianity, he wasn't a brother of Jesus. Peter and John, as we mentioned above, might have been actual church leaders in the developing stages of Christianity at the beginning of the second century. If that's the case, they both received cameos in the gospels as disciples. It would only make sense that a historical James would have been awarded the same gesture.

In all three Synoptic Gospels, a supernatural event called the Transfiguration is presented. During this story, Jesus shines brightly with rays of light, and suddenly the Old Testament characters Moses and Elijah appear and speak with him. The voice of God is heard, and the disciples are amazed - but not all the disciples are in this story. Jesus apparently had a close bond with three of his disciples, and let them in on the best information. These three are there for the majority of gospel scenes. Dubbed "the Inner Circle" by Christians today, this small group consisted of Peter, John, and James.

It would be very odd if the Inner Circle James *wasn't* a cameo from the James that was potentially there at the beginning of Christianity. Yet again, there is a clear distinction in the gospels between the Inner Circle James and James the brother of Jesus. If there was a James involved with early Christianity (and there very well may have been), he was not the brother of Jesus.

So where did the confusion come from?

It seems that James the Inner Circle disciple and James the brother of Jesus listed in the gospels became conflated some time in the second century. During the middle of the century, books were written by warring sects of Christianity with the names of revered characters attached to them. This was done in order to gain a political or theological edge over their opponents. It's also possible that Peter, James, and John were the heads of three different Christian groups. If James can be combined with the sibling of Jesus, then surely that would be the ultimate edge.

Strangely enough, there's nothing within the book of James that alludes to the author being a literal relative of Jesus. Even the book of Jude, which is traditionally believed to be written by Jude the brother of Jesus, doesn't say the author is a "brother of the Lord." The author of Jude just claims to be the brother of James, and depending on when the book was written, that may have been enough for the readers to make a connection to Jesus.

Let's go back to Galatians 1:19. That would be quite the ace in the hole for historicists if it weren't for some major problems.

First of all, the verse likely would have been quoted by Tertullian, the third-century author and staunch defender of Christianity, when he wrote about Galatians in his book *Against Marcion*. Galatians was a part of Marcion's collection that was published in the 140s. This collection, in part, contained ten letters said to be from Paul. That seems to be the first time anyone had ever heard of them. Because Marcion was eventually considered a heretic due to his unorthodox views, later Christian authors would take shots at him, his followers, and the texts he presented.

In *Against Marcion*, Tertullian would have loved to quote Galatians 1:19 in order to show that Marcion's beloved Paul was beneath James in the hierarchy of Christianity. Alas, there is no mention of the "Lord's brother" line. It was most likely added later. This makes even more sense when you remember Marcion published Evangelion, which was based heavily on the Gospel of Mark, and the two James' were distinctly separate.

Secondly, even if someone was to argue that the "Lord's brother" line was in the original text, they would not only have to explain how the word "brother" was meant (it could have meant a fellow male Christian, as we will explain in a moment), but they'd also have to prove the original text was written early enough to even be from someone who could have met an actual brother of Jesus. If we're being honest, if the writings attributed to a man named Paul came from the 120s or later, the author didn't meet James, the Lord's brother, even if he *did* mean that James.

To wrap up the issues with the Galatians line, the word "brother" being used in the verse is also used in 1 Corinthians 9:5 in an instance that doesn't refer to James:

Don't we have the right to take a believing wife along with us, as do the other apostles and the Lord's brothers and Cephas?

The Greek word translated to brothers is *adelphoi*. The verse is mentioning that Christians can have wives like Peter and the brothers of the lord. While one could argue that the word is still separate from the apostles, the Greek text actually has the word for sister (adelphēn) right before the word for wife (gynaika). The use of the word for sister is taken metaphorically, so why not brother? The double standard is unbecoming and is based on a preconceived interpretation. This misapplied definition blossomed into later issues as well.

107

The Iniquities of Antiquities

As we stated in Chapter 3, there is a second potential reference to Jesus found in Josephus' *Antiquities of the Jews*. Below is the quote in context:

*And now Caesar, upon hearing the death of Festus, sent Albinus into Judea, as procurator. But the king deprived Joseph of the high priesthood, and bestowed the succession to that dignity on the son of Ananus, who was also himself called Ananus. Now the report goes that this eldest Ananus proved a most fortunate man; for he had five sons who had all performed the office of a high priest to God, and who had himself enjoyed that dignity a long time formerly, which had never happened to any other of our high priests. But this younger **Ananus, who, as we have told you already**, took the high priesthood, was a bold man in his temper, and very insolent; he was also of the sect of the Sadducees, who are very rigid in judging offenders, above all the rest of the Jews, as we have already observed; when, therefore, Ananus was of this disposition, he thought he had now a proper opportunity. **Festus was now dead, and Albinus was but upon the road; so he assembled the sanhedrin of judges, and brought before them the brother of Jesus, who was called Christ, whose name was James, and some others; and when he had formed an accusation against them as breakers of the law, he delivered them to be stoned**: but as for those who seemed the most equitable of the citizens, and such as were the most uneasy at the breach of the laws, they disliked what was done; they also sent to the king, desiring him to send to Ananus that he should act so no more, for that what he had already done was not to be justified; nay, some of them went also to meet Albinus, as he was upon his journey from Alexandria, and informed him that it was not lawful for Ananus to assemble a sanhedrin without his consent. **Whereupon Albinus complied with what they said, and wrote in anger to Ananus, and threatened that he would bring him to punishment for**

what he had done; on which king Agrippa took the high priesthood from him, when he had ruled but three months, and made Jesus, the son of Damneus, high priest.

In this passage, there is a James, a brother of Jesus, who is said to be stoned under the command of High Priest Ananus. The reference to "Christ" seems like a quick throwaway line, and that's part of the issue.

If you were to read the works of Josephus, it's very apparent he liked explaining foreign or interesting concepts. Dropping a quick line about this Jesus being called "the Christ" would be very interesting to both Josephus' Jewish and non-Jewish readership. He didn't explain what a "Christ" was, didn't explain who the Christians were, and even more importantly, he didn't tie in the Christ line with a callback. Josephus tended to connect passages of his works by saying a variation of "as we talked about already," similar to the first bold print portion of the quote.

No such connection is found here. If that's because the Testimonium Flavianum (discussed in Chapter 3) wasn't originally in his book, that would make some sense, but that doesn't explain why he didn't go into detail on the Christians or the word Christ here.

The biggest issue with this passage is the last bold print section. There's another Jesus in the mix here. Why does that matter? Because that Jesus is the brother of James. Why else would Jesus' appointment to the high priesthood be part of a punishment to Ananus?

Finally, if the traditional timeline of Christianity is to be believed, both the Jews and the Romans would have all but hated the Christians - to the point of violence. Why Josephus would mention Christ but not Christianity is bizarre on its own, but why the Jews would stick up for the Christians and the Roman appointed King

Agrippa would give in to their demands for a punishment drives the story off the rails.

When a Stranger Falls

The earliest Christian authors who wrote about James' death didn't even all agree on how he died. Clement of Alexandria, a Christian writer and theologian who lived from 150 to 215 CE, claimed that James was thrown off the roof of a building and beaten with a club. Other authors claimed he was pushed off the roof, but the fall didn't kill him, so he was then stoned. Josephus mentions nothing about James (and the others who were with him) being sentenced to death by falling, so it appears the death of the Christian James was still being worked out for roughly a century after the story. Sure enough, no Christian author even wrote about James' death until the late second century!

Somewhere in the late 100s, someone came across the story of a James in *Antiquities of the Jews*, and wrote in a little note about Jesus, the son of Damneus, actually being Jesus Christ. "Jesus, the son of Damneus" may have actually been the original line, and this forger may have moved that line later, since Jesus was the actual name of the new High Priest. The forger thereby created the death of James, the brother of Jesus, who was somehow simultaneously *not* a follower of Jesus according to the gospel of John (written around 165) and also so significant as a Christian leader that Ananus targeted him as public enemy number one in his first three months as high priest.

According to early Christian leaders Clement of Alexandria, Hegesippus, and Eusebius, James' death was in 69 CE and (through a judgment handed down by God) was the reason for the Roman siege of Jerusalem in 70. King Agrippa, however, infamously supported the Romans during the First Jewish Roman war, so why he would even bat an eye at the death of a Christian leader just a few years after the fire in Rome and Nero's persecution of the Christians is beyond us. Of course, it's also possible both the persecution from Nero and the James of Josephus' book being the brother of Jesus were later Christian lies created to fill timeline gaps and blame the calamity of war on the perceived persecution of their cult, but that would make the early Christians seem like fallible humans hellbent on destroying any other religion they could if they ever came to power.

For now, we'll just leave it at, "no Christian knew any brother of Jesus - James or otherwise."

"What about all the people mentioned in Acts and the Epistles?"

The amount of people mentioned in the non-Gospel New Testament books is staggering, and one would be right to assume the authors were painting a picture of a religion that was extremely popular among the Jews and the Gentiles of the first-century Roman Empire. Unfortunately, the concept of a wildly popular religion doesn't line up with history or logic.

Timothy, a character from the story of Paul, is said in 2 Timothy 1:5 to have had both a mother and a grandmother who were Christians. The faith assumed to now be in Timothy is spoken of in the past tense for his grandmother (and possibly his mother as well). While his grandmother could have been a convert shortly before her death, the verse implies that Christianity would have been around for quite some time and doesn't really make much sense. Below is the passage in question in context:

I thank God, whom I serve, as my ancestors did, with a clear conscience, as night and day I constantly remember you in my prayers.

Recalling your tears, I long to see you, so that I may be filled with joy. I am reminded of your sincere faith, which first lived in your grandmother Lois and in your mother Eunice and, I am persuaded, now lives in you also.

For this reason I remind you to fan into flame the gift of God, which is in you through the laying on of my hands.

This leads us to another point. The second-century church fathers were nearly all converts of some kind. Obviously there are going to be converts in a new religion, but for nearly all the church leaders to be converts seems odd. Why a religion that has apparently been around for over a hundred years by 150 CE would still be consistently placing people new to the religion in positions of authority is strange. It clearly points to a religion that was recently created, and therefore didn't have as many people being raised in it as children.

This is another place where our theory of Christianity being a "second-century religion" makes the most sense. Pliny the Younger and Emperor Trajan didn't even know who the Christians were in 111 CE, so it only logically follows that most of the leaders in the few decades to follow were recent converts to what Suetonius called "a new and mischievous superstition."

There are plenty of historical figures mentioned along the way, but the authors, either due to running out of names or due to giving away cameos for clout, mention a good number of second-century Christians as well. These are anachronisms, and prove that the books are being written/edited so long after their presented stories they should be dismissed as evidence for the authenticity of Jesus. Here are just a few of the anachronistic cameos found in the New Testament:

Pauline Texts:

Appelles:

A Gnostic (Gnosticism was a second-century Christian movement that was considered heretical) student of Marcion mentioned by Eusebius.

Aquila:

A translator of the Hebrew Bible into Greek who was actively writing during the second century, commonly known as Aquila of Sinope.

Crescens:

A Scribe or assistant of Polycarp in Polycarp's letter written in the second half of the second century.

Hermas:

The brother of Pope Pius I and the writer of Shepherd of Hermas, usually dated to the second century.

Onesimus:

A bishop mentioned in Ignatius' letters.

Philetus:

The Bishop of Antioch around the time of St. Hippolytus (another bishop who died around 236 CE), according to Eusebius.

Rufus:

A Christian mentioned in the Epistle of Polycarp.

Acts:

Dionysius:

Heralded as Saint Dionysius of Corinth, he was bishop of Corinth in 171 CE. In Acts, he is said to be a member of the Areopagus in Athens, one verse before they go to Corinth.

Publius, the chief official of Malta:

A Christian who died around 160-180 CE according to an Epistle of Dionysius of Corinth.

Priscilla:

The Prophetess of Montanus mentioned in the Marcion section of Eusebius, thus dating to the second century.

Theophilus:

The Bishop of Antioch from 169 to 182 CE. Known as Theophilus of Antioch.

Virtually all the characters mentioned in the New Testament who are verified to be from the first century are rulers (i.e., Claudius, Gallio, Pilate, Augustus, etc). If they aren't first-century rulers, they seem to be second-century Christians. Rulers are not only historical, and could help the readers imagine the time the author was trying to place the story in, but they are also much easier to look up. How hard would it be for an author educated in Greek to know when a certain Emperor or Senator was in power and use that information to help manufacture a story?

Obviously, there are going to be some mistakes, such as the timing issue of the census mentioned in the beginning of the Gospel of Luke. But even in that case, it is apparent the author of Luke was trying to use known historical figures to enhance his story.

A Mark-ed Possibility

Speaking of second-century figures found in the New Testament, it's likely that some of the names the gospels are attributed to, specifically Mark and Luke, are not referencing first-century Christians but rather second-century ones.

The names Mark and Luke are mentioned twice in the letters of Paul: Colossians and Philemon. In Colossians, they're a few verses apart. In Philemon, they're in the same sentence. Both of these letters are forgeries dating to the second century, which we demonstrate in Chapter 8. That means the names do not appear in any authentic letters and the only other appearance the characters make is in Acts, which is one of the latest books of the New Testament written in the second half of the second century.

We also know the Gospel of Luke is a rewrite of Marcion's Evangelion, dating to the second century. The canonical Gospel of Mark is also a second-century text, and the first version of it is what Marcion had access to when Evangelion was being written. The names Mark and Luke aren't given to these texts until Irenaeus provides the first naming of them around 180. So where do these names come from?

Marcion's name is actually a diminutive of Mark, and means "little Mark." In fact, it was even pronounced "Mark-ion." We know through later Christian authors Marcion had a student named Lucan or Lucian - pronounced "Lukan" and "Lukian," respectively. According to the Catholic Encyclopedia, "The name Lucas (Luke) is probably an abbreviation from Lucanus, like Annas from Ananus, Apollos from Apollonius, Artemas from Artemidorus, Demas from Demetrius, etc." So Luke comes from Lucanas, a longer version of Lucan. Interestingly, when Irenaeus finally gives us the names of the Gospels of Mark and

Luke he claims these gospels were associated with the heresies of Docetism and Marcionism.

It's possible that the reference to Mark and Luke in the forged Pauline letters are Marcion and Lucan, who would go on to write some of the first gospels or at the very least be involved in the process. The characters Mark and Luke are just throwaway references, the same type that forgeries would leave as marks of authorship as we see happen in 2 Timothy with Polycarp and Crescens (as well as numerous non-Christian forged works), which reveal the second-century date of that text. Why would such insignificant characters who don't show up until small references in second-century texts go on to write two canonical gospels, and be the only two figures to write canonical gospels that weren't themselves disciples of Jesus? If these references were preserving a tradition that Marcion and Lucan played a role in their creation this might make more sense.

Chapter Notes:

1. Clarke, Andrew. "Another Corinthian Erastus Inscription." *Tyndale Bulletin*, vol. 42, 1 Jan. 1991.

As either a second-century cameo or anachronism from the first century BCE, the Erastus Stone lines up very well with whoever was mentioned in Romans. In this journal, however, Andrew Clarke argues that it couldn't possibly be the same person because the century is off. This is a perfect example of researchers simply looking in the wrong century for support.

Religious influence over not only the field of biblical studies but those adjacent to it has made it extremely difficult to venture far beyond what fits within a Christian interpretation of history. This is one reason it is so important to return to all the evidence itself rather than relying on commentary. The Erastus Stone clearly dates to another century based on the surrounding physical evidence, but to propose this would jeopardize one's reputation in academia simply because it goes against the engrained Christian stranglehold on the field.

2. Bar-Ilan, Meir. "Illiteracy in the Land of Israel in the First Centuries C.E." *Essays in the Social Scientific Study of Judaism and Jewish Society*, vol. II, 1992, pp. 46–61. Accessed 15 Dec. 2023.

3. Hezser, Catherine. *Jewish Literacy in Roman Palestine*. Tübingen Mohr Siebeck, 2001.

The literacy rates of the area Christianity evolved in were so low, there's no wonder we can still find cameos and evidence of political infighting in the New Testament books. The authors were more or less writing for fellow authors - they knew the common man couldn't read and therefore could be a bit bolder in their additions.

This lack of access to the texts for the majority of believers proved to be useful for the church later on, and in the Decree of the Council of Toulouse in 1229 the Catholic Church went as far to forbid not only translation of the Bible but even allowing lay members to have access to the books at all.

Further Reading:

1. Trobisch, David. *On the Origin of Christian Scripture.* Augsburg Fortress Publishers, 19 Sept. 2023.

   Dr. David Trobisch, here and elsewhere in his works, argues that the second-century church leader Polycarp, who likely died in either 155 or 165, compiled the first iteration of what would become today's canonical New Testament.

   In Trobisch's view, in response to Marcion's publication of his canon around the year 144, which just contained Paul's letters and his gospel Evangelion, Polycarp compiled a competing, interpolated, and expanded canon. He points to the one letter we have attributed to Polycarp in which the author claims to have organized the letters of Ignatius as evidence that Polycarp had experience and an interest in creating these kinds of collections.

   Furthermore, Polycarp supposedly being a student of John would also make him a good candidate for the verses John 21:24-25, which is a note from the final editor of that gospel. Trobisch presents other evidence, makes a compelling case, and generally puts the range of the New Testament being finalized somewhere between 160-180.

While later in Chapter 8 we make a case for Irenaeus being responsible for much of this role, the date range we present is identical and Polycarp would be a good alternative candidate. Regardless of the specific individuals involved, the evidence clearly points to authorship and compilation of much of the New Testament canon in the later half of the second century.

CHAPTER 5

The Early Church Leaders

Despite so much of the first century called into question, there was still the fact that Christianity existed at *some* point. The second century brought about plenty of faces within the new budding religion. There were Christian churches with varying beliefs, Christian authors writing new books, and theologians trying to decipher the books already written. What did these theologians, authors, and heads of churches have to say about their beliefs? The next stop in the journey was the early church leaders.

"What about Eusebius of Caesarea?"

While our list of Church Fathers will largely be in chronological order, first we need to address the figure who has most significantly shaped the world's understanding of the early Christian church over the last 1,600 years or so: Eusebius of Caesarea.

Eusebius of Caesarea (~260-339 CE), also known as Eusebius Pamphilus, is perhaps the most influential Christian historian to have lived. He was Emperor Constantine's biographer and propagandist, known for writing a number of Christian texts on a variety of subjects but best known for the work *Church History*. In *Church History*, we have our first surviving account of the first three centuries of Christianity, based on a variety of sources including earlier texts that we no longer have access to.

Unfortunately, Eusebius was openly biased and wrote with the agenda of defending the Church. At one point when discussing the martyrdom of a group of Christians, he says,

*We shall not mention those who were shaken by the persecution, nor those who in everything pertaining to salvation were shipwrecked, and by their own will were sunk in the depths of the flood. **But we shall introduce into this history in general only those events which may be useful first to ourselves and afterwards to posterity.*** [1]

When writing an expanded account of the same incident, he said the following:

***I think it best to pass by all the other events which occurred in the meantime**: such as those which happened to the bishops of the churches, when instead of shepherds of the rational flocks of Christ, over which they presided in an unlawful manner, the divine judgment, considering them worthy of such a charge, made them keepers of camels, an irrational beast and very crooked in the structure of its body, or condemned them to have the care of the imperial horses — and I pass by also the insults and disgraces and tortures they endured from the imperial overseers and rulers on account of the sacred vessels and treasures of the Church; and besides these the lust of power on the part of many, the disorderly and unlawful ordinations, and the schisms among the confessors themselves; also the novelties which were zealously devised against the remnants of the Church by the new and factious members, who added innovation after innovation and forced them in unsparingly among the calamities of the persecution, heaping misfortune* upon misfortune. *I judge it more suitable to shun and avoid the account of these things, as I said at the beginning. But such things as are sober and praiseworthy, according to the sacred word — "and if there be any virtue and praise," — I consider it most proper to tell and to record, and to present to believing hearers in the history of the admirable martyrs.* And after this I think it best to crown the entire work with an account of the peace which has appeared unto us from heaven.[2]

He also admitted that no one had done a very good job of documenting all of Christian history before him, opening his *Church History* with the statement,

I am unable to find even the bare footsteps of those who have traveled the way before me, except in brief fragments, in which some in one way, others in another, have transmitted to us particular accounts of the times in which they lived.[3]

In many cases, texts he was dealing with were likely already edited, interpolated into, and their origins had long been forgotten. In other cases, they were entirely destroyed around the time he was writing, meaning few or no original copies would be left intact. In his work *The Life Of Constantine*, Book 3, Chapters 54-56, he documents how books were prohibited and houses of worship by Marcionites and others deemed heretics by the Church were destroyed after Emperor Constantine ordered it be done.

In his *Preparation for the Gospel* Book 12, he cites Plato and the Hebrew Bible as needing to employ the "Noble Lie" - a lie told to convince people to do the right thing and maintain social order, or in the case of the Hebrew Bible, to help people understand and carry out God's will through misrepresenting God's actual nature.

We have a number of other instances in Eusebius that demonstrate inaccuracies or overt biases and he has been criticized for such since the time of his writing. Unfortunately, this is the best we have to work with for a large amount of early Christian history. With so little physical evidence, likely no manuscripts from before the third century, and references to Christians being so scarce outside of Christian texts themselves, it's likely most of actual Christian history was lost.

Eusebius himself states that it was difficult to figure out what happened, and no one had really kept good records of it. So whenever Eusebius makes a claim about early Christian development or certain figures, we have to take it with a grain of salt. He is demonstrably wrong in places, is open about his bias and willingness to stretch the truth, and is writing this down centuries after many of the events are supposed to have happened.

So who were these early church leaders, often called the "Church Fathers?" We've mentioned a few already - Justin Martyr, Tertullian, and a few others. Let's take a moment to get to know these figures and what evidence they provide for the origins of Christianity.

For the most part, we are going to stick to figures who we either have writings from or extensive indirect evidence for rather than addressing every person Eusebius or other later Church Fathers claimed were around at the time. This isn't to say we don't think any of them existed, but rather there is no way of proving one way or another anything about them. We will address lesser-known Christians in a separate section at the end, but much of what can be learned about early Christian history from the early Church Fathers can be gleaned from just a small number of figures.

As a quick heads up, the rest of this chapter gets very in depth. Remember, if you need some extra explanations or resources, visit us online or reach out. A lot of what we talk about in this chapter gets summed up in Chapter 9, alongside a timeline laid out for better clarification.

Jaaron Wingo

"What about Clement of Rome?"

One of the first figures Christians will point to as proof of a tradition going back to the time of Jesus and the disciples is Clement of Rome. Even within Church tradition, we know very little about Clement, and what we have is contradictory. In fact, other early Church Fathers can't even agree whether Clement was the second, third, or fourth bishop of Rome. We also don't seem to get mention of him until Irenaeus around the 180s. As such, there is disagreement on when he lived.

It doesn't help that we have over half a dozen documents attributed to him that even mainstream scholars agree he didn't write. He appears to be another Christian figure that authors latched onto in order to add authenticity to their own writings by attributing them to his name. There is only one letter that is generally considered to have been by Clement of Rome, which is known as 1 Clement. Ironically, the letter itself is anonymous, so it also probably wasn't by this figure. To make matters worse, the letter is a composite letter, making it of very little value and likely a product of the middle of the second century.

The hypothetical value of 1 Clement is that, if it were genuine, it would potentially be our first reference to Peter and Paul, as well as the first reference to one or more of Paul's letters. More conservative Christian scholars put Clement writing in the 60s CE, whereas more mainstream scholarship puts the date of the letter to around the 90s.

Given its composite nature, having been added to over time, and its lack of external citations, even if a layer of the letter were to date to something early, it's likely the references to Peter, Paul, and Paul's letters came about in a later edit. We would date the earliest possible layer to the 130s, with at least one other layer coming decades later.

While it isn't unreasonable that someone with the name Clement existed, it's likely that if he did, he was an early or mid-second-century figure and wasn't responsible for any of the works attributed to him.

"What about Aristides of Athens?"

The death of Aristides of Athens, the second-century Christian apologist, is usually dated to around 133-134 CE, and the extant pieces of his *Apology*, often believed to be delivered in front of Emperor Hadrian, are usually dated between the 120s up until around the time of his death. These dates are according to Church tradition, and in recent years scholars such as Markus Vinzent and William Simpson have questioned these dates, pushing for a date more likely in the reign of Antoninus Pius (138-161) at the earliest.[4,5]

The potential value of Aristides' work for dating early Christian activity is that he seems to know some version of the gospel narrative, perhaps Matthew, and if this were dated to the 120s-130s, it would be the earliest known reference to a number of details about the life of Jesus outside the gospels. However, the manuscript tradition of Aristides' *Apology* is wanting, and all we have to date it to the traditional dates is references from figures like Eusebius and Jerome. The text itself also seems less like an apology delivered in front of the emperor, but rather a text meant for broader distribution using the setting of the imperial court as a backdrop, meaning dating it to any specific emperor might be pointless. We would put this text around the 150s-170s.

"What about the Epistle of Barnabas?"

The Epistle of Barnabas, which received its name around the start of the third century, is an anonymous letter that was so popular among the early church that it made it into the canon among many churches along with the rest of the New Testament for centuries. Barnabas was supposedly a follower of Paul, but most today agree that he was not the author. Some, such as the third-century author Tertullian, believed that Barnabas wrote Hebrews, but the same author is not responsible for both of these texts and aside from a handful of biblical references, we have no evidence for Barnabas having been a historical person.

Mainstream scholars today date the Epistle of Barnabas to the 130s simply because its 16th chapter has a line about rebuilding the temple, which would seem unlikely after 136 at the end of the Bar Kokhba Revolt. However, in our stylometric analysis of the text (which you can read more about in Chapters 7 and 8), we found that Barnabas' chapters 16 through 21 came up as a different author from the rest of the text.

While we can't identify if just some or all of these chapters are from this separate author, chapters 17, 18, and 20 are too short to have had a significant impact on the results meaning it's likely that two or more of chapters 16, 19, and 21 are from another author. It's also telling that the words Jesus and Christ appear over 20 times throughout the text, but never after chapter 15. While we don't have an exact date for either segment of Barnabas, we are confident that it is a second-century text and very possibly later than the traditional dating of the 130s. We estimate that the text was put together sometime between the 130s and the 160s.

"What about Ignatius of Antioch?"

Ignatius of Antioch is another figure that we don't have exact dates for. Ignatius, whose name means "fiery one," also called himself Theophoros, or "God-bearer." We actually have a number of writings attributed to Ignatius available to us today. There are three rescissions, or versions, of Ignatius' letters: the Short Recension, which is only in Syriac and contains three abridged letters, the Middle Recension, which contains seven Greek letters and is generally considered to contain the authentic versions of these letters, and the Long Recension in Greek and Latin which contain thirteen letters and is considered to have a number of spurious letters and edits in it.

The Middle Recension matches what Eusebius has, and was found for the first time in a Latin manuscript by Archbishop James Ussher in the 1600s. Our earliest manuscripts of the Middle Recension date to the 11th century in the Codex Medico Laurentianus, which also contains some of the Long Recension as well.

Ignatius' letters are supposedly written on his trip to Rome after he has been sentenced to death in Antioch. This is where the details get a bit murky. The traditional dating of the death of Ignatius is from Eusebius, who puts him dying during the reign of Trajan from 98 to 117 CE. There is no evidence for this claim, however, and no earlier church leader gives these dates either. The closest thing to evidence is that Ignatius has been arrested and claims to be set for execution. But if Christians are being persecuted across the Roman Empire, it's odd that he's being allowed to meet with and send letters to other Christians without them also facing the same persecution. It would seem that Ignatius is not facing general Christian persecution but instead has been arrested for something he did or was accused of as an individual.

Modern researchers don't believe the authorship or death dates Eusebius gives, either. Figures such as Timothy Barnes, Paul Foster, Richard Pervo, Roger Parvus, Allen Brent, and others put the date anywhere from the 130s and 140s up through the 160s. Other scholars, such as Markus Vinzent, Thomas Lechner, Otto Zwierlein, and others, argue for the letters being forgeries written in the range of the 160s to the 180s. The church structure and other details in Ignatius' letters indicate a more developed structure than would be found around the time of the 110s, too. Ignatius shows traces of Gnosticism or knowledge of it, which was more prominent in the middle and later parts of the second century. Attestation of Ignatius can't be found until Polycarp, dying in either 155 or 165, and then Irenaeus (who is the first external attestation to Polycarp as well) around 180. The arguments for a date during the reign of Trajan are weak and depend almost entirely on Eusebius' unreliable testimony, whereas the evidence for a later date is more extensive. We give a broad range of the 130s-180s for the authorship of Ignatius' letters.

Ignatius seems to be familiar with Peter and Paul, as well as some of Paul's writings, including Ephesians, which is generally considered to be written by another author under Paul's name, and this would make Ignatius one of the first figures to be familiar with these works. Interestingly, he also mentions a figure named Onesimus, who is only mentioned in this time period in two other places: Paul's letters to Colossians and Philemon. Colossians is also generally considered to be falsely written under Paul's name, and Philemon shares many names and characteristics with Colossians. As we'll see in Chapter 8, we will also find out that there seems to be some kind of common author or editor to these Pauline letters and the Middle Recension of the letters of Ignatius.

If the dates for Ignatius are indeed this late, as evidence suggests and numerous scholars attest to, then a peculiar possibility arises.

As mentioned earlier in the book, there are a number of overlapping characteristics between the figure Peregrinus Proteus (as mentioned in the works of Lucian) and the figure Ignatius. Both figures were leading Christians in Roman Syria who were arrested and tried, likely in Antioch in the second century. They were converts to the religion, and both wrote a number of texts while Christians. While we don't have any texts under Proteus' name today, Lucian said he not only wrote Christian scripture, but edited others, as well as sent a number of letters out to other churches after his arrest - exactly as Ignatius wrote letters to churches after he was arrested.

Both write letters to or are visited by Christians from modern-day Turkey after they are arrested, and for whatever reason both are absolutely intent on being martyred and seem to have some kind of death wish, to the extent that part of Ignatius' theology seems wrapped up in the concept of martyrdom. The appointment of ambassadors and couriers by the two is also very similar. Proteus was from modern-day Turkey, a town called Parium, and Ignatius was likely from modern-day Turkey as well, having said to have been a student of John while he was in Ephesus. This would also explain the connection to other church figures, such as Polycarp.

The primary differences are in how they die. Proteus left Christianity after being kicked out, and Lucian assumed his dismissal was due to violating religious food restrictions. He then went on to become a Cynic philosopher and threw himself on a burning pyre in Olympia around 165. Ignatius is said to have died in Rome, being eaten by lions.

How would this be reconciled, as well as the fact that the two characters had different names? If it's true that Proteus was Ignatius and that Proteus left the church yet had written a number of surviving texts, all that would be needed was to change the name of the author. Both figures' stories regarding their arrest and time imprisoned line up well enough that aside from perhaps minor additions and name changes, there wouldn't be much editing needed. On top of that, as we pointed out earlier, Ignatius means "fiery one." Is this a reference to his actual death after the fact, a reference to Proteus' death by fire?

While the evidence is inconclusive here, if Ignatius were Proteus or modeled after him, this would be our first reference to an individual Christian leader outside of the religion's own writings. It would also explain why, despite Lucian's claims that Proteus was such a large figure, how we don't have any of his writings or any references to him within Christianity despite later Christian authors attempting to document lists of bishops, leaders, and writers across the centuries.

"What about Marcion of Sinope?"

Marcion of Sinope, perhaps one of the most important people in the evolution of Christianity, is a man who is only recently getting the attention you would expect for such a pivotal figure. While we have diverging accounts of Marcion's life, the general summary is this: Marcion was from Sinope, a town in modern-day Turkey, and was a "ship-master," likely a relatively wealthy fleet owner. In the 130s, likely after the Bar Kokhba Revolt, he traveled to Rome and became involved in the Christian movement there. After religious disagreements, he was excommunicated in 144, and he published his own writing, *Antitheses*, along with ten letters of Paul and a gospel he called Evangelion, which was effectively an early version of Luke.

Some accounts say he made a large donation to the Roman church which was returned to him upon his excommunication, and after being kicked out, he continued his involvement in the Christian movement which spread his beliefs across the Roman Empire. We don't know exactly when he died, but Justin Martyr, who wrote in the 150s and 160s, seems to think he is still alive at the time of his writing.

Marcion is one of the most attested figures in early Christianity, and the vast majority of sources were opposed to him. Numerous authors wrote texts against him, and we have even more accounts of lost texts written against him. The attacks are so extensive, in fact, that we have been able to reconstruct much of what his Evangelion and versions of Paul's letters looked like.

While these other Church Fathers, such as Tertullian, claimed that his Evangelion was a mutilated, stolen version of Luke, between textual evidence and our stylometric analysis in Chapter 8, we have been able to determine that Marcion's version was actually earlier than our canonical Luke. In fact, it was likely the first gospel most Christians had ever come across, as whatever Proto-Mark, which came before Marcion's Evangelion, looked like was different from our version and didn't seem to cause as much stir as when Marcion published Evangelion.

After 144, when Marcion put out his collection, many gospels started to pop up - Matthew, canonical Mark, canonical Luke, John, Peter, Thomas, a variety of infancy gospels, and so on. We also see, for what is likely the first time, references to Paul's works. It appears that, for some reason, despite having founded most of the key churches outside of Judaea, Paul was an unknown figure until Marcion came around. Tertullian even said Marcion "discovered" Galatians. Taken conservatively, this would mean it was a lost letter until the 130s or 140s, but what Tertullian very likely could have meant is that Marcion discovered Galatians the same way the founder of Mormonism, Joseph Smith Jr., discovered the golden tablets with secret revelations from Jesus and others.

Why was Marcion's work so controversial? While we don't exactly know his theology, we do have enough between the attacks on him and various reconstructions of his collection of works to know that he believed that the god of the Old Testament and the god of the New Testament were not the same god. Speaking of the Old Testament and New Testament, Marcion was not only the first Christian to publish a canon but likely also the first to use the concept of "Testament" for this canon and separate what we now call the Old Testament (or Hebrew Bible) and the New Testament.

According to Marcion, the god of the Old Testament was a demiurge type of deity who created the universe and was possibly even somewhat malevolent and mean. God the Father, who we find in the New Testament, was a different god, who sent his son to effectively ransom believers away from the Old Testament god and provide them salvation. These beliefs were similar, though not identical, to Gnosticism. They also seem to line up relatively well with what we know of Pliny the Younger's testimony regarding Christians in the 110s, supposing it is authentic. Interestingly, Pliny the Younger was a governor over the same region in modern-day Turkey that Marcion was from.

"What about Papias?"

A potentially important figure in early Christianity, Papias of Hierapolis is given a wide range of dates, particularly when it comes to his writings. Unfortunately, we have none of these writings in existence today, nor do we have a very solid date for him. He is generally dated by mainstream scholars to somewhere between the 120s-140s. He is said to have known Polycarp, who died sometime in the 150s-160s, and Ignatius, who we think died anywhere between the 130s-180s, meaning later dates after the 150s would fit Papias better as well.

Papias is said to have written at least five books, but all we have now is a handful of quotes scattered throughout texts from later authors. The most important is likely the one found in Eusebius, in which we find the following:

This also the presbyter [Papias] said: "Mark having become the interpreter of Peter, wrote down accurately, though not in order, whatsoever he remembered of the things said or done by Christ. For he neither heard the Lord nor followed him, but afterward, as I said, he followed Peter, who adapted his teaching to the needs of his hearers, but with no intention of giving a connected account of the Lord's discourses, so that Mark committed no error while he thus wrote some things as he remembered them. For he was careful of one thing, not to omit any of the things which he had heard, and not to state any of them falsely." These things are related by Papias concerning Mark. But concerning Matthew he writes as follows: "So then Matthew wrote the oracles in the Hebrew language, and every one interpreted them as he was able." And the same writer uses testimonies from the first Epistle of John and from that of Peter likewise. And he relates another story of a woman, who was accused of many sins before the Lord, which is contained in the Gospel according to the Hebrews. These things we have thought it necessary to observe in addition to what has been already stated.[6]

People have written entire dissertations on this brief segment alone. If it were an accurate quote and true, it would more or less confirm Church tradition. However, there are numerous problems with this quote. First, Eusebius is a rather unreliable source, as we discussed earlier in this chapter. We have no way of verifying if the quote was actually from Papias - it could either be faked by Eusebius or Eusebius could've incorrectly identified the source. Second, it's also dependent on Papias both existing, which is less certain than many figures of the time, and telling the truth to the best of his knowledge as well. And these are just the issues with the transmission of the information.

There are problems within the actual quote itself, as well. First, our Gospel of Matthew found in the New Testament was originally written in Greek. This has been proven in a number of ways, and no serious scholar today believes it was written in Hebrew originally. There are no signs of translation from Hebrew to Greek and Matthew uses the Gospel of Mark and Marcion's Evangelion, which were both originally written in Greek. It wouldn't make any sense to use Greek texts to write a Hebrew text only to translate that text back into Greek and then leave no textual or historical evidence there was ever a Hebrew version. On top of this, the name Matthew being attributed to the Gospel of Matthew was likely done much later, after the authorship of the gospel. We don't hear about this name being used for the gospel until Irenaeus around 180 CE.

Another issue is that Mark wasn't written by a follower of Peter. The evidence suggests that the first version of the Gospel of Mark wasn't written until sometime in the first few decades of the second century, and our canonical version of Mark with the Little Apocalypse (which we discussed in Chapter 2) in which Jesus predicts the destruction of the Temple didn't come around until the middle of the second century. There also doesn't seem to be any disorder to Mark's gospel in a way that would indicate what the Papias quote suggests regarding it being "not in order" and not being a "connected account." Just as the information about Matthew seems incorrect, so does the information about Mark.

Furthermore, Eusebius says Papias quotes from 1 John, 1 Peter, and the Gospel of the Hebrews. This, too, reveals a later date for Papias. As we see in Chapter 8, 1 John has stylometric overlap with the Gospel of John, the last canonical gospel to be written likely somewhere in the 150s-160s. 1 Peter is a forged document not written by Peter but written by someone responsible for some of the fake Paul letters as well, also written in the second century. Worse yet, from what we know of the Gospel of the Hebrews, it appears to be a later adaptation of the Gospel of Matthew, which would then also date to after the 150s.

There are other claims about Papias, such as that he was a student of John. This claim we find in a number of sources, as they say that Papias, Ignatius, and Polycarp were all students of John. There's also an interesting quote in the Vatican Library text *Vat. Reg. lat* 14 in the preface to the Gospel of John which claims:

The Gospel of John was revealed and given to the churches established by John while he was still alive, as John's dear disciple Papias of Hierapolis reported in his last five exegetical books. He [Papias] wrote down the gospel while John dictated. But the heretic Marcion, after he had been rebuked for contrary matters [or possibly Antitheses], was cast out by John. But with him he [Marcion] had brought writings or letters by John to the brethren who were in Pontus.

The text is unclear, but all of this also indicates later dates for Papias and likely John. We know Marcion went to Rome in the late 130s, and he wasn't excommunicated from the church there until 144. Even if a similar incident had happened in the 130s in Asia Minor and somehow news of this didn't make it to Rome until at least 144, this would mean John was still alive in the 130s, placing him around the age of 130-140 years old if he were actually a disciple of Jesus. The quote would also imply Marcion was a student of John, which does not work for a number of reasons. One good reason being that if he had access to the Gospel of John, it's unlikely that he wouldn't have used any of John's material when he published Evangelion. The preface also could be read as implying Marcion wrote his work *Antitheses* while in Asia Minor, which is also problematic. This is just another example of an unreliable piece of information supposedly transmitted through Papias.

Ultimately, nearly everything we have attributed to Papias seems to be internally contradictory or conflicts with external evidence. In many cases, these quotes also put Papias in the second half of the second century, which means even if these quotes were accurate, they were written so late they provide little help in discovering what actually happened. The quotes and paraphrases also conveniently seem like attempts to create an older source for what would later become church tradition, yet for some reason, no one managed to save a single copy of at least one of his five books. Papias is yet another unreliable witness in the search for a historical Jesus.

"What about Justin Martyr?"

Justin Martyr is another turning point for Christian history. Born somewhere around 90-100 CE in Samaria, Justin converted to Christianity probably sometime in the early 130s. During the reign of Antoninus Pius (138-161), he went to Rome and started his own Christian school. Despite growing up in Samaria, Justin seems to not have known Hebrew or Aramaic and was likely a native Greek speaker. He fancied himself a philosopher, and his writings reflect this. Tradition has it that after a dispute with a Cynic philosopher he was beheaded between 162 and 168 CE. He was a very prolific writer, with his main surviving works being his *First Apology* (151-157 CE), *Second Apology* (~157 CE), and the *Dialogue with Trypho* (155-167 CE). Some also believe he wrote the Letter to Diognetus, as it was found in a manuscript with his other works.

The most important thing Justin brings to the table for us is that he is the first early Christian author with a solid, reliable date to seem to know something that looks like the Synoptic Gospels. While it's unclear what exactly he had - he calls them "memoirs of the apostles" - we can be pretty confident he didn't have exact copies of what we have today. He might have had drafts or earlier versions of what we know as Matthew, Mark, and Luke, and his quotes and paraphrases seem to indicate he had other traditions that didn't make it into our current New Testament that he considered on par with those works. He might have even had a "gospel harmony," a book that combined multiple gospels into one.

Interestingly, he doesn't seem to know the Gospel of John. He knows a man named John wrote Revelation, but doesn't say anything about him writing a gospel or letters. He also doesn't seem to quote from any of the John works, either. This is likely due to the fact that while the John tradition had been around in his time, the Gospel of John itself had likely not been written or spread during his lifetime.

More surprisingly, he doesn't seem to know of anything from Paul. In fact, he doesn't even mention the *name* Paul, which is odd because Paul supposedly wrote about half of the New Testament, is mentioned in 2 Peter, and has an extensive section of Acts dedicated to his travels. Paul was also considered one of the founders of the church of Rome, where Justin spent roughly 20-30 years of his life.

This is why Justin is so important. With Marcion in Rome in the 130s-140s and publishing Evangelion and the Pauline letter collection in 144, we would expect what we see - relatively slow adoption and the lack of acknowledgement by contemporary authors. Justin doesn't even mention Paul, much less reject him, but you would think if the mainstream theory of a historical Paul were true, Justin would be indebted to his works to some degree. While we don't know whether word of Paul never reached Justin or he just outright chose to ignore what was supposedly authentic, near-canonical level religious texts around for a century by the time of Justin's life, we can't be sure. But either scenario is indicative of the fact that Paul and his works were not as well known or taken seriously by all early Christians during the time of Justin Martyr.

Likewise, the publication of Evangelion spurred on a gospel rush around its time, and this being the case, Justin would likely be privy to some of the early versions of these texts. We know Mark and Evangelion were already in existence by the time of Justin's writings, and Matthew being a response to these gospels, it was likely in the early stages or perhaps being added into a gospel harmony when he was writing in the 150s and 160s. This is supported by the nature of the potential references Justin has to these texts. While they don't perfectly line up with our canonical texts, there seems to be some kind of overlap in traditions. If these texts had been written in the late first century or early second century as mainstream scholarship purports, these variations would be less likely and the texts would be more directly quoted.

After Justin in the 150s-160s, though, we start to see references to the Pauline letters and, eventually, more direct, reliable references and quotes from the canonical gospels. Why is this? It's simply because the canonical gospels were written during or even after his lifetime and the letters of Paul were not accepted by many Christians until later. This is because Paul wasn't an apostle to the first-century Gentiles, but rather to the second-century Gentiles, and the struggles we see throughout the New Testament actually take place in the second century itself.

"What about Tatian?"

Tatian, a student of Justin Martyr who would later get labeled a heretic by other Christians, is well known for having created the *Diatessaron*, one of the most significant as well as one of the earliest gospel harmonies. His version included versions of all four of the canonical gospels and is generally dated to around 170. Interestingly, he did not include the intro to Theophilus in Luke 1:1-4, which could be further indication that our canonical version of Luke is actually addressed to an individual, particularly Theophilus of Antioch, and could even date to after Tatian's *Diatessaron* itself.

Also important about Tatian is that his gospel harmony included John and thus contains one of (if not *the*) earliest references to the Gospel of John that we have. His teacher, Justin, doesn't seem to know of it, but with an estimated publication date for the *Diatessaron* at 170, we can determine the Gospel of John was completed sometime closer to the end of Justin's life in the 160s.

"What about Polycarp?"

Polycarp of Smyrna, another Church Father who claimed to be a student of John, was Bishop of Smyrna until his death in the 150s or 160s. We have one extant writing attributed to Polycarp, but it has internal contradictions indicating, at the very least, it is a composite letter. The contradictions could even indicate that the document is a forgery in Polycarp's name. There is also a document known as the Martyrdom of Polycarp, which has numerous additions at the end and was likely heavily edited over the years. In this account of Polycarp's death, he is first burned at the stake, but immediately after miraculously surviving the fire, he is stabbed to death.

The exact date of Polycarp's death is uncertain. Eusebius puts Polycarp's death somewhere around the years of 166 and 167. An addition to the Martyrdom of Polycarp after Eusebius puts his death in 155 to 156, however. Neither of these sets of dates are particularly reliable, so we prefer to use a date range from the 150s to the 160s.

As previously stated, only one writing we have today is attributed to Polycarp. The letter, known as Polycarp's Epistle to the Philippians, has a number of issues. First, even mainstream scholars agree that the letter is a composite work. In one section, he is writing as if his friend Ignatius is alive, and then in another section he talks about Ignatius having recently died. The letter itself is actually a preface to the collection of Ignatius' letters and says so in the text itself. Our first reference to it is Irenaeus, a self-proclaimed student of Polycarp, who encourages readers to also read Polycarp's letter (which itself does the same for the letters of Ignatius). The letter is also full of New Testament quotes - it almost looks as if someone stitched the letter together by piecing verses together in places. This doesn't rule out authorship by Polycarp, but it could indicate either a forgery or possibly a later editor that pieced two letters together and added in content.

It's also possible that we have other writings of Polycarp, however. The Pastoral Letters (1 Timothy, 2 Timothy, and Titus), which are internally and traditionally attributed to Paul, have been agreed upon by scholars across the last few centuries to be much later forgeries. Usually, mainstream scholars will put these letters sometime in the early second century, but increasingly there has been a trend to see these letters as later - perhaps even been written by Polycarp and his associates.

We can see a general date for the Pastorals reading 1 Timothy. In 1 Timothy 6:20, we get a direct reference to Gnosticism and a direct mentioning of Marcion's text *Antitheses*. Unfortunately, this is hidden in most English translations, with the word *"antitheses"* being translated into something like "contradictions", "opposing ideas", or another synonym. The Greek text, however, explicitly tells people not to be convinced by the *Antitheses*. This means the earliest 1 Timothy could've been written is 144 CE. Gnosticism, a heretical version of Christianity which taught, among other things, that the Old Testament god was different from the New Testament one, was seen as a problem for some early Christians around the same time. 1 Timothy elsewhere attacks common practices of "heretical" groups of the second century, such as vegetarianism and the incorporation of women in church leadership.

Likewise, as we mentioned in Chapter 4 when discussing this text, 2 Timothy 1:5 mentions Timothy's grandmother and mother were Christians before him. In other words, Timothy is a third-generation Christian in what is supposedly just around 60 CE. This clearly makes little sense unless Timothy was a child, and even then it's a stretch. What's more likely is that the author is imagining Timothy as a fully grown assistant to Paul, though somewhat younger, and forgetting to back-date his thinking. In the author's day, there are plenty of third-generation Christians given it's in the second half of the second century when this is being written. We will see later how Irenaeus, another second-century Church Father, is one of the only Christian writers in the second century who was born into a Christian family and not a convert, and he was born somewhere around the 130s-140s.

But how does this tie into Polycarp? In 2 Timothy, we get an almost direct name drop telling us who is responsible for the letter. 2 Timothy 4:10-13 mentions a list of names, some of which never appear anywhere else in the Bible. Two in particular stick out: Carpus and Crescens. Of the thirteen names in this section (Demas, Crescens, Titus, Luke, Mark, Tychicus, Carpus, Alexander, Prisca, Aquila, Onesiphorus,

Erastus, and Trophimus), these are the only two that do not appear somewhere else in the New Testament. Who are these figures?

Polycarp in Greek was actually Polycarpos, or Latin Polycarpus. In 2 Timothy, Carpus is said to have been loaned Paul's cloak and Paul wishes it returned, as well as his books and parchments, which Carpus also has. Carpus is suspiciously close to what one would imagine is a shortened version of Polycarpos/Polycarpus. Interestingly, thanks to the work of Patricia Rosenmeyer, we know that these kinds of minor one-off appearances of a character were ways for authors to insert themselves in epistolary fiction and fake letters. In fact, the very usage of having a cloak returned by the author was used in at least one other work, which is not surprising, as the cloak would often be the outer image a person would see when concealing themselves.

If this weren't suspicious enough, the name Crescens making an appearance is arguably even stronger evidence, particularly when alongside what appears to be a variation of Polycarp's name. The name Crescens appears nowhere else in the Bible nor in any Christian literature in the first or second century except in one place: the Letter of Polycarp to the Philippians. Who is Crescens? In chapter 14 of Polycarp's epistle, we find out that he is Polycarp's scribe and assistant. There is almost no other explanation as to how these two unique names appear side by side only in these texts other than they were written by the same people around the same time.

Others, such as German scholar David Trobisch, go as far to say they believe Polycarp might have been the person who did the one of the final rounds of edits and compiling of what we know as the New Testament. We see other signs of editorial remarks across the New Testament, such as Luke and Acts referencing a Theophilus (a contemporary of Polycarp) and the ending of the Gospel of John clearly indicating a layer of edits as well. Regardless of the exact extent of Polycarp's involvement in writing, editing, and developing the New Testament, we can be confident that he or those associated with him were directly involved in the latter half of the second century.

"What about Theophilus of Antioch?"

Theophilus, whose name means "God-lover," was bishop of Antioch from around 169 to around 182 CE, and he likely died shortly thereafter. He was a pagan convert to Christianity born somewhere near the Tigris and Euphrates rivers (which stretch into modern-day Turkey) and is best known for his single surviving work, *Apology to Autolycus*. In this text, he attempts to convince his pagan friend Autolycus to convert to Christianity, but he never mentions the disciples, Paul, or even the title or name Christ. Jesus is mentioned twice near the end, and the word Christian is used several times. This is one of the early usages of the word that we know is separate from the word "Chrestian" as Theophilus talks about anointment as the meaning of the label.

While this does inform us of how some early Christians thought and what texts they had access to, it also helps us identify the recipient of the Gospel of Luke and Acts.

If you read the first chapters of both these texts, you will see the author addressed the books to Theophilus. Knowing that Evangelion, effectively Proto-Luke, came in 144 and Theophilus was a convert to Christianity likely sometime in the 150s to 160s, we can be confident that these books were written to Theophilus of Antioch. While some will try to claim Theophilus was a general title of any God-loving Christian, these dates and the fact that Theophilus of Antioch was a convert in need of further instruction in the religion seem to solidify Theophilus of Antioch as the person canonical Luke and Acts were written to.

"What about Irenaeus?"

Finally, we get to Irenaeus, a Greek Christian who lived from around 130 or 140 to 202 CE and the last significant Christian author of the second century. Originally from Smyrna or the surrounding area in modern-day Turkey, Irenaeus considered himself a student, or at least a hearer of Polycarp. From Polycarp, he connected himself to John, and thus considered himself directly in the line of the apostolic tradition. Unique about Irenaeus is that, as opposed to most of the Christians we know of in the second century, Irenaeus was born a Christian as opposed to converting to it as an adult. While this might sound surprising, when one considers the idea that Christianity was not really a structured movement until the second century, it makes sense that the majority of church members, leaders, and authors were converts.

Irenaeus wrote multiple books, but the most important that has survived (largely via Latin translation rather than original Greek) is his *Against Heresies*. This five-volume work covers topics ranging from Marcion, Valentinus, and other figures described as heretics going all the way back to the supposed origin of these heretical texts, Simon Magus. *Against Heresies* was written sometime between 174 and 189, and we actually have a small fragment of the text from around 200-250 known as P. Oxy. 405. This fragment also contains a quote of Matthew, making it not only one of the earliest fragments of Christian writing in general but one of the earliest fragments containing New Testament material.

Irenaeus is also important in that he is the first author to cite a number of texts that would become the New Testament canon. Irenaeus quotes from 21 of the 27 books in the New Testament, leaving out 3 John, 2 Peter, James, Jude, Hebrews, and Philemon (though some contend he might have referenced Hebrews and James). He is the first Christian who definitely cited the Pastoral Epistles, 1 Timothy, 2 Timothy, and Titus, and considered them authentic Pauline texts. He also cites 1 Clement and the Shepherd of Hermas.

Irenaeus is also where we get the names of the canonical gospels from. Prior to Irenaeus, we know of no one who gave the names Matthew, Mark, Luke, and John to these gospels found in the New Testament today. He is also the first to argue for four gospels being used specifically. He wrote in *Against Heresies* that four heretical sects each had misused or mutilated each of the gospels respectively, with the Ebionites or conservative Jewish Christians using Matthew, Docetists or those who believed Jesus never had a physical existence using Mark, Marcion using Luke, and Gnostics such as the Valentinians using John.

While this was no doubt an oversimplification, there is some truth to it. We know that Luke is actually an adaptation of Marcion's Evangelion, and also know that Matthew was an anti-Marcionite adaptation and combination of Mark and Evangelion, which used more Jewish scripture than any of the other canonical gospels. The idea that the Gnostics used the Gospel of John goes back at least to Irenaeus, and the text itself is more spiritually oriented than the other canonical gospels. Mark, the earliest gospel, had quite a bit of content added and edited over the course of the second half of the second century, and the original version had Jesus as less historical and more spiritual, making it reasonable that Docetist groups would have found it appealing (and likely could have been descendants of some of the "original" Christians who understood Christ as entirely a deity rather than a historical figure).

One of the most important things for Irenaeus was the idea of apostolic authority- that truth and leadership should be passed down from the disciples and those who had followed them. This is part of why Irenaeus wanted to associate names with each of the gospels he used, and why these names are either disciples themselves or followers of disciples, according to Irenaeus. The concept of apostolic authority became a keystone in proto-Catholic and Catholic arguments for centuries following Irenaeus and is still part of the core of the Catholic Church today.

Irenaeus also had a particular emphasis on certain other concepts. One example is his emphasis on order and certain numbers, both of which were common to the time and drew from Greek and Jewish philosophy, respectively. He was also insistent on the importance of elders, and was at an older age himself when he wrote *Against Heresies*. Irenaeus took this argument quite seriously and actually used it, along with scriptural quotes such as John 8:56-57, to justify his belief that Jesus was actually crucified at the age of around 50 rather than the age of 30, as most Christians believe today. All of *Against Heresies*, Book 2, Chapter 22 is dedicated to this argument and arguing against Jesus' death being at or around age 30. It's interesting that even in the time Irenaeus was writing this text somewhere in the 170s-180s, such details regarding Jesus' life had not been agreed upon by the church.

We don't know exactly what happened to Irenaeus. After becoming bishop, we hear little of him except from Eusebius, who claims he was involved in the Easter Controversy in the early 190s, in which early Christians argued when the correct date for Easter was. Beyond that, we don't have much regarding Irenaeus. It's possible he died in old age, and the earliest attestation to him possibly being martyred was Gregory of Tours in the 500s and is thus unreliable.

"What about the church leaders after the second century?"

By the time we reach the end of the second century, most, if not all, the New Testament texts have been written. The majority of them have been referenced, as well, giving us some form of external attestation. While Christianity at this point still hasn't fully developed into what it would become once it truly gets centralized and doctrines solidified, it's become recognizable in many regions by the end of the second century. However, there are a few important figures up until the end of the fourth century that provide commentary on the second century who we should briefly mention.

Clement of Alexandria

Clement of Alexandria lived from around 150 to 215 CE. His main works (*Protrepticus*, *Paedagogus*, and *Stomata*) were written between 195-203. He covers a range of topics in these works, as well as a handful of other documents we have fragments of. Clement does document a number of useful details regarding the second-century development of Christianity, and his writings also indicate that he accepted a number of non-canonical Christian texts as scripture, including the Infancy Gospel of James.

Tertullian

Tertullian is perhaps the most important author of the third century when it comes to understanding the second-century development of Christianity. Born in Carthage in 155, Tertullian is now known as "the father of Latin Christianity" and was one of the earliest Christians to write extensively in Latin rather than Greek. He was a convert to Christianity, converting relatively late in life around the year 197.

Of all Tertullian's works, perhaps his most important work for our study is his *Against Marcion*. Written around 207 or 208, *Against Marcion* is a five-book collection entirely dedicated to critiquing and rebuking Marcion and his teachings. We find a brief biography of Marcion, a description of his split with the church in Rome, his theology, and then a near line-by-line comparison between Marcion's Evangelion and the canonical Gospel of Luke.

Tertullian makes a number of other interesting claims, such as Marcion finding or discovering Paul's letter to Galatians and that Marcion had brought a large sum of money to Rome in a story that seems to parallel Paul's fundraising of money for the church in Jerusalem. Interestingly, in Tertullian's analysis of Marcion's versions of Paul's letters and Evangelion, Tertullian seems to only imply one visit of Paul to Jerusalem rather than two, not only in Marcion's text but his own supposedly correct and canonical version. The visit not mentioned in Tertullian contains the oft-cited reference to "James, brother of the Lord," and between the odd structure and flow of this visit in the text and lack of references not only in Tertullian but authors prior have led some to believe this visit was a later addition to the text likely in the third century.

Tertullian wrote a number of other texts, including a similar but shorter attack on the Valentinian Gnostic sect. He used the majority of what would become the New Testament canon except 2 and 3 John, and also used other non-canonical texts which he held as of similar value to those that became canon. After his life, a number of spurious works were attributed to him, which, while falsely attributed, do have some value as insight into early Christianity. Tertullian himself was drawn to a sect known as Montanism around the time of completing

Against Marcion. As far as we can tell, Tertullian lived to an old age and died sometime around the year 220.

Origen

Origen of Alexandria lived from 185 to 253 CE. He wrote upwards of 2,000 religious documents and, despite being a controversial figure during his own time and afterwards, played a significant role in the development of Christianity in the third century. Origen's contributions are so significant, in fact, that it is hard to summarize them all here even in regard to our singular topic at hand. Most importantly, however, is that Origen is one of the earliest sources that gives us a glimpse at what would become the New Testament canon. Origen accepted 1 John, 1 Peter, Jude, and James as authentic, but doubted the authenticity of 2 John, 3 John, and 2 Peter. Origen is actually the first to mention 2 Peter, as all Christian writings and authors dating to the second century never quote or mention it.

Epiphanius

Epiphanius is the latest figure that has a significant impact on our study. While there are a number of other figures in the fourth and fifth centuries that also add details to some of what we have now about previous centuries, there are diminishing returns on their accuracy and closeness to the events and source material. Epiphanius of Salamis lived from around 310 to 403 CE.

Epiphanius' most famous work and most relevant to understanding what happened as Christianity developed in the second century is the *Panarion*. This text documented eighty heresies, pagan religions, and philosophies of his time and before. The number was selected based on Song of Songs 6:8, in which the text mentions "eighty concubines," which Epiphanius interpreted as 80 sects or heresies that might tempt Christians away from what he considered the truth.

While Epiphanius wrote the *Panarion* with an obvious bias and is quite aggressive regarding his disdain for certain groups, it nonetheless has historical value, as he often quotes, paraphrases, or summarizes the beliefs and histories of a number of groups, including Marcionites. While his account differs a bit from Tertullian and others, it is nonetheless another attestation of the group, their beliefs, and some aspects of their history.

"What about the various heretics and people mentioned by early church leaders?"

A number of figures get mentioned by Irenaeus, Eusebius, Epiphanius, and other later church figures, but in many cases these figures have nothing more than a reference or at best a placement in a lineage which gives us some general idea as to when they might have lived. In a few cases, we get paraphrases or even quotes, but beyond that, we usually have no writings associated with these figures.

Quadratus, who supposedly wrote an apology during the reign of Hadrian (117-138 CE) is a good example of this. We have a couple of paragraphs about him in Eusebius, writing in the 310s, and he quotes a sentence from Quadratus' apology. We get another reference to Quadratus in Jerome's writings in the 390s. Another, to pick a single name out of many in this situation, would be Musanus. Musanus is mentioned in two sentences in the works of Eusebius and another even smaller section in Jerome, which says he lived during the reign of Marcus Aurelius (161-180). Despite supposedly being an important author, we have no quotes, no specific dates, no locations, and not even titles of his works.

We also have a number of heretical figures who are in a similar situation: they get mentioned, perhaps get paraphrased or quoted, and beyond that are lost to history. Valentinus, a Gnostic author, is a figure we have more work from in this category. He is estimated to have lived from around 100 to 180 and was active in Rome. We have a number of texts of his quoted in the writings of early Christian authors and possibly a translation of a gospel attributed to his school of thought, but this is uncertain. On the other end of the spectrum, we have Theudas, the supposed teacher of Valentinus, who we have no dates for, no surviving texts or fragments from, and only get references to the name in Clement of Alexandria and some Valentinian works.

With all of these figures, there's just not enough to go off of. The best we have in most cases is hearsay coming decades and often centuries after these people supposedly lived. The evidence, their own writings, has been lost or even in some cases destroyed. The dates are often questionable, and as we've seen with more well-attested figures, are often fudged to push the origins of Christianity earlier. And all of this is assuming these figures even existed. While we would usually have little reason to doubt the authenticity of such figures in an ancient text claiming to be writing about true events, just as we have with the dates of said figures, we have seen instances where entire people were fabricated to promote a theological agenda.

It's also important to note that even with the questionable dating methods used with many of these name-dropped Christians, the vast majority of them date to the second century. There were certainly Christians prior to the writing of the canonical books of the New Testament, and it's possible that some of those mentioned in the works of Eusebius and others actually were around taking part in the evolution of what would become Christianity at some point in the early or middle second century. But because we have little to no evidence for the majority of them, we have to simply acknowledge the limitations of how much we can verify in regard to them.

"What about other non-canonical texts?"

Some will attempt to claim that certain non-canonical texts that did not make it into the New Testament still trace back to the first century and sometimes even to the disciples of Jesus. There's even a fake letter from Jesus himself to King Abgar V of Osorene. While the majority of these are already dated to the second century by most mainstream scholars and agreed to also be forgeries, there are a handful of texts we will briefly address that some claim to be earlier.

Doubting the Gospel of Thomas

The Gospel of Thomas is a sayings gospel which is hotly debated. Some will claim an early date for it, such as back to Jesus' lifetime, and others will claim a late date in the second century. There are even some who claim it dates back before Jesus and was adapted to Christianity after the fact. Others claim it was something like the hypothetical Q source, or even Q itself. There are a number of reasons that the text is clearly a second-century production, though.

Our first attestation to the Gospel of Thomas is Origen of Alexandria, writing in the 230s. At this point, most of our canonical second-century texts have been attested to decades earlier. Even a number of our latest canonical documents have been referenced and quoted, and we've been given lists of and quotes from a large number of non-canonical texts at this point too. Had Thomas been early, we should have seen references to it earlier than Origen.

Second, the overlap between Thomas and the Synoptic Gospels seems to indicate that Thomas used Matthew and Luke, not the other way around. There are harmonizations where Thomas has been written to reflect a combination of quotes from Matthew and Luke, such as in Thomas' sayings 10 and 16. There are other places where it uses a Lukan version of a quote instead of the Markan version, despite the Markan version being older. This again indicates the author of Thomas knew either Luke or Marcion's Evangelion, which was effectively Proto-Luke.

There are also indications that the author of Thomas was familiar with a particular gospel harmony found in Roman Syria, which would put the date in the 160s-170s at the earliest. This date range matches not only with the use of Matthew, Mark, and Luke, but also for attestation by Origen. It gives the document enough time to circulate and be adopted by a sect that drew enough attention to be worthy of mention by the time Origen is writing in the third century.

The use of Thomas himself, a character who does not play a major role in earlier gospel content, Paul, or elsewhere in early Christianity, shows that there has also been enough time for various groups to start to latch onto figures found in the earlier gospels. This also happens with Mary, Peter, and even more obscure figures such as Nicodemus. Had the Gospel of Thomas been an earlier text with Thomas being such a central figure, we would likely see him play a more prominent role in other content. Given that we don't, it's likely that the use of the figure Thomas is similar to that of other names found in the gospels who had stories expanded over time, not the other way around.

What the Didache Didn't Say

The Didache, also known as The Lord's Teaching Through the Twelve Apostles to the Nations, is a short, anonymous Greek text that did not make it into the canonical New Testament. For centuries, scholars correctly dated the text to the late second century, but the drive to push all Christian texts earlier during the 20th century has resulted in erroneous dating attempts as early as the first century. The longer title gets its name from the first line: "The teaching of the Lord to the Gentiles (or Nations) by the twelve apostles." The content is divided into three sections: ethics, rituals, and church organization.

Our first reference to the Didache is Eusebius in the 300s. We get a couple other references to the text in the later 300s as well by Athanasius and Rufinus. All of them listed it as non-canonical, with Eusebius placing it alongside documents like the Apocalypse of Peter and the Shepherd of Hermas.

While some attempt to claim the church organization is underdeveloped in the Didache and thus the document is early, the usage of positions such as deacons and bishops in the text clearly indicate that the earliest the document could've been written was the middle of the second century. We find the word for bishop used most in Acts and the Pastoral letters, some of the latest canonical texts we have. It's also found in 1 Peter, a fake letter attributed to Peter written in the style of Paul and also dated to the second century. Many have also pointed out overlapping concepts and vocabulary between the Didache and the Gospel of Matthew, which was also written in the middle of the second century. Ultimately, all signs point to the Didache being written in the second century along with much of the rest of early Christian literature.

The (Not So Good) Shepherd of Hermas

The Shepherd of Hermas, a Christian text that was popular during the second century, contains the recounting of five visions, twelve mandates or commandments, and ten parables. It is another text some claim either fully or partially dates to the first century. The author identifies himself as Hermas and claims to have been a contemporary of

Clement, thus where the idea of first-century authorship comes from. However, as we noted earlier in this chapter, Clement was actually a second-century author (if he wrote at all). Interestingly, the *Muratorian Canon*, a list of Christian texts considered to be canonical and often dated as early as the 180s, attributes the Shepherd of Hermas to the brother of Pope Pius I, who was Pope sometime between 140-154. This lines up with the rest of early Christian literature but would also open the possibility of identifying a real Clement of Rome around this time as well. Many early Christian leaders considered the Shepherd of Hermas as canonical, but ultimately it was not selected to be in what we now know as the New Testament.

Shepherd of Hermas is a peculiar Christian text in the fact that it never mentions the name Jesus. It also only mentions the word Christ in one manuscript of the many we have. There seems to be no conception of a historical Jesus, a death and resurrection, or much of anything we would consider central to the idea of a historical Jesus. Instead, it talks of the Son of God, which is pre-existent and entirely metaphysical and spiritual. The closest we get to anything that sounds like the concept of a human Jesus comes in Parable 5, in which it talks about "the flesh." However, the conception laid out there is obscure, unclear, and doesn't fit with the theology of canonical Christian scriptures.

The Shepherd of Hermas is likely another mid-second-century text and, given its obscurity, placing it earlier would do nothing to indicate the possibility of a historical Jesus. In fact, if anything, it would further prove the idea that early Christians did not have the concept of a historical, human Jesus but rather had more abstract and philosophical understandings of a deity. Given there are only a handful of possible references to canonical Christian texts, the consideration as scripture by relatively early sources, and its lack of references to a historical Jesus, the date range attributed to it by the Muratorian Canon between the 140s-150s seem reasonable.

Various Other Gospels and "Gospel Sources"

As we stated earlier, there are dozens of other gospels that didn't make it into the Bible. Some, such as the Gospel of Truth, are directly linked to second-century heretics. Others, such as the Gospel of Peter, the Gospel of the Hebrews, and others, are effectively competing Synoptic Gospels. Given the date for our canonical Synoptic Gospels being in the 140s CE at the earliest, this date also applies to these non-canonical gospels which use the same sources. It also lends credence to the idea that Marcion's Evangelion is what started the gospel boom - even others that did not make it into the canon tried to copy and create their own versions of it.

There are also gospel fragments, such as Oxyrhynchus 1224, the Egerton Gospel, and others that we only have a few sentences or even phrases from that don't seem to match our canonical gospels. The fragments themselves usually date to the third century or later, and given that our third-century fragments of canonical texts are of texts written in the second century, this is a reasonable date for these texts as well. In fact, mainstream scholarship usually dates these gospels in the second century. When they don't, they use the logic of their early dating of the canonical gospels to justify an early date for these fragments, too.

Then we have supposed "gospel sources." The most well-known one is the supposed "Q" source, but there are hypothetical sources for the Passion of Jesus, various Gospel of John sources, and others. Most of these supposed sources are ideologically motivated and fabricated to push the date of Christian texts closer to the time they assume Jesus lived.

Q, for example, is just Marcion's Evangelion - that was the first iteration of these stories and sayings and Luke, Matthew, and numerous non-canonical gospels used it as a baseline. Yes, someone did write these before it was published, but likely no more than a few months or years beforehand, just as it is with any book. To assume a lost sayings source or a century-old oral tradition is to already assume Jesus is historical and that these things must go back to him or his followers. There is no trace of Q in other earlier texts, no fragments of a Q source, and no reason to assume it other than to push content back closer to the supposed life of Jesus.

The same goes for the Passion source and similar sources - what really happened is someone wrote the first version of Mark, and from there various authors used it and made creative additions of their own. Even with a hypothetical older source, at some point someone had to come up with it. Pushing the dates back for its creation beyond the initial use of them is purely speculative and ideologically motivated. It presumes the answer it wants - a historical Jesus.

When it comes to the Gospel of John, our stylometric analysis in Chapter 8 does find a number of different authors responsible for the text, but this does not mean there is some lost source text that was floating around for over 100 years before the gospel was written. Just like the supposed Q material that was really just content added by Marcionite authors in the 130s-140s, the various parts of John are just different authors from the same community with a final editor who pieced it all together. Given John is our latest gospel, likely being written in the 160s, our oldest source in it is likely the Synoptic gospels themselves dating to a decade or two earlier. The biggest outstanding piece of the text beyond the author who adapted the synoptics to John would be the *Discourse Source* or *Farewell Discourse*, which is simply a speech Jesus gives from chapters 14-17 of John. It was just content written by someone in the John community in the second century, which got added into the Gospel.

"Don't we have an abundance of manuscripts/copies used by the early church?"

You might hear some historicists say something along the lines of, "We have more manuscripts of the New Testament than any other text." While this might be technically true, it's a very misleading statement. "Manuscripts" can mean anything from whole texts down to literally less than a full line of text on a scrap of parchment or papyrus.

Most of these manuscripts come from the fourth century or later, and that's really where the hundreds of texts come in. In fact, our oldest full New Testament manuscripts, Codex Vaticanus and Codex Sinaiticus, are dated to around the middle of the fourth century. Even these two manuscripts don't perfectly match our current Bibles - both have various verses missing or added, for example. Vaticanus is damaged and doesn't have four of the Pauline letters, and Sinaiticus has the non-canonical Epistle of Barnabas and Shepherd of Hermas at the end. Even in these relatively complete manuscripts, the canon was very much still undecided. Some of the manuscripts we have might even be evidence for entirely different versions of the texts we have today. The fragment known as P69, ostensibly one of our oldest fragments of Luke, could very well be a fragment of Marcion's gospel and has a different reading than our version of Luke.

On top of that, the manuscripts we have don't even agree with each other all the time. There are hundreds of thousands of variants - with differences as big as omissions or additions of entire verses and as small as changing a single word or letter - in the manuscripts of the New Testament. Scholar Eldon Jay Epp estimated that as of 2014

159

there are up to 750,000 variants across the current manuscripts we have today.[7] Peter J. Gurry, another scholar writing about the New Testament, believes that when excluding spelling errors, the number of variants is in the range of 500,000.[8] More conservative scholars, such as Bart Ehrman, estimate that the number is closer to 300,000 to 400,000. Regardless of the exact number, the scale of how many variants we find attests to the unreliability of the scribes transmitting the information. There are only around 138,000 words in the Greek New Testament, so even with the low estimate of 300,000 variants, there are more than double the number of variants than there are actual words in the New Testament.

To make matters worse, the most reliable methods aren't usually used to date our manuscripts. Rather than using carbon dating, for example, the most common method used is paleography. Paleography is basically the use of handwriting to determine the dates of ancient manuscripts. If you've ever watched police dramas, you'll know handwriting varies from person to person. However, the hypothesis underlying paleography is that some handwriting trends stick around from generation to generation, and thus if we have some reference points we can use those to date the texts in question. Paleography is usually considered a last resort method due to its lack of reliability, but unfortunately that's the main method used to date New Testament manuscripts due to a desire not to destroy parts of our oldest copies of the Bible (carbon dating requires the destruction of some of the paper). This is why you see such a wide range for manuscript dates. As scholars such as Brent Nongbri point out, this method and some of its problems lead to skewing dates earlier than they should be. So, while it's possible for Codex Sinaiticus, for example, to be in the early to mid-fourth century, it's also possible that it's later up into the early fifth century. The same goes for Vaticanus and other key manuscripts.

All manuscripts earlier than the 300s, with the exceptions of a few of Paul's letters, are in fragments. Fragments can be large, containing multiple chapters, or they can be very small, not even containing full sentences. Not only are our fragmented manuscripts few before the 300s, we actually only have around a dozen or so that we confidently date before around the 250s, with perhaps another dozen or two dating from around 250-300.

Earlier than that, we really aren't sure. All manuscripts from potentially earlier dates haven't been carbon dated and advances in paleography keep moving things further back. In fact, the John Rylands Library out of the University of Manchester, which houses our oldest known manuscript known as P52, says that despite P52 having previously been dated to 125-175 using paleography, "Recent research points to a date nearer to 200 AD, but there is as yet no convincing evidence that any earlier fragments from the New Testament survive."

Why does this matter? The most important takeaway is how late and scarce our physical evidence for the New Testament and Christianity is. The manuscripts vary quite a bit, showing that the texts were still being rewritten in different ways for centuries after they were supposedly authored. The manuscript evidence we have is also another argument in favor of our second-century authorship of these texts. What is more likely: the New Testament is written in the first century and we don't have any manuscripts or texts for 100-200 years, or these texts are written in the second century and we have our first manuscripts around that time? It's true, we don't have originals either way, but it makes more sense to base our understanding of history closer to the date of the physical evidence rather than closer to the date that is theologically convenient for the religion in question in spite of the evidence.

The Sacred Names

As we talked about in Chapter 4, the words "Jesus" and "Christ," along with a few other words like "Lord," never get spelled out until the third or fourth century. To put it another way, no manuscript says the name Jesus until the 300s or later. All of these manuscripts use what is known as nomina sacra, Latin for sacred names. Nomina sacra are effectively Christian runes and abbreviations made of two to three characters substituted in place of these names or words.

We don't know exactly where the use of nomina sacra came from, but it wasn't simply for saving space. There are other times authors and scribes could've used more common abbreviations or abbreviated other, longer words and chose not to do so. While there are some deviations, the standard approach was to take the first and last letters of the word to create the nomina sacra for the various words abbreviated. In a few cases, the first and second letters were chosen, but these are outliers. Most nomina sacra also had a line over them, similar to how Roman numerals have lines over them. We also know that it wasn't a carryover from the Jewish tradition of abbreviating Yahweh, as a number of Greek manuscripts carry over the full name and others use a distinct abbreviation for it that does not follow the pattern of the nomina sacra but rather the pattern of the original Hebrew.

There were four core nomina sacra, specifically the nomina divina - divine names. Greek has a number of grammatical cases, but for the sake of simplicity, our chart will stick to the nominative case.

Here are the nomina sacra most commonly found in early manuscripts:

English	Greek	Nomina Sacra
God	Θεός	ΘΣ
Lord	Κύριος	ΚΣ
Jesus	Ἰησοῦς	ΙΣ
Christ/Messiah	Χριστός	ΧΣ

A number of other words would be transformed into nomina sacra in various texts, including things like heaven/heavens, savior, man/human being, Israel, and others, but the above four were the most common and consistent. After the original practice of abbreviating these four, it expanded into a variety of other words.

We don't get manuscripts spelling any variation of Christ out, for example, until the fourth century. In Codices Vaticanus and Sinaiticus, "Christian" (or some variation of it) is spelled out one time each in 1 Peter and Acts, and anti-Christ in 1 John and 2 John. But these aren't as straightforward as it would seem, a simple spelling out of these words.

Yet Another E for an I

For Christian, Vaticanus uses an "ei" spelling - χρειστιανος - Chreistians. This matches the fifth-century Codex Bezae and some others in its spelling. Sinaiticus, however, spells it χρηστιανος with just the "e" - "Chrestians." Likewise, we get this e/ei spelling when these texts spell out anti-Christ.

Slight spelling variations are to be expected. There's even a term for this in biblical studies: "itacism" (or iotacism - when the vowels in Greek shifted). But this actually could have significant theological implications. We assume based on certain theological references that

163

Jesus was the Christ, "the anointed one," as the word means. But when the word is spelled with an *e* instead, it becomes "the good one."

In fact, it would seem that certain groups actually specifically used Chrest instead of Christ, such as the Marcionites. The oldest inscribed reference to Jesus that we have anywhere is in Deir Ali, Syria, from around 318 CE and says:

The meeting-house of the Marcionites, in the village of Lebaba, of the Lord and Saviour Jesus the Good [Chrest] - Erected by the forethought of Paul a presbyter.

This is our oldest inscribed reference to Jesus, and it calls him Jesus Chrest - not Jesus Christ. The usage is quite extensive in the manuscript tradition, as well. For example, The Nag Hammadi codices, some of our oldest manuscripts, specifically have 147 instances of abbreviated nomina sacra, 27 instances of Chrest, and only 2 uses of Christ - both in the Gospel of Philip which uses all spelling variations through the text.[9]

Here is a brief list of early manuscripts which use Chrestian:

Manuscript	Word	Date/Century
SB XII 10772	Chrestian	3rd-4th Century
P. Laur. II 42	Chrestian	3rd-4th Century
P. Oxy. XLIII 3149	Chrestian	5th Century
SB XVI 12497	Chrestian	3rd-4th Century
P. Oxy. XLII 3035	Chrestian	3rd-4th Century
P. Oxy. XLIII 3119	Chrestian	259-260 CE

Greek Magical Papyrus IV. 3007-86	Chrestian	4th Century
Kellis Manuscripts	Chrestos	4th Century
Codex Sinaiticus	Chrestos	4th Century
Nag Hammadi Codices	Chrestian and Christian	4th Century

Chrest was also more common outside the Christian world. Chrestus, like the name written by Suetonius which we covered in Chapter 3, was a common name among slaves. It was also a title affixed to individuals, such as Phocion the Good (Greek Φωκίων ὁ χρηστός), the fourth-century BCE Greek politician. Various gods from a variety of religions were given the title Chrest, from Isis to Apollo to Mithras. Multiple Jewish apocalyptic texts of the time also would talk of a "righteous one" or Chrest.

The word Chrest is used throughout the New Testament manuscripts we have, much more than the Christ version of the spelling. Furthermore, whenever we see something described as "good" it is often some variation of Chrest. For example, in 1 Peter 2:2 when it says, "The Lord is good," The Greek is literally, "χρηστὸς ὁ Κύριος" or "Good/Chrest the Lord." Even non-canonical material has instances of Chrest. The manuscript Papyri Graecae Magicae IV.1227-64, a collection of spells and magic from the 100s BCE to the 400s CE, cites "Jesus Chrest" in the incantation to drive out a demon, for example.

We know by the third century CE, authors such as Tertullian are correcting others for using the spelling and pronunciation Chrest and Christian. Prior to this, we do get a mention in Justin Martyr's *First Apology* chapter 4, which says "For we are accused of being Christians, and to hate what is excellent (Chrestian) is unjust." He goes on to elaborate further, talking about deeds and actions - something that "excellence" and "good" would matter more to than a concept of being "anointed." It looks like he was defending it or making wordplay based on Chrest rather than saying it is wrong. If the text is read with Chrestian in place of Christian in the chapter, we get a much more coherent argument. Our earliest manuscripts for Justin's works come almost 1,000 years after they were written, and by that point Christ and Christian was the spelling across the whole religion. It's possible that the later scribe making this copy of Justin *corrected* him, but in doing so messed up the original wordplay in the text. Nonetheless, we know that even if this was a later title, some groups such as the Marcionites used the Chrest variant up into the fourth century.

The church leaders from the late-second century and later definitely had their hands full trying to rein in all kinds of offshoots and sects, all while trying to whitewash their religion's mystery cult past and history with the spelling variants we now see today.

Chapter Notes:

1. Eusebius, and Christian Frederic Crusé. *Eusebius' Ecclesiastical History*. Peabody, Mass., Hendrickson Publishers, 2009. bk. 8.2.3

2. Bishop, Eusebius. *History of the Martyrs in Palestine*. Legare Street Press, 26 Oct. 2022. bk. 8.12.1

   This book is actually an appendix to Eusebius' work *Ecclesiastical History* (also referred to as *Church History*). It appears to have been found later in a Syriac manuscript of *EH*, which would make sense, as over sharing Eusebius' admission of bias probably wouldn't make for a very convincing argument.

3. Eusebius, and Christian Frederic Crusé. *Eusebius' Ecclesiastical History*. Peabody, Mass., Hendrickson Publishers, 2009. bk. 1.1.4

4. Vinzent, Markus. *Writing the History of Early Christianity: From Reception to Retrospection*. Cambridge, Cambridge University Press, 2019. ch. 4 (Kindle version pp. 205-216)

5. Simpson, William Alexander. *Aristides' Apology and the Novel Barlaam and Ioasaph*. Studia Patristica Supplements, 2017.

6. Eusebius, and Christian Frederic Crusé. *Eusebius' Ecclesiastical History*. Peabody, Mass., Hendrickson Publishers, 2009. bk. 3.39.15-16

7. Epp, Eldon Jay. "Why Does New Testament Textual Criticism Matter? Refined Definitions and Fresh Directions." *The Expository Times*, vol. 125, no. 9, 28 May 2014, pp. 417–431, www.doi.org/10.1177/0014524614530796. Accessed 10 Nov. 2023.

8. Gurry, Peter J. "The Number of Variants in the Greek New Testament: A Proposed Estimate." *New Testament Studies*, vol. 62, no. 1, 2015, p. 113, www.cambridge.org/core/journals/new-testament-studies/article/abs/number-of-variants-in-the-greek-new-testament-a-proposed-estimate/0D19A713ACD4AC530525A1E12BF2106C. Accessed 16 Dec. 2023.

9. Linnsen, Martijin. *ChrEstian all over the Nag Hammadi Library*. 2021.

Further Reading:

1. Rosenmeyer, Patricia A. *Ancient Epistolary Fictions*: *The Letter in Greek Literature*. Cambridge; New York, Cambridge University Press, 2008.

We cite Rosenmeyer in Chapter 2, but we wanted to list *Ancient Epistolary Fictions* again due to the common signatures of ancient times. Keep in mind that the people who were educated enough to write books complete with theological arguments likely studied older texts as part of their schooling.

2. New Advent. *The Fathers of the Church*. https://www.newadvent. org/fathers/.

The Catholic website New Advent has a large number of English translations of many of the works of the early church leaders. Despite the translations often being old and the scriptural references being overly generous in places, it's a useful resource. While you'll have to search around for some others not found here, we do recommend reading the works of each to see for yourself how Christianity developed in the early years.

CHAPTER 6

The Theological and Rational Issues

Many people take a logical approach to the Bible. Not only in regard to the historicity of Jesus, but in the way that Christianity itself was formed. These people are more concerned about the rational side of the early followers. After all, it must have started somewhere, but where? What did the early Christians believe, and can we learn more about if Jesus was real by understanding them? In this chapter, we look into those concerns.

"What about the Jewish prophecies that were fulfilled?"

The arguments for the historicity of Jesus based on the "prophecies" alluded to in the New Testament are nothing short of strange. As we mentioned earlier in Chapter 2, most of the assertions claimed as prophecies in the Gospels aren't really actual prophecies at all. They are just stories of Jesus doing something that another character had already done in the Old Testament. There's nothing prophetic about that. If someone were to write a story about former NBA player Michael Jordan, mention that he is bald "as foretold in the books of history," and reference 2 Kings 2:23 as a prophecy, the creator of such a story would be soundly and reasonably mocked. That is, however, exactly what a massive portion of verses in the Gospels do. They take random descriptions of people and events (even some that are allegorical in the original context) found within the Old Testament books and use them to create characters and craft a narrative. The authors don't just use these arbitrary Old Testament lines for prophecies of the miraculous works of their main character, but also the mundane events and basic information for their "natural" Jesus. But it's infinitely easier to construct a work of fiction when the source material is laid out in front of you.

A Sound Defense

That brings us to an interesting situation. It's worth noting at this point that some people would point to parts of our theory as false equivalencies. Because of some mistakes of the mythicist claims in the past century, it can be tempting to point at any of our allegations of parallels between the Gospels and prior works in an attempt to paint us as insincere. Many of our critics personally believe that the prophecies Jesus supposedly fulfilled are a testament to not only his divine nature, but, in some way, his historicity as well. However, we have worked hard to rid our theory of any sense of the outlandish claims some mythicists make, and we feel that our theory fits perfectly with reality and actual history - in a way that the ecclesiastical history the Bible presents doesn't. Furthermore, the parallels we draw are based on what we know from different cited books, while the seemingly random parallels drawn in the Gospels and lauded as "prophecies" are based on little more than an author's creativity and the magnitude of their collection of known myths. To put it bluntly, if the parallels we point out with Jesus can be dismissed as anything close to deceitful, the parallels drawn by the authors of the Gospels should be evidence of the inaccuracy of even the natural life of Jesus in their stories.

While on the topic of both prophecies and defending our position, it's a good time to explain another critique of our theory. As explained in Chapter 2, we show that the ill-timed Capernaum reference found in the Gospel of Luke is proof of its authorship being after Marcion's gospel, Evangelion, in roughly 144 CE. Some historicists to whom we have presented our case argue that the authors of the gospels were not concerned with writing a story in chronological order. They claim that the Capernaum error found in Luke is nothing more than an accurate quote from Jesus placed before where one would expect it - but with no issue at all! Not only is that a very convenient card for the historicists to have in their back pocket (being able to dismiss all continuity errors and light anachronisms whenever they feel), but it is also a demonstrably incorrect statement with proof to the contrary. Generally all the narratives in the New Testament are presented in chronological order, and the few exceptions have a reason for their deviations.

Where To Plant A Tree

One such example, which involves a "prophecy" being carried out by Jesus, perfectly illustrates our points of both ridiculous prophecies and chronological concern: In Mark 11:12-21, Jesus and his disciples come across a fig tree. The passage, in its entirety, is below:

The next day as they were leaving Bethany, Jesus was hungry. **Seeing in the distance a fig tree in leaf, he went to find out if it had any fruit. When he reached it, he found nothing but leaves, because it** *was not the season for figs. Then he said to the tree, "May no one ever* *eat fruit from you again."* *And his disciples heard him say it.*

On reaching Jerusalem, **Jesus entered the temple courts and began** **driving out those who were buying and selling there. He overturned** **the tables of the money changers and the benches of those selling doves,** *and would not allow anyone to carry merchandise through the temple courts.* *And as he taught them, he said, "Is it not written:* '**My house** *will be called* *a house of prayer for all nations'? But you have made it 'a den of robbers.'"*

The chief priests and the teachers of the law heard this and began *looking for a way to kill him, for they feared him, because the whole crowd* *was amazed at his teaching.*

When evening came, Jesus and his disciples went out of the city.

In the morning, as they went along, they saw the fig tree **withered from the roots. Peter remembered and said to Jesus, "Rabbi,** **look! The fig tree you cursed has withered!"**

This story is based on a passage in the Old Testament. Jesus simply acts out what the old scripture says, but the verses don't ever claim a particular person would ever do that in the future. It's not really a prophecy, it's just lines of metaphorical writings about the Jews being used as a blueprint for what the author of Mark wanted to have his main character do. This is done in other verses in the Gospels as well and claimed as fulfillment of prophecies, but in this particular case, the author of Mark didn't feel the need to claim it as a prophecy. That led to an unintended reaction. Here is the Old Testament passage the above story was taken from, found in Hosea 9:10-16:

"When I found Israel, it was like finding grapes in the desert; **when** **I saw your ancestors, it was like seeing the early fruit on the fig** **tree.** *But when they came to Baal Peor, they consecrated themselves to that* *shameful idol and became as vile as the thing they loved. Ephraim's glory*

will *fly away like a bird*—*no birth, no pregnancy, no conception. Even if they rear children, I will bereave them of every one. Woe to them when I turn away from them! I have seen Ephraim, like Tyre, planted in a pleasant place. But Ephraim will bring out their children to the slayer."*

Give them, Lord—what will you give them? Give them wombs that miscarry and breasts that are dry.

"Because of all their wickedness in Gilgal, I hated them there. **Because of their sinful deeds, I will drive them out of my house.** *I will no longer love them; all their leaders are rebellious. Ephraim is blighted,* **their root is withered**, *they yield no fruit. Even if they bear children, I will slay their cherished offspring."*

Notice that the sections we've put in bold print are in order of tree-bird-house-root. There's a specific reason for that. The author of Mark was obviously using the Hosea passage as a model. What we don't know for sure is whether or not he intended for the origins of the story to be discovered, because he failed to mention them. The author of Matthew, copying from Mark (sometimes even word for word), completely failed to realize what the author of Mark was doing or referencing, and so in his edition of the story, he fixes what he sees as a weird chronological error. To the author of Matthew, it must have seemed odd to have Jesus deal with a fig tree only to return to it later after his temple outburst. Instead, in Matthew 21:12-20, he has Jesus drive out the temple salesmen, go out of town for a night, then come back in the morning to take care of all his important fig tree business:

Jesus entered the temple courts and drove out all who were buying and selling there. He overturned the tables of the money changers and the benches of those selling doves. *"It is written," he said to them, "'***My house** *will be called a house of prayer,' but you are making it 'a den of robbers.'"*

175

The blind and the lame came to him at the temple, and he healed them. But when the chief priests and the teachers of the law saw the wonderful things he did and the children shouting in the temple courts, "Hosanna to the Son of David," they were indignant.

"Do you hear what these children are saying?" they asked him.

"Yes," replied Jesus, "have you never read, 'From the lips of children and infants you, Lord, have called forth your praise'?"

And he left them and went out of the city to Bethany, where he spent the night.

Early in the morning, as Jesus was on his way back to the city, he was hungry. **Seeing a fig tree by the road, he went up to it but found nothing on it except leaves. Then he said to it, "May you never bear fruit again!" Immediately the tree withered.**

When the disciples saw this, they were amazed. "How did the fig tree wither so quickly?" they asked.

The authors of the Gospels were trying to construct a chronological narrative that made sense to them and their readers. Contradictions in continuity or issues with congruence among the Gospels are not proof of the authors' extraordinary and convenient intent - they are simply errors and/or purposeful changes. In the case above, the lines and stories are so incredibly similar that the only logical conclusion would be a deliberate alteration - here, we see an author's attempt at correcting what they see as a chronological mistake. There is no proof of the New Testament authors abstaining from putting a non-prophetical biographical passage in chronological order.

The Disappearing Divination

Continuing with the issues with prophecies, something seemingly out of place is the lack of them outside the Gospels. While bountiful in the first four books of the New Testament, they all but disappear afterwards. The prophecies in the Gospels are not only fulfilled by the main character, but the secondary and some tertiary characters as well. For example, John the Baptist gets plenty of the prophetic spotlight despite only really being a main plot point of three different scenes. And of those three scenes, he is only alive for two of them. Contrast John the Baptist with the figure of Paul, the prophecy-free supposed author of half the New Testament, and it seems odd that no more prophecies are doled out later to much larger characters. We attribute this to John the Baptist being a real historical person with a real following, so prophecies are cast upon him in the Gospels to elevate him to a level *just* below Jesus in an attempt to woo his leaderless followers. Paul, on the other hand, was viewed as a lower level letter writer whose few short texts were expanded and edited with no regard for his status. With no concern for literary integrity nor for prophetic elevation, the writings attributed to Paul and his subsequent fabricated biography were used as a scolding tool - not a marketing ploy.

Absent hyperbole, the Jewish prophecies references in the New Testament provide no evidence for the existence of Jesus, and, in fact, only add to the evidence that the authors used these old lines from the Jewish scriptures to manufacture their stories.

"Didn't Jesus' prophecies come true?"

The prophecies presented in the gospels and the surrounding New Testament books offer nothing more than a glimpse into the social hopes and feelings of an era of Ancient Roman Empire. Even the mainstream dates don't really consider the prophecies to be actual clairvoyant statements. The Gospel of Mark, thought by scholars to be the first book with the Little Apocalypse (explained in Chapter 2), is typically dated to the immediate years after the destruction of the second temple in Jerusalem in 70 CE.

The only way that a non-religious scholar would advocate for a pre-70 date would be if they argued that the tensions between the Jews and the Romans had grown worse, and the belief of imminent destruction was the main motivation behind writing the gospels. There's nothing intrinsically wrong with that approach, but it definitely tries to stifle the supernatural fortune telling abilities of Jesus, and that's our point. Even scholars who think the Gospel of Mark was written earlier than we do try to come up with a natural explanation for Jesus' statements that could be taken as supernatural prophecies.

The "wars and rumors of wars" prophecy is one that is repeated to this day, and for a staggering amount of reasons. It seems that with every potential military conflict dating back to the second century, the Christians have expected the world to end. However, just as there were wars and rumors of wars prior to the writing of the gospels, there will unfortunately continue to be. Jesus didn't actually make any prophecies (it's difficult to tell the future when you don't exist), and even if he did, they have no connection to modern life and should have been fulfilled within a few decades of his supposed lifetime.

"Didn't Christianity start with Jesus?"

Even from a conservative Christian standpoint, the technical answer to this question is no. The Bible itself states that the term "Christian" started getting used in Antioch years after the supposed death of Jesus, and groups of followers are recorded as meeting in churches on the first day of the week sometime after the gospel stories end. More or less, this question, which mythicists get asked more than one might expect, is flawed to begin with. However, taking it to be a sincere quandary of whether or not Christianity was around prior to Jesus, we can attempt to answer it better.

If Jesus really had existed, then to some extent you might be able to claim he was the starting point for the religion. But, depending on your definition of Christianity, there's just too much evidence of outside influence to say that the religion started with Jesus or even from the very same people who wrote the books.

Let us explain.

Nonlinear Inequalities

In tumultuous times, cults (and religions, their synonymous larger counterparts) splinter into groups. It's only natural; not everyone sees eye to eye, so when things get tough and questions get asked, different answers are given. Even the most riveting of figureheads and leaders can't instill a perfect doctrine inside their faithful for too long. When the inevitable happens, and the founder of a cult dies, we almost immediately see differing sects form from the first.

It's usually based on who the sect believes is the next true leader. Joseph Smith Jr., the founder of The Church of Jesus Christ of Latter-Day Saints, also known as Mormonism, died in 1844. Not counting the nine during his lifetime, there were 18 sects (each with a different leader) that split from the original cult during the 20 years after Joseph's death. Two more followed within the next few years. Without their beloved charlatan to lead them, the Mormons fell into disarray and the throne was up for grabs. We're not counting the most popular sect that we in America are most familiar with, as it is considered to be the truest continuation after Smith's death, with Brigham Young at the helm. We see this lack of perfect cohesion in Judaism, Islam, Buddhism, and really any religion that gets big enough to start to see a reasonable amount of diversity.

Starting in my teenage years, I was fascinated by the teachings of the Mormon Church. Not because I felt they were somehow correct, but rather the opposite. Being raised in a Baptist household, I was taught that the Mormons weren't real Christians. Trying to see if this claim was true or not, I spent years looking into their books and beliefs, and spent time meeting with missionaries, elders, and bishops. I very quickly realized that the Book of Mormon (and subsequent texts stemming from Joseph Smith Jr.) was absolute fiction. Anachronisms are rampant, and nothing is substantiated by logic, history, or archaeology. I started to try to explain these findings to the missionaries I had become friends with, but they "pulled the faith card" and said they believe the Book of Mormon is completely true, regardless of how much proof I had that it wasn't. It was at this point that I wondered if I ever "pulled the faith card" myself, and decided to try to only believe things that can be explained without blind faith. I'm definitely familiar with the story of Mormonism, and studying the rise of an obviously fabricated offshoot of Christianity can help understand the beginning stages of Christianity as a whole.

Jaaron Wingo

Diversity is not evidence against Jesus, however, a lack of diversity would be. We don't see different sects of Christianity until nearly the middle of the second century. In our theory, different cults and splits from bigger religions come together to form Christianity, but based on what we have found with stylometric analysis and dating of the texts, there's no evidence of sectarian beliefs stemming from one church until roughly 135-140 CE.

Church leader Clement of Alexandria, writing book seven of his work known as *Stromata* between 198-203 CE about the origins of Christianity and trying to fill in the gaps between the Gospels' narrative endings and the first Gospel authors, implies that the first

100 years or so were perfect because of the divine nature of the message and unity of the church. Until Marcion, the oldest of heretics, came onto the scene and messed it all up, that is. Doesn't sound too divine if a shipowner from Sinope can derail the literal words of a god!

This is telling. Not only for dating the New Testament authorship in the second century, but for the reality of a founder actually dying roughly 90 years prior. Depending on how much credibility you want to give to the gospel narrative, Jesus supposedly had a number of close followers and family. Dispersed around the Roman Empire, the Twelve Disciples would have very quickly started twelve different denominations (at a minimum) within their lifetimes. With no unifying book to tell the story or keep the congregations in line, Christianity would have faded into the dust by the middle of the first century. The only times a religion has kept cohesion as well as the Christians claim they did are with the threat of death for apostasy.

But if you turn your attention back to the second century, our theory once again lines up with reality. If Proto-Mark was completed around 120-125 CE, uniting pockets of mystery cults into one brotherhood, splinter groups show up right when expected: just a decade or so later. The floodgates open, and Gospels get written left and right. Letters are "found," faithful friends to the church get special guest and cameo roles in new books, and reimagined history is presented to the 97% illiterate flock.

So what does all of this have to do with finding out if Jesus started Christianity? To put it simply, it (like the rest of our book and theory) shows that the character named Jesus wasn't created until the second century. That means Christianity didn't "start" with Jesus. However, even without a historical Jesus, there is still some version of a Christ myth floating around before the Gospels were written. There's potential proof of that in the books of Tacitus and Suetonius. Couldn't those just be pre-gospel Christians? Yes and no. It depends entirely on what you consider Christianity to be, and at the risk of turning this trial into some sort of Scopes Monkey Trial 2.0, let's take a final dive into the Synonym Problem.

The Synonym Problem: Evolution of a Cult

Charles Darwin was not the first person to contemplate or write about the theory of evolution. He is, nevertheless, the most famous man to do so. Building upon the work of others, he wrote his *Origin of Species* after observing the results of natural selection in the Galapagos Islands. When researching what early church leaders had to say about the beginnings of Christianity, a very peculiar account caught our attention. It appears a couple of texts from Ancient Rome may give us clues to what the earliest form of "Christianity" was.

We placed Christianity in quotation marks above because, similar to the evolution of humans, the different stages of the evolution of Christianity technically have different names. Just as it doesn't go directly from "ape to human," Christianity is not simply "Jew to Christian." Not to mention, Christianity may mean something different to different people. If you take it to simply mean the belief in a savior or messiah of some kind, then Christianity could extend to just about any apocalyptic Jewish belief or many Greek cults longing for a savior from oppression. You could even extend it back in time (or forward in time) to any religion that has ever existed with a savior as the main focus. The more you add qualifiers and requirements to what Christianity is, the more it pushes the start date forward through time until you reach the turn of the second century.

Jaaron Wingo

According to Philo of Alexandria, a Jewish philosopher from Alexandria in Northern Egypt who lived from 20 BCE to 50 CE, there was a sect of what he described as Jewish philosophers called the "Therapeutae" living near Lake Mareotis outside of Alexandria. He explains that they live very peacefully in very basic quarters, and they commune together one day out of the week to eat a meal and listen to an elder preach. Women, while still technically separate from the men, were allowed to join to some extent in the meetings and listen to the words of the elder.

Comparisons with the Christians have been drawn, and a couple of fairly early Christian writers actually claimed the Therapeutae as the earliest Christian monks or simply Christians. Epiphanius, who lived from 315 to 403 CE, actually claimed that the Therapeutae were a Christian group called the Jessaens. He claimed that the early Christians were called Jessaens due to Jesus being from the lineage of Jesse (through his father, Joseph). Other than this claim, clearly made no less than 200 years after the first Gospel was written, there is no other evidence of the term Jessaen being used.

Philo writes about the Therapeutae beliefs and teachings, which look to be a blend of Buddhism and Judaism more than Christianity. They place heavy emphasis on Moses, which isn't really anyone the Christians would be too overtly concerned about - especially if they had their own, much more recent leader to follow. Philo does indicate that the Therapeutae were scattered among the Roman Empire, but says they are primarily located in Alexandria and undertake pilgrimages to the Lake Mareotis site.

With their community-centric customs and beliefs being similar to the practices listed in Acts 2:45-47, the Therapeutae seem to have a bit in common with the Christians, but only as a group that would one day evolve into Christianity. Interestingly enough, their connection with Alexandria (as well as the early Christian church leaders' claim of a connection with the city) lines up with a letter from Emperor Hadrian (quoted by a later scribe) where he claims that the worshippers of Serapis in Alexandria call themselves Christians. Some scholars have even considered the Therapeutae to stem from the "healers" (as the name Therapeutae translates to) from the cult of the Greek healer-god Asclepius (who, as we mentioned in Chapter 2, gets an interesting semi-cameo in the Gospel of John through the inclusion of a supernaturally healing Asclepion pool). Scholars have even pointed to second-century BCE inscriptions on the Greek island of Delos claiming Therapeutae as followers of none other than Serapis.

The Therapeutae would have been a very good starting point for what would evolve into Christianity. The missing ingredients are simply a messianic figure, knowledge of Hellenistic religious tropes, and someone educated in Greek to write it all down.

As luck would have it, multiple people during the 100 years surrounding Philo claimed to be the Messiah. According to Origen, a Christian scholar who lived from 185 to 253 CE, Dositheos was a Samaritan religious figure in the first century CE who claimed to be the Messiah. Origen goes on to list John the Baptist, Theodas, and Judas of Galilee as others the Jews called the Messiah. The Messiah seems to come and go quite a bit!

All three of these later listed men are mentioned in both the New Testament and Josephus. While the author of the book of Acts doesn't pick up on it, Judas of Galilee was seen in Josephus' writings as the catalyst for the rebellion that would become the First Jewish War. Along with another violent group called the Sicarii, Judas of Galilee's Jewish-nationalist followers carried out terroristic acts throughout Judaea, and I believe he was likely the reason for the inclusion of an adversarial character named Judas "called Iscariot."

Theodas, interestingly, is referenced out of chronological order in Acts. This is due to Acts not being written by an author who lived in the first century. As historical fiction, there are going to be some errors with dating people and events. This is far from the only time the author of Acts and Luke makes errors like this. Using sources and stories from other people, the author writes a very good historical fiction story of Paul and the disciples, but an obvious fiction nonetheless.

Jaaron Wingo

Simon bar Kokhba, the leader of what is considered the third Jewish-Roman War during 132-136 CE, was considered by some Jews to be the Messiah. He was crowned the ruler of the temporary Jewish separatist state and died at the hands of the Romans in 135.

Some scholars understand the surviving accounts of Athronges, a Jewish shepherd who lived during the reign of Herod Archelaus between 4 BCE and 6 CE, and Simon of Peraea, a rebellious former slave of the first century BCE's Herod the Great, as stories of people the Jews considered to be the Messiah. Both men were crowned as kings, and led numerous people into battle for the Jewish people.

A stone tablet found sometime around early 2000 on the banks of the Dead Sea contains 87 lines of Hebrew, telling portions of a story of a messianic figure. The story, which we only have a small, broken portion of, is called "Gabriel's Revelation." It involves the angel Gabriel of Jewish lore and a man who is considered by some experts to be the aforementioned messiah figure Simon of Peraea. The phrase "three days" is consistently important in this narrative, and according to its initial English translation, it states the main character will "rise" after the three days. Subsequent translations now read as after three days there will be "a sign," but even that is strikingly similar to the "sign of Jonah" mentioned by Jesus in the Gospels of Matthew and Luke. This stone tablet is dated to the late first century BCE or the early first century CE - before Jesus' supposed ministry, but just in time for a concept to develop with the cults of the day.

The concept of the "suffering servant" messiah or even a dying and rising messiah don't seem to be foreign to the Jews, as a scroll dated to 200 BCE found among a collection of scrolls hidden in a cave by the Dead Sea talks about a messianic figure known as Joseph, who refers to YHWH as "my father and my God."

According to Alan Avery-Peck, a professor of Judaic Studies at the College of the Holy Cross, another Dead Sea Scroll talks about the Old Testament leader Joshua (a variant of the name Jesus) in what should be taken as a messianic way. There were a plethora of Messiahs being discussed and followed during the time of the Therapeutae and the writing of the Gospel of Mark.

During the evolutionary process that brought about the Christians, the cult-like writings from Paul would have likely been fused in, using what would become the nomina sacra. If he was indeed a worshiper of Julius Caesar or the state religion, it seems words, phrases, and beliefs that were swirling around at the time were borrowed to form Christianity.

Found in the ancient cities of Priene, Apamea, and Eumeneia (located in modern-day Turkey), an inscription of an official edict in 9 BCE from the proconsul Paullus Fabius Maximus calls Caesar Augustus "savior" and "god," and specifies his birth as "the beginning of the gospel." The quote in context is below:

It seemed good to the Greeks of Asia, in the opinion of the high priest Apollonius of Menophilus Azanitus: "Since Providence, which has ordered all things and is deeply interested in our life, has set in most perfect order by giving us Augustus, whom she filled with virtue that he might benefit humankind, sending him as a savior, both for us and for our descendants, that he might end war and arrange all things, and since he, Caesar, by his appearance (excelled even our anticipations), surpassing all previous benefactors, and not even leaving to posterity any hope of surpassing what he has done, and since **the birthday of the god Augustus was the beginning of the gospel for the world that came by reason of him,**" *which Asia resolved in Smyrna.*

Compare that last sentence, along with what is written about Augustus in book six of Virgil's *Aeneid*, "Here is the man, here he is, whom you heard was promised to you rather often, **Augustus Caesar, son of god**, who will found the golden age again in Latium throughout the fields once ruled by Saturn," with the first verse in the Gospel of Mark that says, "**The beginning of the gospel about Jesus Christ, the Son of God.**"

There are four basic principles that come into play for the process of evolution: Variation, Inheritance, Selection and Time. There were various mythical beliefs throughout the Eastern Roman Empire. The Jews and the Christians did not exist in a philosophical vacuum. Generation after generation taught these beliefs to their children, and, in some cases, spread the beliefs through word of mouth or at the tip of a spear. Some beliefs were stamped out and didn't catch on - either by a failure in marketing, the aforementioned spear, or lack of a loyal (yet exceedingly gullible) fanbase. The messiah stories of the Jews and the healings of Asclepius stretched from centuries into BCE, and could have culminated during the turn of the second century CE into a mystery cult that found a home within the capricious Greeks of Turkey and the daydreaming Jews without the Temple. This natural process of religious evolution possibly brought forth what we now point to as the start of Christianity, a cult that didn't start with a Jesus, but soon after invented one to retcon their own origin story into history.

The Chicken or the Egg

The evolution of Christianity has many observable phases. Christology, which we very briefly discussed in Chapter 2, is generally a linear concept. As the character of Jesus is fleshed out and more stories get added with each gospel, we see greater and greater detail regarding his background, characteristics, and divine nature. The part of his background that we have placed under the microscope the most during our research is his hometown. Earlier, we shared some of our findings on the difference between the terms Nazarene and Nazoraean. We believe Nazareth (and its potential links) to be one of the most helpful keys to unlocking the dates of composition for all four canonical Gospels.

As a recap of what we have so far, Nazarene and Nazoraean are two similar words that are used in a couple of different ways in the New Testament. The Gospel of Mark only uses Nazarene to describe Jesus, while the Gospels of Matthew and John use Nazoraean. Luke uses both terms. As for the term Nazareth, the Gospels of Matthew, Luke, and John all use the term multiple times, while the edited, canonical version of Mark mentions it once (and, as we've pointed out, it likely wasn't in the original version).

Epiphanius claims the Nazoraeans were a particular sect of Christianity, but he also claims that all the Christians were called Nazoraeans at one point. The reason he gives for this is that the hometown of Jesus must have been the most clever nickname people could come up with. He doesn't mention anything about the term Nazarene, so that leaves the possibility that Nazarene and Nazoraean mean the same thing. That is the position of most English translators of the Bible.

There are problems with this assumption, however. If Nazarene and Nazoraean mean the same thing, one has to wonder just why the different variants were used by certain authors, while Luke flopped between both. Another issue is just what exactly they would all mean. If they mean what the Christians claim (a person from Nazareth), then not only would it be weird that Mark doesn't really mention Nazareth at all, Nazareth doesn't show up in any writings whatsoever (Christian or non-Christian) until the middle of the second century when we know Luke and Matthew were written.

Matthew specifically says that Jesus was called a Nazoraean because he was not only from Nazareth, but he was fulfilling prophecy by being from there, too. But we don't have any prophecy that statement seems to be based on. We would also expect for Nazareth to not only be mentioned in the days of the prophets, but also be a relevant town by the time of Jesus, if not solely due to said prophecy.

If the town was actually so important for the hundreds of years since the prophecy could have been made, why do we never see it until the second century? Why do so many of the earliest gospels not include Nazareth? Why does no one think anything good could come from there if it's literally part of prophecy?

As far as we can tell, the first potential mention of Nazareth is the town of Nasara, which is the name given in Marcion's Evangelion. If the town is so important that it's in a prophecy, why are there multiple variants of how it's spelled in the gospels? Why is there no mention of it in the Old Testament? Why aren't people living in the town with the hopes of *their* child being the Messiah? Why isn't Nazareth mentioned by any other New Testament authors other than the ones who wrote the gospels?

If it's just that the town's too small to be mentioned by anyone other than the gospel writers, how do Jesus' critics in the Gospel of

John know enough about it to make comments about how nothing good can come from there? Despite being very rare in the first century before the siege of Jerusalem in 70 CE, Nazareth is said to have a synagogue in the gospels. Synagogues in Galilee during the time Jesus supposedly lived are borderline anachronistic, so if Nazareth had one, the city would definitely be on a map before the second century.

As an aside, the prophecy Matthew might be alluding to is the Old Testament verse about Samson being a Nazarite. But Nazarite means something completely different than someone from Nazareth, and it being an allusion to Nazarite would also remove the entire connection to the possible town - wiping Nazareth off the map for good, and invalidating any New Testament book that claims Jesus came from Nazareth. It would also mean that the author is really bad at making connections, and could have been aiming at Nasaraean, which would be a Jewish group that existed prior to Jesus' supposed life. Epiphanius was very quick to dismiss any connection to both Nasaraean and Nazarite.

The connection to the Nasaraeans actually makes the most sense. If the author of the Gospel of Mark was trying to draw a connection to the Nasaraeans, that wouldn't be much of an issue. The earliest form of Mark very likely didn't have Nazareth, so that theory seems to hold up. Our theory is that Evangelion used the term Nazarene, and the author of Matthew introduced the term Nazoraean to Jesus. Since the author of the Gospel of Luke used Evangelion and the Gospel of Matthew as his sources, the usage of both Nazarene and Nazoraean is explained. The usage of Nazarene was clearly not the author of Luke's preference, as in their later book, Acts, the word Nazoraean is used solely.

Obviously, there is a possibility that the terms don't mean the same thing, but that causes even more issues. According to the Gospel

190

of Matthew, Jesus is called a Nazoraean due to prophecy. That means Mark's four references to Jesus being a Nazarene are a complete waste of ink.

"Why didn't the Romans or Jews refute the claims?"

As we know from experience, proving a negative can be a very hard thing to do - at least, to the standard that the opposing side sometimes desires. For instance, proving the nonexistence of Bigfoot seems easy enough, as the lack of hard evidence makes most people scoff at the very idea of a bipedal ape roaming the countryside. But a lack of evidence isn't enough to sway the most hearty of Bigfoot claimants. It's not impossible, but you would need sufficient contradictory evidence to persuade the people currently searching the forests of North America that their belief is unfounded.

As a result of these difficulties, we would expect the majority of early refutations to the claims of Christians to have been pointing out the lack of evidence or silliness of the claims. When we examine the earliest secular references to Christianity, they did just that. Suetonius (possibly borrowing from Tacitus, who said the same thing) called Christianity a "mischievous superstition." Pliny explained Christianity and said he did so because he's never dealt with one before. Lucian said Christians were "misguided creatures" and that "all this they take quite on faith."

While Suetonius and Tacitus should have dove deeper into the claims from the Christians, they clearly just took the word of the believers in regard to their history, as the Judaean crucifixion records from over eight decades prior were probably hard to find - especially after the Great Fire of Rome. It seems that explaining that the cult was new and mischievous was good enough in their opinions. To these historians, Christianity was new and, by all accounts, looked to be based on silliness. In short, the Romans *did* refute the claims, but they did so in a very light and dismissive manner.

As for the Jewish refutations, depending on which book you'd like to point to and how big of a date range you'd be willing to accept for authorship, the Jewish Talmud talks about different people named Joshua/Yeshua/Jesus who lived around the first century CE and caused trouble or practiced magic. While some of these people may have existed, it's possible the passages are responses to the Jesus of the Christians, written in an attempt to explain where some of the ideas may have come from. Overall, the lack of the Jesus of the Christians is telling, and places the Jewish refutations in the same category as the Romans. There just wasn't anyone there to point to, so it's hard to prove a negative.

Unfortunately for historicists, a mid-first-century CE writer and philosopher from Rome named Seneca wrote an essay attacking every religion known to the populace. This essay, *On Superstition*, is now lost, but was quoted by Christian theologian Augustine in 426 CE. Augustine explains that Christianity was not mentioned by Seneca.[1] We have one of the best candidates for an excellent Ancient Roman refutation of Christianity, and there is nothing but silence. Some mythicist writers, such as David Fitzgerald, have pointed to this silence as evidence against the historicity of Jesus, but a question remains: even if Jesus hadn't existed, where was the talk of the Christians? Our theory that Christianity simply wasn't there at the time, of course, explains why.

The silence of authors and the missing pages of Ancient Roman history books don't just lack the stories of Jesus. They are completely clueless about Christianity as a whole. We have shown repeatedly throughout this book that there can be Christianity without the character of Jesus, but there can *absolutely* be no Jesus without

Christianity. The Romans and the Jews of the second century didn't need to prove the negative further, because thanks to the deafening silence, it seems (as our theory suggests) that we see not even the claimants of Jesus Christ existed in the first century. A new and mischievous superstition indeed.

"Isn't Jesus one of the most attested to people from Ancient Times?"

Historicists consistently rely on this argument to dismiss mythicist claims. While theists can fall back on the idea of Jesus' divinity to underwrite this phenomenon, to the atheist, agnostic, and non-religious historicists we ask, why do you think that is?

Though we're sure there might be a couple of atheist outliers somewhere out there on the planet that would subscribe to some strange version of Jesus' sanctitude, the vast majority of them don't believe Jesus was divine. Atheist historicists are generally of the opinion that Jesus was a normal human being from Judaea who amassed a following from his teachings and travels. Unless you are presenting a theory we're not aware of, Jesus was not a politician, military leader, member of royalty, famous writer, famous entertainer, or rich member of the elite. Under normal circumstances, there's really no reason for him to be one of the most attested to people from Ancient Times.

Except this isn't normal circumstances. We briefly discussed the argumentum ad populum in Chapter 2, but this goes beyond just the writings of the various gospels. The horrible destruction of history and art in the name of Jesus and the installation of theocracy after theocracy are the very reasons why he is one of the most attested to people. Countless pages, books, and voices from antiquity are lost, but the faithful followers of the group that overtook every other cult in the

Roman Empire held onto fragments of their books. That's no surprise whatsoever.

It simply makes sense that he is one of the most attested to people in antiquity. If he's divine, you'd definitely think he'd be attested to, and if he isn't divine, it's undeniably due to the fact that Christianity became the largest religion in the world.

But that is where it stops. Just because we don't have tons of documents from Christianity's opposition or from non-religious voices in antiquity, doesn't mean that the direct and indirect quotes from people within Christianity were true. The aftermath of the removal of dissenting voices and interpolation of history by the most virulent of Christianity's lot over the last 1,700-1,800 years shouldn't, in our opinion, be used as an argument for Jesus' historicity.

"Why would the early Christians lie?"

This question is easily the most common question religious people ask when confronted with any sort of criticism directed towards Jesus. It's one of the main ways they defend the supernatural parts of the Gospels against the atheistic historicists who grant Jesus an existence. As we said in Chapter 1, the mainstream consensus is that Jesus probably existed, and that statement is used as the foundation the religious need to build a case for resurrections, miracles, and virgin birth.

The question of why the early Christians would be motivated to lie is generally rooted in the idea that there was a massive downside to believing in Jesus in Ancient Rome. While that, at times, was absolutely an accurate statement, the question itself isn't as logical as one may think.

Despite the fact that the persecution and killing of Christians seems to have started rather quickly into the start of the religion, the reasons for the punishments against them weren't as easy to point out. Traditionally, the early Christians were thought to have been killed simply for believing in a religion other than the state religion. If that's the case, literally any other non-state cult would have been killed as well. Are we to believe that all the cults of the day were true in their teachings and beliefs simply because they were killed, too?

The Roman government tended to frown upon new cults, which is why the Ancient Roman historians emphasized the fact that Christianity as "new" whenever they discussed it. If the Christians were being killed, it could have very easily been for that reason. In contrast, the Jews were allowed to carry on with their religious practices and even hold their own tribunals due to the longevity of their religion. Despite government organized attempts to stamp them out, new ideas flourish naturally in any society, and beliefs evolve from prior ones. Just as with the argument that the Christians were killed for being different, literally any cult that was new would have also been met with disdain, but that is not an argument for its authenticity.

The same goes for the fact that "assembly" was not allowed unless a group obtained an official permit. Permits had to be requested, and were sometimes denied to anything from religious groups to volunteer fire departments out of concern that the meetings would turn political.[2] If the Christians were meeting every week in secret, it was true that they were literally breaking the law to do so. The punishments mentioned in Pliny's letter to Emperor Trajan specifically mention that Pliny found out the Christians met together once a week. That discovery being mentioned is both proof that neither he nor Trajan had any prior knowledge of the new cult, and also proof of their crimes. Again, any religious or political group meeting together would have also been punished, and punishment for committing crimes is in no way an indication the goal of the group committing said crimes is superior or legitimate.

If the stories of Nero slaughtering the earliest evolutionary forms of Christians are correct, it makes us wonder how on Earth he knew who they were and why he chose to attack them. There would have been little to no Christian contact with the Roman government unless there were issues with violence or rebellion previously, or the fire was indeed their fault.

It seems to us to be more likely that the Christians regarded suffering as a virtue. After all, if they're claiming their Jesus had been killed by the government, going to the grave singing hymns in his name would be considered an honor. Look no further than the New Testament books themselves for proof that persecution and even death were taught to be viewed as nothing more than stepping stones to a reward:

James 1:2-4

Consider it pure joy, my brothers and sisters, whenever you face trials of many kinds, because you know that the testing of your faith produces perseverance. Let perseverance finish its work so that you may be mature and complete, not lacking anything.

Philippians 2:5-11

In your relationships with one another, have the same mindset as Christ Jesus: Who, being in very nature God, did not consider equality with God something to be used to his own advantage; rather, he made himself nothing by taking the very nature of a servant, being made in human likeness. And being found in appearance as a man, he humbled himself by becoming obedient to death — even death on a cross!

Therefore God exalted him to the highest place and gave him the name that is above every name, that at the name of Jesus every knee should bow, in heaven and on earth and under the earth, and every tongue acknowledge that Jesus Christ is Lord, to the glory of God the Father.

Romans 8:14-18

For those who are led by the Spirit of God are the children of God. The Spirit you received does not make you slaves, so that you live in fear again; rather, the Spirit you received brought about your adoption to sonship. And by him we cry, "Abba, Father." The Spirit himself testifies with our spirit that we are God's children. Now if we are children, then we are heirs—heirs of God and co-heirs with Christ, if indeed we share in his sufferings in order that we may also share in his glory.

I consider that our present sufferings are not worth comparing with the glory that will be revealed in us.

The apocryphal book of 2 Maccabees, written somewhere between the second and first century BCE, tells of a Jewish woman who had seven sons. According to the story, they were all commanded by the Greek king Antiochus IV to eat pork to show their allegiance to him instead of God. After their refusal, he had each of the men brutally tortured and killed in front of their brothers and mother. They were called the Maccabean Martyrs and were highly regarded due to their faith until death. Whether the story is true is beside the point, but the concept of dying for your faith was not created with the Christian religion.

As a quick aside, the idea of a savior, god, or son of god dying wasn't a new concept developed by Christianity, either. There are some people who claim the death of Jesus is proof of the authenticity of the Gospels because, as they say, "no one would write a story about how your savior ended up being killed." The idea is that Jesus being killed by mortals would be too embarrassing to share if it wasn't just a historical fact. Not only is it demonstrably false to claim no savior god had been said to die, but the gospel story has Jesus coming back to life anyway, so coupled with the high regard for the Maccabean martyrs, the "criterion of embarrassment" falls flat on its face. Even stories today of political prisoners and people dying for what they believe in are incredibly popular. Not to mention, on the topic of embarrassment, plenty of Greek and Roman gods of the time also had embarrassing moments, occasional mistakes, and bad traits. People still believed in them.

Jaaron Wingo

So far, we've only really covered the people who believed the Christ claims. As for the people who made them up, it's a bit of a different conversation. It's hard to pinpoint exactly what each person thought at what time when you're dealing with an evolving set of beliefs. Just as the last person at the end of the game of telephone believes wholeheartedly in what they heard, that doesn't mean it's anything like the initial message. If the Teacher of Righteousness preached a sermon a few centuries prior, and the attachment of his sermon to a Christ figure had happened decades prior, then if a person already believed a man named Jesus was the Christ, connecting Jesus to the sermon from the Teacher of Righteousness seems as natural as anything else.

But there are still some downright lies being told. Not every claim of Jesus' story was pieced together over time as smoothly as how we just presented it. Early church leaders routinely warred with each other and "found" letters (the Epistles) to support their claims on a seemingly regular basis. What about their lies?

It's possible the first gospel written was nothing more than an allegory of the fall of Jerusalem or Judaea (hence the strong use of Josephus' *Wars of the Jews*). If that's correct, the initial story of Jesus wouldn't have been meant as historical, but someone could have taken it as such. The Epistles, showing constant political infighting among the church leaders, would have been more of an attempt to keep the growing congregations under control than to outright change history. Of course, just like with the Gospel of Mark before, people may have just accepted the Epistles as historically accurate documents too (despite their issues and contradictions).

If that wasn't the case, the possibility of keeping power and control would have served as the perfect motive for lying about Jesus. While yes, the idea of death sounds awful, history has shown us that with numerous cults (Mormons, Branch Davidians, etc.) and professions (pirates, cartels, etc.), some people risk it all for the possibility of money and power. Some of the most successful people to take such a risk are the ones who completely convince themselves the risk is trivial or even non-existent. As we wrote about in Chapter 3, Lucian of Samosata told of the celebrity lifestyle Peregrinus Proteus was given due to his lying and grifting of the early Christians. Proteus died setting himself ablaze, partly due to his beliefs, but, as Lucian hints at, mostly due to his love for attention.

Depending on the reward, a risk is worth taking. When people get desperate enough, the risk is barely considered.

Death of the Salesmen

As tradition has it, ten of the original twelve disciples were put to death for their beliefs, with John being exiled and Judas killing himself. The manners of which their deaths supposedly occurred vary quite wildly, with little in common other than gruesome violence. Most of these stories of martyrdom come from church tradition that is found outside of the canonical books. Only two deaths are even recorded in the New Testament: Judas and James.

The disciples are said to have spread out across the Roman Empire, and their deaths are generally attributed to harsh reactions from whatever the local governing body of pagans happened to be in their purported missionary communities.

It seems highly unlikely that so many people who claimed to be eyewitnesses were put to death, and still no one outside of Christianity mentioned them, their savior, or their religion for decades after their murders. We postulate that the bulk of the disciples were completely fictional characters, allowing for the extravagant deaths to be conjured up later. Through the spread of these stories of suffering, the disciples would have been given fully developed backstories, and the early church leaders would have painted false histories of perseverance and victimization. Perhaps the dreadful stories of the martyred disciples was a way to justify or seek vindication for the tearing down of buildings, persecuting of other religions, and self-righteous wreaking of havoc the Christians carried out as they rose to power in the early fourth century.

A peculiar set of problems arises with these backstories, however, and it's here where we start to see through the nearly two-thousand-year-old veil. Throughout the first five hundred years of Christianity, revisionist history tactics seem to have been used liberally to fill gaps and holes in the story. But as you will see shortly, the church's ability to extend itself over these gaps stretches it too thin.

The mainstream dating of the New Testament books has the apocalyptic book of Revelation (called Apocalypse in the Catholic Bible) written in about 95 CE. Irenaeus, the first church leader to assign names to the anonymous gospels, attributed Revelation to John the disciple. In fact, quite a few second-century church leaders, such as Papias, Justin Martyr, Melito, Clement of Alexandria, and the author of the Muratorian Canon (a *potentially* second-century list of the books of the New Testament) made that claim. That would seem to flow logically if one assumes the source of the Gospel of John was actually named John, and, to be fair, the author all but says he is by saying "the disciple Jesus loved," while he never says the name of John the disciple. John the disciple was named in the Gospel of Mark (which was used as a blueprint for all the gospels), so not having him named in the Gospel of John is pretty much a dead giveaway.

The book of Revelation has the word "John" written in it four times, with all the passages very clearly making the claim that John is the name of the author. Now for the twist: scholars today maintain that Revelation wasn't written by the same John, which makes sense, as he would have been nearly 100 years old. More on that in Chapter 8.

Still, the issue remains: why did the early church leaders believe it was John the disciple? Proving it wasn't him who authored it doesn't explain why so many people who lived closer to the date of its authorship thought he did. This is a massive problem for Christianity. Why were so many leaders wrong? A few second-century church leaders were even said to be students of John. How could these leaders be trusted to present an accurate picture of a story so fraught with all the errors and issues we've discussed in this book so far, if they all seemed to agree on the wrong author (one said to have lived into the second century) based on practically nothing at all? Is it possible the early church leaders made a habit of claiming certain books were written by certain individuals? Scholars have known for decades now that Paul wasn't the author of all the texts the church leaders said he wrote. How many of these problems do we run into, and why? Is it possible to determine which of the books were actually written by who the leaders claimed (and maybe verify some of the claims and evidence we've presented in this book at the same time)?

Chapter Notes:

1. Augustine, et al. *The City of God (de Civitate Dei)*. New City Press, Cop, 2012. bk. 6 ch. 11

According to Augustine in the sixth book of *The City of God*, the reason Seneca lambasted the Jews in his mid-first-century essay *On Superstition* but never said a word about the Christians is because he apparently liked them. In Augustine's mind, if Seneca would have spoken ill about the Christians, then perhaps "he should do so against his own will."

There's also just the very real possibility that Christianity wasn't around in the middle of the first century. That could explain why Seneca, who lived from 4 BCE to 65 CE, not only failed to mention them in *On Superstition*, but also never said a word about them in his 14 other essays, 9 tragedies, and 124 letters. The majority of those writings deal with philosophy and morals, and are preserved in collections of his works today. You'd think someone who wrote about different beliefs so often and had a soft spot for Christianity would eventually name-drop the religion founding Jesus who was supposedly alive at the same time as him.

2. Pliny the Younger, and P G Walsh. *Complete Letters*. Oxford, Oxford University Press, 2009.

In multiple letters to Emperor Trajan found within the cited collection, Pliny explains issues with illegal assemblies. In fact, in the letter that is cited as one of the very first mentions of Christians in secular history, Pliny makes it clear that his issue with the Christians lies with their assembly without permission. He likens the cult to a "secret brotherhood". Evolving out of other mystery cults, this would have been an apt description of Christianity.

Further Reading:

1. Epiphanius, and Frank Williams. *The Panarion of Epiphanius of Salamis, Book I (Sects 1-46).* Brill, 2009.

For some of the most compelling evidence that the early Christian authors made an effort (and came close to succeeding) to retroactively modify history in order to strengthen the credibility of their religion, you need only refer to Epiphanius' *Panarion*. The book offers accidental peeks over the wall of Christian revisionism thanks to Epiphanius' bumbling attempts to explain the different sects of Christianity and Judaism. When compared with historical markers, it's easy to see the second-century formation of Christianity and the blossoming of its numerous sects. To put it bluntly, the early church leaders shouldn't have let Epiphanius anywhere near a pen.

Panarion isn't the only book from the early church with such inadvertent issues. The constant complaining and disparaging of Marcion in the writings of early Christian authors allows modern-day researchers to reconstruct what he wrote in his gospel, Evangelion. If the authors had just kept their opinions to themselves, a good portion of the work we are presenting in this book wouldn't have been possible. Those authors would have never guessed people would have been able to collect all their writings and piece it back together. A classic case of "I would have got away with it, if it wasn't for those meddling advancements in technology, libraries, and the internet!"

CHAPTER 7

The Stylometric Analysis

After doing a significant amount of reading of the New Testament texts and the history surrounding the first few centuries of Christianity, we wondered if there was a more unbiased, concrete way to find out more about the origins of the New Testament. We had a very strong working theory, but juries want to see more than just a detective's hunch and some accusations. They need to see the prosecution lay out the case beyond a reasonable doubt.

Turn on your TV. Scroll through Netflix, Hulu, or just about any other streaming subscription. You don't have to search for very long before you find a plethora of true crime series. Some of the most popular are the cold case stories: the crimes that sat unsolved for years, only to have the cases blown open by DNA evidence. That's usually the path the stories follow. They start off with a heinous crime committed so long ago the culprit believes they got away. Then, after sitting in an evidence locker for years, some of the collected blood/hair samples are reexamined using modern DNA research. By digging deeper than the culprit probably ever thought forensic scientists could, the investigation continues and the correct arrests are made

Forensic science has been around for centuries. The first guilty verdict based on an early form of forensic science was in 1325 in medieval China. The examination of hair, footprints, and fingerprints are all examples of this field of science, but DNA analysis first led to an arrest in 1986. Just like advancements in DNA research have led to the truth, we needed something more than throwing out our opinions and hoping they were right. We needed hard evidence to point to that would solidify our theory. We also needed to correct parts of it that we may have initially got wrong. Our theory wasn't perfect, so we needed to know what we had missed and what we had caught. This led us to look into stylometry.

"What is Stylometry?"

Stylometry is the mathematical analysis of style in writing. Style can come in the form of word choice and vocabulary, spelling, punctuation, grammatical usage, and other factors. People have been looking at the style of the New Testament books for nearly as long as they've been in existence. Early Church Fathers, for example, debated over the style of Hebrews and if Paul was the author or not. However, our very limited ability to navigate Koine Greek meant we would have to find another approach to stylometry. This is where computerized stylometry comes into play.

Computerized stylometric analysis of the New Testament goes back to the 1980s with Anthony Kenny's *A Stylometric Study of the New Testament*. However, even to this day, the majority of stylometric analysis done on New Testament texts makes the assumption that looking at them alongside second-century texts would be of no avail. Because of this, we saw an opening to potentially prove or disprove our hypothesis that most, if not all, of the New Testament canon was written in the second century.

Unsurprisingly, stylometry has come a long way since the 1980s. Recently, researchers have been able to be as precise as knowing whether Donald Trump wrote a given tweet or one of his interns did,[1,2] and identifying J. K. Rowling as the person behind the pseudonym Robert Galbraith.[3] But we aren't programmers, nor do we have an extensive knowledge of Koine Greek as mentioned above. Plus, even if we did have that knowledge, it would be inaccessible to most people and they would just have to take our word regarding our findings.

But then we came across Stylo, a stylometry package for the programming language called R (just the single letter). R is generally used for statistics, and a package is basically an extension of extra code that can do even more things. R is frequently run in RStudio, an integrated development environment (IDE) which makes R easier to use.

Stylo provides not only stylometric analysis, but also a graphical user interface (GUI), which means for the most part you don't really have to code anything yourself. Once you get it running, it's basically a software inside of RStudio. Stylo was created by Maciej Eder, Mike Kestemont, Jan Rybicki, and Steffen Pielström as a project of the Computational Stylistics Group, which is based out of several universities in Europe.

The way Stylo works is it uses a mathematical formula to compare the Most Frequent Words (MFW) in each text to other texts.

Here is Eder's Delta, the formula developed by one of the creators of Stylo which, along with the other formulas Stylo has built in, can be found in the Stylo guide:[4]

$$\Delta_{(AB)} = \frac{1}{n} \sum_{i=1}^{n} \left(\left| \frac{A_i - B_i}{\sigma_i} \right| \times \frac{n - n_i + 1}{n} \right)$$

Obviously, this math could all be done by hand if you really wanted to, but the computer can do it quite a bit faster than we can. This is even more so the case when you're looking at dozens or even hundreds of texts with thousands of words. What the formula does is measure the distance between various texts based on the most frequent words (or strings of words or characters). Stylo will then create a graph to represent these distances from one another.

There are a number of different formulas you can use, and some work better in certain scenarios than others. We found that Eder's Delta and Eder's Simple Delta tended to provide us with the most reliable results when looking at Greek texts of varied lengths from antiquity. What does reliable mean here? Before diving into the New Testament, we developed our methodology based on using texts in Greek (and other languages) with known authors to determine the most effective way of testing texts. Thus, most reliable means most accurate and likely to attribute texts correctly. This isn't to say other formulas or different variables such as different most-frequent-word numbers are useless, but that each has their place and purpose. Our approach is specifically tailored to Greek texts from around the 200 BCE to 300 CE range.

Stylo also lets you look at other factors, such as strings of letters or words. These strings are called n-grams. A 2-gram would be two words together, such as "two words" and a 3-gram would be something like "three words total." The idea behind using n-grams beyond single words is that authors use strings of words uniquely in their writing. Even at the single-word level, though, our usage of vocabulary is different enough to be able to tell the difference between authors in many cases.

Stylo has a number of other functions, and if you are interested, there are guides online as to how it works and how to use it. We recommend anyone interested in this subject learn to use Stylo as the more research and work is put into these texts, the more likely we are to learn more about the development of early Christianity. While we think we have made a number of discoveries or at least confirmed using stylometric analysis the discoveries and theories of others, we know there is more to be learned from the various documents we have from the first few centuries of Christianity.

The best part about all of this is that, aside from the legwork of collecting texts and the learning curve regarding the software, this is all free, open-source, and repeatable to every person reading this book. None of our data, methodology, or tools are behind paywalls or inaccessible.

If you want to repeat our tests, try to disprove us, or improve upon what we've done and make further discoveries, you can. If we are wrong or lying, you can catch us, and if we are right, you can confirm it yourself. We have nothing to hide and we encourage others to pursue this research further.

Matthew Britt

Stylo Demo

For those that are curious about how accurate it is or are better visual learners, or those who just want to know more before moving forward, we want to provide some examples of what Stylo can do in other contexts before jumping into early Christian documents.

When you download Stylo, on the organization's GitHub, a website used by developers to store and share software, they have two collections of novels as test corpuses (collections of texts) - one in English and one in German. We will be looking at their English test, a Latin test we created, and a Greek test we created. While the images here are abbreviated versions of the tests due to the full results graph being too large to read in book format, we will first look at one full test: this book, *Christ Before Jesus*. We will use the results from this test to go over the layout of a Stylo dendrogram, the type of graph it produces.

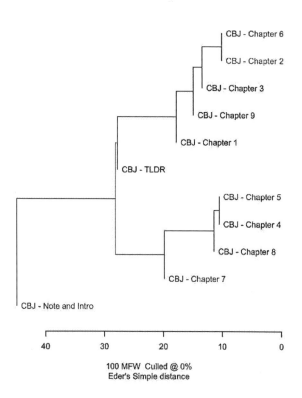

Before jumping into the explanation, I want to say that this graph is accurate. We ran this test near the very end of the writing process when the book was in review. While the entirety of the book was collaborative and we wrote some parts in the chapters attributed to each other above, the divide above is an exact split of which chapters we were each responsible for. It was fun to test Stylo on our own writing and made us reflect on which words and phrases we each use more often and in certain ways than each other.

Matthew Britt

At the top of the graph we see the name of the graph and the type of analysis Stylo ran, in this case cluster analysis (an analysis for determining groups or clusters within a dataset). At the bottom we see it says "100 MFW Culled @ 0%" and "Eder's Simple distance." 100 MFW means we analyzed the 100 most frequent words used - the program counts the usage of every single word and makes a list, then in this case took the top 100 used to work with. Stylo allows for culling, which asks the program to only look at words that show up in a certain percentage of the texts. Because we just ran the chapters of the books as a demo here, we didn't apply any culling. Eder's Simple distance is the name of the formula we used in this specific run. The formula for this can also be found in the Stylo guide. Above these two lines, we see a list of values ranging from 0 to 40. These are the distances; the higher the number, the further apart things are.

Now let's get into looking at the results. The Note and Intro section is the most distant from the other texts, and this is likely due to how short it is. When a text or number of texts are too short for Stylo to analyze, they will cluster together far away from everything else. In this case, this was the only part too short for it, so it put it further away from the rest of the chapters.

Then, around the 25-30 distance range, we see a split in the branches of the dendrogram. This split, being the furthest split on the overall tree excluding the Note and Introduction, is the split between the two authors, Jaaron Wingo and Matthew Britt, respectively, on the graph. While there are only two larger branches here, when there are multiple authors, there will be more branches and clusters on the graph. Sometimes, when the texts are more varied than two authors who grew up in the same town and went to the same school, the first division will indicate larger differences - sometimes time periods, sometimes translations, or something else. It depends on the specific texts you use in your test.

Note that our TL;DR section is very short, but Stylo is still able to determine Jaaron wrote the majority of it. This chapter, written by Matthew, is the most technical and formal section of the book, thus removed somewhat from that grouping, but Stylo still correctly identifies it as well. This points out something important: regardless of the topic, Stylo correctly identifies the author. It doesn't look at the theme, theology, opinion, topic, or anything like that. It looks at most frequent words, and these words are usually function words like "it," "be," "the," and so on. There may be differences in our word choices when writing formally, casually, or in certain other situations, but even then, an author's specific "fingerprint" of style shines through.

We should note when reading Stylo results that the colors are attributed in alphabetical order and will eventually circle back around. Stylo will attribute colors based on the text before an underscore such as Paul in "Paul_1Corinthians" and "Paul_Romans." In our book, we have made all images black and white so while you won't see color here you will if you run the test yourself on your computer.

As mentioned above, we had to crop our results images simply due to the size of the graph produced when we look at large numbers of texts. Because *Christ Before Jesus* only has 11 chapters and sections combined, the full graphic is legible. Our English, Latin, and Greek tests all had a minimum of 100 texts. Our runs with early Christian texts also usually had too large a number of texts to present the full graphics, but rest assured - if you doubt any of our results or think we're hiding something, you can test it on your own computer.

Now let's look at our modified version of Computational Stylistics Group's English demo:

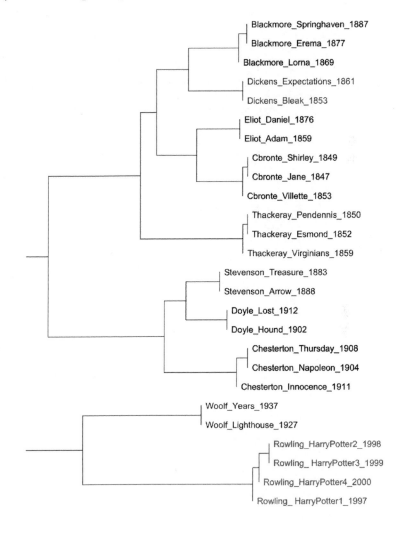

As mentioned above, the first underscore is what determines text color if you are running it yourself. The word before the underscore acts as the user-applied label but does not affect the results. If we had incorrectly named a text from Rowling as being from Dickens, for example, that incorrectly attributed text would have Rowling's name but show up near the Dickens text. Alternatively, if somehow Dickens had secretly written something from Rowling and it had Rowling's name on it, it would be located near the Dickens texts.

Also note that each author has their own branch. In this run, we have a variety of authors but it still correctly groups the texts based on authorship. Rowling is the most distant from the others, likely due to writing almost a century later than many of the other authors. The closest in style to her is Woolf, who is the second-latest author on the graph.

We now move on to our Latin test:

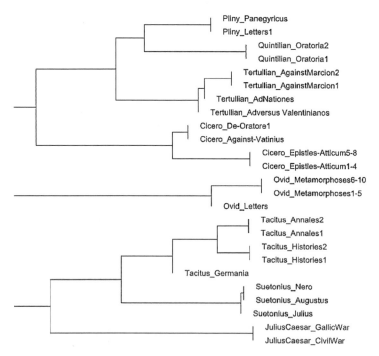

This test we created ourselves and originally ran over 100 texts. This shortened version demonstrates how accurate Stylo is with Latin. Notice that genre does not matter. We have letters and formally written works from Pliny, Cicero, and Ovid, but they show up correctly attributed to the author rather than grouped by genre. If Stylo detected genre, the letters from these authors should show up in a group with just letters rather than correctly attributed to their respective authors as they do here.

We then created a Greek test corpus to get a feel for how it would run in Greek. We tested our methodology against a run of 100 Greek texts, though when starting out we ran upwards of 500 texts just to test our entire corpus of Greek works from the era. We also learned that we could divide texts up into relatively small sizes and get accurate results, and were able to determine the minimum text size that could be run in Greek and still be accurate. Here is a shortened version of our Greek test:

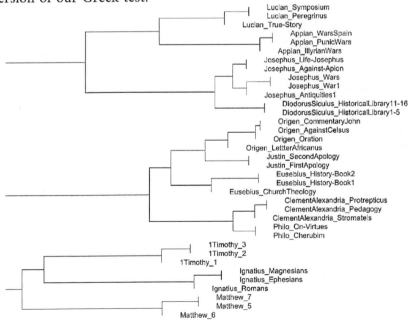

The most important takeaway other than the accuracy of Stylo when analyzing Greek texts is that it can correctly attribute Greek texts as small as a chapter of a New Testament book. Note at the bottom of the graph that we selected three chapters from 1 Timothy and three chapters from Matthew and all of them were correctly attributed to the same group. This doesn't mean the authors were actually Paul and Matthew, respectively, but that the same person is responsible for the chapters of each text above. The author of 1 Timothy wrote those three chapters of 1 Timothy, and the author of Matthew wrote those three chapters of Matthew and Stylo can tell.

Potential Concerns

We want to address a few concerns we anticipate before we finally get into the results. While we have done our best to be rigorous and thorough, we know there will be people who are skeptical and want to provide assurance that we aren't making things up or doing things incorrectly.

"Aren't the texts too small?"

We almost didn't run our chapter-level analysis due to this concern, but it turns out that at least in Greek, Stylo still finds reliable results at the chapter level for the gospels, which is about an average of 700 words. Chapters for the Pauline Epistles and other texts tended to have closer to an average of around 400 words. In some cases, such as 2 John, 3 John, and Philemon, there were less than the average, meaning we are less reliant on stylometric analysis for these texts when by themselves. We ended up combining 2 John and 3 John to give us a better opportunity to more accurately attribute these texts, given that they are considered to be by the same author as one another.

In the early stages of developing our methodology, we tested Stylo's ability to place these small texts accurately. As we show in our demonstration below, Stylo is capable of correctly detecting authorship at a chapter-by-chapter level for New Testament texts. While the size of some of the texts is a valid concern, Stylo is still generally able to handle most New Testament texts. While we hope to follow up with a study using pericopes rather than chapters, we do think what we find here is relevant and reliable despite the limitations of the source material.

"Shouldn't you run x n-grams, x Most Frequent Words, x Delta, etc.?"

Stylo allows you to run tests in a variety of ways. We could pick any number of combinations of variables and try to find something that fits our hypotheses, and this, to a degree, is a valid concern. But we started out not trying to prove ourselves correct, but just to see what we would find and if it would give us evidence one way or another.

As such, the way we approached selecting our setup was based on our trial runs and a number of academic papers regarding Stylo. With our English, Latin, and Greek test corpuses, we ran every delta option in Stylo with different numbers of character and word n-grams and MFW values when developing our methodology. Given that we knew the authors of the works in our test runs, we were able to determine the most effective way for each language and not publish an image in this book that uses a method lower than 96% accuracy.

We then took what we learned from the papers and our broader tests and applied it to a broad collection of early Christian documents, including the New Testament, without doing anything to the books to compare it to what the scholarly consensus is. For example, there are 13 letters attributed to Ignatius of Antioch. Scholars believe seven of those are authentic and the other six are later forgeries, which Stylo confirms. Scholars also believe the Pastoral Epistles are written by a different author than the rest of the Pauline letters and should show up as such, which they do. We also know that Paul did not write any gospels, Matthew didn't write any letters, and so on, so we should see this as well, which we did.

We are confident that our results are reliable and accurate and how we ran the texts was one of the best ways possible given the various limitations, such as text size and limited texts from authors. Regardless, we encourage others to follow up on this and potentially improve on our research where there is opportunity to do so.

"Shouldn't you use random sampling?"

First, in case you're wondering, why would one want to use random sampling? Hypothetically, it would allow you to balance the size of the texts and apply the other benefits of randomized samples, such as the removal of bias. Random sampling is very common in statistics.

The answer as to why we don't use it, though, is in relation to the two above. In some cases, the texts are already really small and most reasonable random sample sizes would still lead to unbalanced (though less so) samples. Furthermore, because numerous New Testament texts have multiple layers of redactions and edits to them, there's no guarantee you would get a good read on a particular book.

For example, if our theory about Luke 1-3 being added later by another author is correct, there's a chance the random sample would come from there or come from another part of the text, and then "Luke" could show up in one of these places when the rest of it should be in another. It's even worse in some of the Pauline letters where there seem to be line-by-line additions and edits. If we could guarantee the texts were written by one author throughout their entirety, it would work well, but this just isn't the case with the New Testament.

"Are you just making up these results?"

One of the best parts about Stylo is that you can run these tests yourself. We spent months gathering texts and checking the data quality of them before running tests, but as we went along, we got much quicker at the entire process. While it takes time, this is a very democratized process in which you can confirm the research yourself. And, ultimately, there's no way to make up these graphs without doing something like falsely labeling files or Photoshopping the whole graph. If you are concerned we did something like this, again, you are welcome to try the test yourself.

"If stylometric analysis is used to find authorship, how are you using it to find dates?"

It's true that stylometry doesn't give you dates per se. However, because we are able to identify some authors and use textual, manuscript, and other evidence to identify dates and authors of some texts, we are able to reconstruct a general idea of when many Christian documents were written. For example, we know Ignatius of Antioch was writing during the second century. While there is debate as to the exact dates of his letters, the second century is agreed upon by most scholars. When another letter or document shows up right alongside Ignatius, it means he or someone with a very similar writing style to him, perhaps a student, had a hand in writing that document. As such, we can date that document to the second century as well.

"Didn't the apostles use scribes?"

While it was common to use scribes back in the era we are looking at, there is too much variance between texts to be able to claim a "scribes in the gaps" argument against our results. We do have an author who admittedly used scribes and other sources to write his books: Josephus. But except for a handful of sections out of all the content he wrote, it all shows up as his writing. A good scribe would not make the orator's vocabulary and style come off so different as to make it look like texts were coming from an entirely different author or even a different century. The only time the scribe's style would come through so significantly is if they were completely forging a document using someone else's name and their own style came through.

"Could the stylometric analysis be picking up theology, genre, or theme instead of authorship?"

A human stylistic analysis might look at things like theology or theme, but the computer does not see this beyond the word choice of the authors. Genres may come into play at a broader level, but we have tested authors who have letters, historical documents, philosophical pieces, recorded speeches, and a variety of other works and Stylo is able to accurately detect authorship despite these differences. Even though we use different words in different formats and genres (like writing a text versus writing an essay), there are still patterns like fingerprints that are unique across our writings as individuals.

The program we use looks at the most frequent words, and usually theological words do not come into play at the level we look at. For example, according to the Oxford English Corpus the top ten most common words in English, in order, are: the, be, to, of, and, a, in, that, have, I. The list continues with words like that, with the 90th-100th most common words in English being: way, even, new, want, because, any, these, give, day, most, us. The 100 most common words in English account for around than 50% of the words we use on a regular basis. Greek, and every other language, works more or less the same way. Theological words come way down on the list.

What matters and what makes the program work is how we all use words with different frequencies. Someone with a PhD, someone with a high school diploma, and someone for whom English is a second or third language will use even simple words such as those top 10 or 100 words differently and with different frequencies. It might be the case that two people with PhDs might use words more similarly to each other than a non-native English speaker, and this would be detected, but these two PhDs would have other differences in style between themselves that would make it where we could still likely detect which is which with adequate writing samples. People have had different teachers, come from different regions, and even just have stylistic preferences that create a unique fingerprint of style.

Consider the following parallel passage from the Synoptic Gospels regarding the Parable of the Sower in the American Standard Version, which provides a more direct word-for-word translation:

Mark 4:13-20

And he saith unto them, Know ye not this parable? and how shall ye know all the parables? The sower soweth the word. And these are they by the way side, where the word is sown; and when they have heard, straightway cometh Satan, and taketh away the word which hath been sown in them. And these in like manner are they that are sown upon the rocky places, who, when they have heard the word, straightway receive it with joy; and they have no root in themselves, but endure for a while; then, when tribulation or persecution ariseth because of the word, straightway they stumble. And others are they that are sown among the thorns; these are they that have heard the word, and the cares of the world, and the deceitfulness of riches, and the lusts of other things entering in, choke the word, and it becometh unfruitful. And those are they that were sown upon the good ground; such as hear the word, and accept it, and bear fruit, thirtyfold, and sixtyfold, and a hundredfold.

Luke 8:11-15

Now the parable is this: The seed is the word of God. And those by the way side are they that have heard; then cometh the devil, and taketh away the word from their heart, that they may not believe and be saved. And those on the rock are they who, when they have heard, receive the word with joy; and these have no root, who for a while believe, and in time of temptation fall away. And that which fell among the thorns, these are they that have heard, and as they go on their way they are choked with cares and riches and pleasures of this life, and bring no fruit to perfection. And that in the good ground, these are such as in an honest and good heart, having heard the word, hold it fast, and bring forth fruit with patience.

Matthew 13:18-23

Hear then ye the parable of the sower. When any one heareth the word of the kingdom, and understandeth it not, then cometh the evil one, and snatcheth away that which hath been sown in his heart. This is he that was sown by the way side. And he that was sown upon the rocky places, this is he that heareth the word, and straightway with joy receiveth it; yet hath he not root in himself, but endureth for a while; and when tribulation or persecution ariseth because of the word, straightway he stumbleth. And he that was sown among the thorns, this is he that heareth the word; and the care of the world, and the deceitfulness of riches, choke the word, and he becometh unfruitful. And he that was sown upon the good ground, this is he that heareth the word, and understandeth it; who verily beareth fruit, and bringeth forth, some a hundredfold, some sixty, some thirty.

Just a surface-level look at these texts shows us that the style of these authors are different. For example, Mark starts almost every sentence with "And." But let's look at what Stylo tells us and how it determines authorship.

The first thing Stylo does is identify the most frequent words set at the numbers you ask it to look at. The ten most frequent words in the selections above are: the, and, word, that, they, are, of, he, sown, in. It runs a count for each passage for the number of words and then uses these frequencies and the formula above to create distances. So when you ask Stylo to look at the 100 most frequent words, it does this counting for each document for each of the 100 words. We'll look at the word "he" as an example of the frequencies because it's easy to see above. Mark uses "he" one time, Luke zero times, and Matthew ten times.

After it runs it through the formula, which uses the frequencies to determine distance, it creates a distance table. After that, it provides a visualization based on the data in the table. Here is the table for the passage above, rounded to the nearest whole number for simplicity.

	Mark	Luke	Matthew
Mark	0	65	49
Luke	65	0	78
Matthew	49	78	0

The smaller a number is, the more similar it is. The larger the number is, the more the "distance" between texts is, and therefore, the more dissimilar they are. Each text, when run against itself, shows 0 distance because it is identical. In the table above, Mark and Matthew are the most similar because the distance between them is the smallest

49. Luke is the most different from the others, being a distance of 65 from Mark and 78 from Matthew.

Of course, when we run this in Stylo, we are running it based on the original Greek and not English translations. We're also doing much larger amounts of text, meaning a larger and better sample size. But even with this tiny sample in an English translation, we see what many scholars already agree upon: Matthew uses sections from Mark more closely than Luke does. It has nothing to do with theology, genre, or theme, as these are the exact same passages just written by different authors in their own style.

Divide and Concur

We did not alter the texts in any way, but in some cases did divide texts to see if there was any merit to certain theories. For example, 2 Corinthians is widely agreed upon by mainstream scholars to be multiple letters combined into one. The same is true of Philippians. We explain our divisions later when they appear in Chapter 8's results, but all divisions were based on either scholarly work or chapter divisions. We did not make any of our own divisions or changes to the texts. As mentioned above, there was a single instance where we combined texts - 2 John and 3 John. Scholars usually agree these were written by the same person, but both are extremely small. Combining them allowed us to get a more accurate read on them.

We also did divisions based on chapters for a number of non-canonical texts, as you will see in Chapter 8. This was done to allow us to see differences within the text and if there was any merit to further research into the possibility of multiple authors for certain texts. Most notably, this is the case for 1 Clement and the Epistle to Barnabas, which get discussed in the following chapter.

Corpus Selections

We initially included everything we could find to get a broad overview of the situation. This meant almost every Jewish and Christian writing in the Greek language we could find from the first century CE up through the third century. We also added in a number of earlier and later texts as controls. From there, we were able to get a general idea of what to exclude in later runs. For example, we usually removed authors from before the 1st century BCE because they were irrelevant - there was no connection between them and Christian texts. Likewise, we also removed authors from beyond the third century. The New Testament is all attested to by the first half of the 200s CE, so anything beyond that will probably not be relevant.

If you are wondering where a specific text shows up or why we don't have it shown in one of our images, it's likely that the results were not significant to determining the dates or authorship of the texts of the New Testament. While these results might be interesting to some, to cover the results of every text we ran would be another book.

There are numerous opportunities to apply Stylo to this era's literature and delve deeper into the texts not only of the New Testament but other works as well, and we hope others will be encouraged to continue where we leave off. There is a lot of interesting information we saw that goes beyond the scope of this book, not only in Greek, but in the other languages we tested, such as Latin, as well.

Final Disclaimer

If you do attempt to do this yourself, keep in mind that the corpus size - the number of texts you add in - will affect the branches of the graph it creates and the distances between texts. The more unique authors and content you add, the further things will be. The

227

fewer the texts and authors, the more minor differences may stand out and affect results.

This means that we must look at broad strokes of results at times. Yes, you may have a significant finding in your run, but that result needs to be replicable and repeatable. Test it a few other ways. Make sure it isn't due just to corpus size, or that your n-gram selection isn't appropriate for the size of texts you're running. We worked hard to confirm we aren't just seeing a fluke, and all our findings are also backed by the evidence seen elsewhere in the book.[5]

Chapter Notes:

1. "Text Analysis of Trump's Tweets Confirms He Writes Only the (Angrier) Android Half." *Variance Explained*, 9 Aug. 2016, varianceexplained.org/r/trump-tweets/. Accessed 18 Dec. 2023.

2. "RPubs - Trump Twitter Analysis (Updated: 2017/12/11)." *Rpubs. com*, rpubs.com/jwgrieve/340342/. Accessed 18 Dec. 2023.

3. Juola, Patrick. "How a Computer Program Helped Show J. K. Rowling Write a Cuckoo's Calling." *Scientific American*, 20 Aug. 2013, www.scientificamerican.com/article/how-a-computer-program-helped-show-jk-rowling-write-a-cuckoos-calling/. Accessed 15 Dec. 2023.

4. Eder, Maciej, et al. "Stylometry with R: A Package for Computational Text Analysis." *The R Journal*, vol. 8, no. 1, 2016, p. 107-121, https://doi.org/10.32614/rj-2016-007. Accessed 15 Dec. 2023.

5. Computational Stylistics Group. *Publications.* https://computationalstylistics.github.io/publications/.

The Computational Stylistics Group is the organization responsible for creating Stylo. On this webpage, you can find numerous studies about and using Stylo. You can also visit their GitHub preprint page (https://github.com/computationalstylistics/preprints). Between these two sources, almost any question you have about Stylo should be answered.

We realize that for many people Stylo might be a stumbling block, yet the results it provides in the following chapter are vital to understanding what really happened regarding the creation of the New Testament. If you are a Christian or even a non-religious person who believes in a historical Jesus and don't want to accept our Stylo results, we recommend you go see how it has been used in numerous peer-reviewed academic studies. If you're a professional scholar or amateur interested in understanding how it works or want more detailed answers to some of your questions, the resources provided by the Computational Stylistics Group are great.

What we presented in this chapter is (hopefully) an accessible introduction to stylometry and Stylo without getting too far into the weeds. For those who need more answers, though, we highly recommend reviewing the various works made available by the Computational Stylistics Group. Everything you need to replicate and possibly even improve upon our research is freely available and the details as to how it works are as well.

CHAPTER 8

The Results from Stylometry

"What are the main discoveries of the stylometric analysis?"

Running the New Testament alongside other texts from the era revealed a number of things, and below, we walk through the main findings step-by-step. For those looking for a faster, more digestible read, we have a list of findings following this section.

Marcion, Luke, and Acts

In Exhibit 1, we see what is perhaps the most important result of our stylometric analysis and this is why we are starting with it. Not only is it the most important, but the most well-attested and controversial in the second-century church. This single finding, which is backed by textual evidence in the New Testament itself as well as documents from other early Christians, undermines the mainstream dating of almost all New Testament texts.

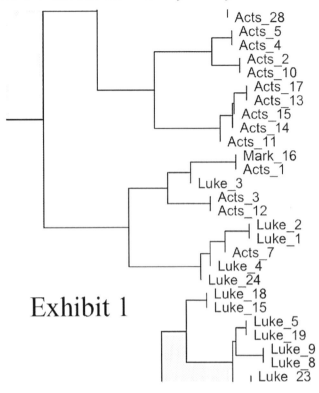

Exhibit 1

Irenaeus is the first that claims Luke the Evangelist, the supposed author of the Gospel of Luke, also wrote Acts of the Apostles. As we discuss earlier in the book, the reality seems to be that Evangelion, Marcion's gospel, came before the Gospel of Luke in 144, and the author of Acts went back and added content to Evangelion to make Luke's gospel. While our textual argument makes a good case for this, and this was the position of Marcion and his followers, our stylometric analysis definitively proves it.

In the image, you'll see that most of Luke is at the bottom of its own tree. The passages found there overlap with the chapters taken from Marcion's Evangelion. At the top of the image, you see Acts on a different branch. In the middle, but connected with Acts and not with Luke, are the following chapters of Luke: 1-4 and 24. These are the main chapters added and expanded upon in Luke that are not found or are significantly shorter in Marcion's Evangelion. It is proof that Marcion's version came first and Luke was a later text.

Let's walk through the logic here. If the Gospel of Luke and Acts were written by the same person as tradition claims, then there would likely not be the separation we see here between the two in the first place. Second, and more importantly, the chapters not found in Marcion's Evangelion would not act any differently than the rest of Luke. However, if the author of Acts did not write most of Luke but rather edited it and wrote 1-4 and 24, then what we see is exactly what we would expect. Luke 1-4 and 24 match the style of Acts, not of the bulk of Luke taken from Evangelion.

This means Evangelion was the original publication of the content in most of Luke, which happened in 144, and that both the canonical Luke and Acts had to have been written after this. The 144 date explains why in Marcion's version of Luke 24:9 we see the phrase "Redemption of Israel" the same as seen on Bar Kokhba coins minted in the 130s. This phrase is not found on coins or slogans around the time of the First Jewish-Roman War from 66 to 73 CE, but we have physical evidence of it being used in the 130s. You can see the coins for yourself online on page 19 of the *Handbook of Biblical Numismatics*. This discovery also explains to us why Luke and Acts are addressed to Theophilus - they're written to Theophilus of Antioch, who was a bishop starting in the 160s.

If this is the case, Matthew (which reacts to Evangelion) and John (which reacts to content in Luke and Matthew), also came after 144. It also means Matthew and Luke did not need to draw from a hypothetical Q source, but from Marcion's Evangelion. While we don't have Matthew shown in the image above, our stylometric analysis showed that it acted similar to other New Testament texts that show up in the second century. This aligns with the various evidence presented elsewhere in the book that Matthew copied from Evangelion. Interestingly, we also have evidence that Matthew also took from Marcion's *Antitheses*. For example, one of the most attested to lines of Marcion's writing, which is not specifically found in Evangelion, yet is formatted like an antithetical statement, is Matthew 5:17. The canonical version says, "Do not think that I have come to abolish the Law or the Prophets; I have not come to abolish them but to fulfill them." However, *Dialogue of Adamantius* (an anonymous third or fourth century anti-Marcionite text), Isidore of Pelusium (fourth and fifth century Christian apologist), and others say that the Marcionite *Antitheses* reverse this phrase, claiming Christ did come to destroy (or abolish) the Law rather than fulfill it. Irenaeus and Tertullian also discuss this verse and those coming after it as if they are affiliated with Marcion. What seems to have happened is Matthew's author took Marcion's *Antitheses*, kept it where it fit his theology, and reversed it where it did not - another piece of evidence for Matthew being a reaction to Marcion's Evangelion.

Originally in our theory, we believed that Luke 1-3, which is almost entirely absent from the Marcionite version of the gospel, would be the only ones strong enough to show up as written by a different author. Chapters 4 and 24 also show up here, and have over half of their content added after Marcion's Evangelion. This means that Stylo performed beyond our original expectations and confirmed that the content added later into chapters 4 and 24 is so distinctly not original to the rest of the text, that they also show up closer to Acts than the content found in Evangelion. When the later editor added content into chapter 4 and moved things around, he slipped up and messed up the original order found in Evangelion regarding Jesus' stay in Capernaum. Both the textual evidence and stylometric evidence show that our version of Luke comes after Marcion in 144, and this is devastating to mainstream positions that attempt to date the gospel to the first century. In general, it is a major blow to the idea that the gospels relied on some form of reliable oral tradition, as well, because now instead of one generation or two between the events and the story we're looking at over a century of silence for much of the material.

Matthew Britt

Acts itself is not mentioned until Irenaeus in the late 170s to early 180s, which would also fit with the dates we have for Theophilus of Antioch, who both canonical Luke and Acts are dedicated to. There are other hints that Acts is a later text. For example, in Acts 16:7 we see that Paul is not allowed to go into Bithynia - the Holy Spirit, in fact, prohibits it. This is the only time this happens to any region, so why is this the case? Bithynia is part of the region in which Marcion's hometown is located. Marcion is the first to introduce Paul in the 140s, and this seems to be an attempt to say that he couldn't have actually had the true teachings of Paul because Paul never even went to where he was from. As mentioned earlier in the book, there are also a number of second-century figures who get referenced in Acts as well. It's these anachronisms, along with various others, that align with the stylometric analysis showing that Acts is a later second-century construction.

Also note that Mark 16 is found alongside Acts. This is because the original ending of Mark was Mark 16:8. As we mentioned in Chapter 2, in many Bibles (especially the NIV), you'll see a footnote at the end of the verse saying that many manuscripts end there. What our results show is that the same person who wrote Acts and edited Evangelion into the Gospel of Luke also added the longer ending of Mark. Textually, this makes sense too, as both the longer ending of

235

Mark and the added ending of Luke both have Jesus "taken up into heaven" in what is known as the Ascension. The other two canonical gospels do not have this scene, nor did the shorter ending of Mark.

The Irenaeus Irony

As we mentioned above, the Gospel of Luke was not given its name until Irenaeus. In fact, Acts of the Apostles is not named or definitively quoted until Irenaeus either. Acts goes from no direct quotes from any church leaders to over 50 quotes in Irenaeus' *Against Heresies*. This made us wonder, could Irenaeus or someone affiliated with him have had a role in the creation of Luke and Acts?

Of course, hard evidence like stylometric data is preferable when looking to answer these questions. Unfortunately, we have no surviving Greek manuscripts of the works of Irenaeus. The best that is available is W. Wigan Harvey's reconstruction, which was published in 1857. As we will see later with Marcion's Evangelion, we have reconstructions from within the last decade available to us. There are also reconstructions of Evangelion from over a century ago, but there is a marked improvement and refinement in the more modern ones that are available. Harvey's reconstruction is not only old, but what is available of it is also proportionally much less of the original work than what has been reconstructed of Evangelion.

So while we felt confident with our modern reconstructions of Marcion's Evangelion, the reconstruction we have of the works of Irenaeus leaves much more to be desired. Nonetheless, we still ran the reconstruction of *Against Heresies* in hopes of being able to confirm or deny any connection Irenaeus might have to the works of the New Testament. Surprisingly, it frequently showed a direct connection with Acts and the added sections of Luke when we ran it at the chapter level.

We then ran it with whole texts and once again, *Against Heresies* showed up in the same branch with Luke and Acts even more consistently.

Could this mean Irenaeus was the author of the Gospel of Luke and the book of Acts? While we have our doubts about the available reconstruction of Irenaeus' works in Greek, there is actually quite a bit of evidence that would support his authorship of the books. As discussed, Irenaeus was writing in the 170s to 180s, and became bishop of Lugdunum (now Lyon, France) around 177. Prior to that, he was the second-highest in the church of his region. Theophilus of Antioch was bishop of Antioch from 169 to around 182. Irenaeus addressing Luke and Acts to Theophilus, whether as a second-in-command in Lugdunum or as bishop, then makes perfect sense.

Likewise, in the introduction of Luke, the author states that he has taken other sources and made a more orderly account - a parallel to Irenaeus' claims in *Against Heresies* about Evangelion being a mutilation of Luke's gospel. His insistence on the importance of apostolic authority and having leaders who can trace their authority directly back to the apostles also lines up well with the broader goal of Acts of the Apostles. While churches throughout the Roman Empire are founded in Acts, the story explicitly says in Acts 16 that the apostles (and specifically Paul) were not allowed to enter Marcion's home province, thus explicitly undermining any apostolic lineage for that region. Much of *Against Heresies* attacks Marcion and his church, and we see anti-Marcionite jabs throughout Luke and Acts. From the direct lifting and rearranging of Marcion's gospel to the diminishing of Paul, the apostle Marcion claimed authority from, in Acts from the figure we see in the letters attributed to Paul, the overall goal seems to establish an orthodox claim on all apostolic authority.

Irenaeus spends an entire chapter in *Against Heresies*, Book 3 Chapter 14, building up the character of Luke and in the surrounding chapters he uses Acts, which he attributes to Luke, to undermine opposing views on Paul, such as the one that the Marcionites held. Prior to Irenaeus, Luke is never mentioned by any other church leader and is only found in three brief references in Philemon, Colossians, and 2 Timothy. The latter two are broadly considered inauthentic late texts, and as we demonstrate below, Philemon is inauthentic as well. In this one work of Irenaeus, Luke goes from someone who only gets mentioned in three fake letters of Paul to his most loyal companion, who was divinely inspired to write the two longest books of what would become the New Testament.

The use of 2 Timothy to bolster Luke and his general presence in it are particularly interesting. Irenaeus is the first to mention or quote 2 Timothy, and the text itself name-drops Irenaeus' anti-Marcionite teacher Polycarp who died in either 155 or 165, as well as his assistant Crescens. The specific mention of Luke comes in 2 Timothy 4:11, right around the mention of Polycarp and Crescens, saying:

Only Luke is with me. Get Mark and bring him with you, because he is helpful to me in my ministry.

Here, Luke has gone from only being a friend, physician, and fellow-worker of Paul to the last remaining follower. This is then used by Irenaeus to make Luke Paul's most important student, and thus validate the canonical Gospel of Luke and Acts. He claims that if you accept any of Luke, which is drawn from Evangelion and thus something Marcionites generally accept, then you must accept Acts, as it was written by the same author, and therefore this would include claims such as how Marcion's home region never received the true gospel from Paul.

This brings us to the names of the Gospels themselves. We know no one attributes names to them until Irenaeus and they're all anonymous works. We suggest earlier in the book that Mark derives from Marcion and Luke derives from the name of his student Lucan or Lucian (all pronounced at the time with a hard "c" sound). These texts were perhaps so well-known to be associated with these figures, or at least the general movements they represented, and Irenaeus might have in turn used the names to create the characters Mark and Luke found in today's New Testament, whitewashing them while still acknowledging the origins. It's interesting that these two are also not attributed to direct disciples but rather the following generation, in a way making them "lesser" than the other two, John and Matthew.

There seems to be a second-century figure named John, as he is referenced multiple times by a number of other second-century figures. At the very least, the name stuck with a particular sect, and was then placed onto the gospel produced by them. In fact, Irenaeus traces his apostolic authority to this John, so it's important that his forefather has a gospel to his name.

Then we're left with Matthew. Of all the disciples to pick, this one is an interesting choice given his minor role. Perhaps it was because he was one of the few that might have been literate given his role as described in Matthew. In Luke and Mark, Levi is a tax collector and not explicitly identified with Matthew, so perhaps the more explicit change to Matthew in the Gospel of Matthew inspired its name. Or maybe it's another play on words. The Greek for Matthew is *maththaios*, and the Greek for disciple or student is *mathētēs*. Given it's one of two gospels attributed to direct disciples of Jesus, this might have played into Irenaeus' decision to give it the name.

The timing, textual evidence, motive, and even the hard evidence of stylometric data seem to indicate that Irenaeus is the author of Luke and Acts. This also makes sense with the cohesion of what we consider orthodox Christianity around this time and shortly after. While we still have Christians in the 170s such as Tatian using a harmony gospel instead of the fourfold collection of gospels, Melito of Sardis claiming Christianity had its origins in the reign of Caesar Augustus (27 BCE-14 CE), and even Irenaeus himself with claims such as Jesus being aged around 50 when he died, we begin to see a select number of texts regarded as canonical or near-canonical from this point onwards. Irenaeus had the goal of refuting those he considered heretics, and in the process played a large part in defining what orthodoxy would be.

If Irenaeus is behind the creation of Luke and Acts, this would likely mean that he is also behind the compilation of what would later become the New Testament canon we find in the Bible today. However, some scholars such as David Trobisch believe this was done by Polycarp, Irenaeus' teacher. If this is the case, it's possible that Polycarp wrote the bulk of additional material in Luke-Acts and he or Irenaeus wrote the introductory lines to Theophilus. With Polycarp as the possible author, this would move the authorship of most of canonical Luke and Acts only a decade or two earlier, into the 150s at the earliest. If there were any genuine, direct quotes from canonical Luke not found in Marcion's gospel prior to the time of Irenaeus, this would likely explain how it might be the case.

While we had already established Luke and Acts after the date of 144, along with Matthew, canonical Mark, and John, this seems to push our canonical version of Luke and Acts as late as the 170s. All our gospels and material regarding the early church is thus a product of late second-century edits and authors, making any potential information about supposed first-century Christian figures show up a century or more after the alleged stories. That leaves us with documents that claim to be products of these very figures - the letters of Paul, Peter, and other disciples found in the New Testament. As such, these are our next stop in our stylometric investigation.

Paul's Prison Letters

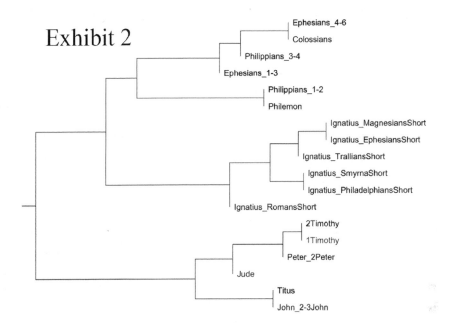

Exhibit 2

While the above image is not chronological, we are going to start with the top of the image: Paul's Prison Letters. These four letters (Philippians, Ephesians, Colossians, and Philemon) are given this name due to them being the only letters Paul supposedly wrote from prison. Mainstream scholarship considers Ephesians (which we split to test the theory that the first two chapters were used as an introduction to Pauline texts given they cite them more than the following chapters) and Colossians to be inauthentic and Philippians to be a composite work of at least three smaller letters. Each of these smaller letters was generally too small to run, so we split the text along chapter lines due to inherent limitations in the text's size. Philemon, given it is only 25 verses long, is usually ignored and considered authentic.

However, Philemon shares an almost identical list of names with Colossians. While some will claim Colossians used Philemon as a template and claim Philemon is authentic, we can see here that the same author group that wrote Ephesians and Colossians, both forgeries, also wrote Philippians and Philemon. Given the common theme of the author being in prison, this is not surprising - whoever wrote it liked the idea of their characters going through this form of struggle. But even disregarding the stylometric results, there are a number of things that indicate Philemon is a forgery.

First, personal letters are the most likely to be fake. What easier way to introduce a new, previously unknown or "lost" letter than to say it was a personal letter to only one individual? There are three other personal letters attributed to Paul - 1 Timothy, 2 Timothy, and Titus - and all of them are considered to be forgeries. Philemon is the only personal letter of Paul anyone considers authentic, and usually it's just because it's so short, there seems to be no reason to question it.

Second, the list of names found in both Philemon and Colossians is very similar. Colossians was likely the template for Philemon, and we know Colossians was not written by Paul - even mainstream scholars generally agree on this.[1] There are also overlapping themes with Colossians aside from it being a Prison Letter. Just as with the later additions to parts of Colossians 3-4, in which certain social hierarchies such as slavery and patriarchy are reinforced, some of those same social hierarchies are reinforced in Philemon: specifically slavery.

Third, in verse 19, we see a "signature" from Paul himself, with the verse saying:

I, Paul, am writing this with my own hand. I will pay it back — not to mention that you owe me your very self.

Usually when these "signatures" are added into the letter, it's an attempt to fool readers. The forger knew that the reader would be reading what they would assume is a copy and thus believe the original letter actually had different handwriting. In reality, had there been different handwriting, there would be no need for the author (supposedly Paul) to point out that it was different handwriting. The goal is to give the illusion of an original with different handwriting because all of your readers are reading copies. There would have been only one original, and given that these letters were explicitly meant to be encyclicals (documents shared around the various churches) almost all readers would be getting copies anyways - all without the actual signature but a later scribe adding in the supposed "authentic" reference to one.

Finally, there is Onesimus. It's likely he is actually the reason the letter was faked in the first place. Whether the letter was real or fake, why was it included in a collection of religious letters? Philemon has little to no religious value and even the other fake personal letters attempt to pass along some kind of instructional content. Philemon is only 25 verses, and nearly half of them are either introductory or closing content. The rest is dedicated to arguing on behalf of Onesimus. Paul puts his reputation on the line and offers to cover any cost Onesimus incurred his master Philemon - that's some serious vouching for! Paul must have really been impressed with and cared about Onesimus. As we will discuss later, Onesimus turns out to be an important figure in the second century.

If the letter is fake, that's exactly the point. What better way to build the reputation of a living person than to have a letter from one of the founders of the religion speaking on his behalf? We know Polycarp and his students (such as Irenaeus) were insistent on the importance of being able to trace one's religious lineage back to the original apostles themselves, and this seems to be an attempt to do that. Philemon has escaped scrutiny longer than any other Pauline letter simply due to how short it is, but once it's put under the microscope, it becomes clear that it's just a second-century forgery and attempted power grab.

The Ignatius Collection Connection

We now look at what comes just below and connected to Paul's Prison Letters: the letters of Ignatius. Depending on the dating of the Ignatius Letters, they could be one of the earliest references to Peter and (more importantly) Paul that we have outside of the New Testament.

Ignatius' letter collection consists of seven letters - six churches and one to an individual - while he was being taken to Rome to be executed. There are a number of unique themes in the letters of Ignatius, including the themes of martyrdom, suffering, and imprisonment. As we discussed in Chapter 5, it is possible that the letters of Ignatius are actually reworked letters from Peregrinus Proteus, a Christian author whose story and emphasis on his own death and imprisonment seem very similar to that found in the letters of Ignatius. We're told by Lucian of Samosata that Proteus wrote his own works (likely including letters to churches just as Ignatius did) and also edited Christian scriptures. While this sounds like something unprovable, our stylometric analysis did add a twist to the situation.

As far as we know, Ignatius is the only Church Father to be writing while imprisoned during the second century. It then becomes more interesting that the letters stylometrically match with Paul's Prison Letters. To make things even more interesting, they share a common character: Onesimus.

As we just mentioned, Onesimus is mentioned in Paul's letter to Colossians and is one of the main characters of Philemon. In Philemon, we learn he is a runaway slave who Paul had converted to Christianity. In Colossians, he is going with Tychicus to deliver the letter to the

Colossians. In Ignatius' letter to the Ephesians, not to be confused with *Paul's* letter to the Ephesians, Onesimus is bishop of Ephesus and Ignatius feels the need to praise him and insist that the believers there respect him.

We now have overlapping stylometric data, overlapping themes, and even a recurring character in letters that should be generations apart.

What are the dates for these texts? Ignatius' letters are somewhere between the 130s-160s, with mainstream scholars preferring a date range of 130s-140s. What about these four letters of Paul? The first time we see all of Paul's letters (excluding the Pastoral Epistles) is in Marcion's canon published in 144.

What does this all mean? While it's difficult to say for certain, it looks like the letters of Ignatius and Paul's Prison Letters either had a common editor or a common author. What seems most likely is that someone involved in editing or writing the Prison Letters went on to write or edit the letters of Ignatius.

We have two main suspects: Ignatius (whoever he was) and Onesimus. If Ignatius was Peregrinus Proteus, then the story told by Lucian of someone editing Christian scriptures, and also writing his own, fits perfectly. The date range is also reasonable for this possibility. Proteus could have edited the Pauline letters sometime in the 130s working with Marcion's school, the letters were taken by Marcion to Rome, and then Proteus went on to get arrested and write what would become the letters of Ignatius.

On the other hand, if we consider Onesimus, we have a bishop both authors mention from a city they both write letters to despite supposedly being a generation or two apart. It was commonplace for authors writing fiction or forging works in ancient times to name-drop themselves in relatively minor roles - as letter carriers, guests, and bits like that. If we look at the letters from their ostensible chronological order, we almost see a story of Onesimus running to Paul, eventually working for him, and then going on to become bishop. Both authors also go out of their way to show respect for the character despite his minor role. If Onesimus didn't play a role in the editing or writing of these letters, he was close to someone who did.

Before moving on, we want to bring up one final thing regarding Ignatius. If you counted, you likely noticed only six letters from Ignatius, though it's accepted that there are seven authentic letters. The letter to Polycarp, the only personal letter in the collection, shows up so far away from the rest of the writings attributed to Paul and Ignatius that it would not fit in the image.

As we discussed with Philemon, personal letters are the most likely to be faked. If any of Ignatius' letters were likely to be faked, it would be the one to Polycarp. Interestingly, the recipient, Polycarp, has a single letter which is possibly a forgery, as well. This letter seems to have been presented as an introductory letter to Ignatius' letter collection, making the single personal letter Ignatius sent a bit more suspicious. It's possible that both these letters were created to serve the purpose of bolstering the credibility of both authors and tying Ignatius closer to another, more orthodox figure such as Polycarp.

The Latter Letters

Next, we get a number of letters that come later in the evolution of Christianity. Of this group, 1 Timothy, 2 Timothy, and Titus are falsely attributed to Paul. The vocabulary, church structure, and other content in these letters are so vastly different from the rest of Paul that they have been known to be inauthentic for centuries. They were also not part of Marcion's letter collection in 144, meaning they were not written by that time.

As mentioned in Chapter 5, it would seem that Polycarp and his scribe Crescens make a cameo in 2 Timothy and 1 Timothy mentions Gnosticism, as well as Marcion's work called *Antitheses*, so we can confidently date these letters to the 150s-160s at the earliest.

Continuing down the image, we see 2 Peter and Jude.

Jude, supposedly written by the brother of Jesus, despite the author never outright claiming to be, seems to be mentioned by Athenagoras in the 170s and then later by Clement of Alexandria in the 190s. It's one of the shortest books of the New Testament, and given its length, it can be hard to get a good stylometric read on it.

2 Peter, on the other hand, is a little longer and often quotes verbatim from Jude. We don't get attestation to 2 Peter until the third century, and Origen says that some doubt its authenticity. The writing of 2 Peter is drastically different from 1 Peter. Neither of which could have been written by the apostle Peter, and 2 Peter also seems to know of a letter collection attributed to Paul. We don't get mention of Paul's letters or a collection until 144, so we know this text is late. Given their late first references outside of the Bible, it's reasonable Jude was written sometime between the 140s-160s and 2 Peter from the 160s up to nearly the end of the second century. In fact, it's quite possible 2 Peter is the latest Christian text that made it into the Bible.

We then have Titus, 2 John, and 3 John. Titus was most likely written by the same group of authors as 1 Timothy and 2 Timothy, and 2 and 3 John are very short personal letters with very little theological content. Ostensibly attributed to the disciple John, the texts actually never mention the name of the author. They just say "the Elder," which in Greek is "presbyter." This was a title given to a certain John the Elder, but whether he was actually a disciple of Jesus is not clear and different church fathers give different answers to the question. It's possible, though, that another elder wrote the text, as elder often was used for those over the age of 50.

2 John and 3 John are the shortest books in the New Testament, with 13 verses and 15 verses, respectively. They are the length of actual letters of the era, and unlike most of the works attributed to Paul, were probably genuine letters rather than religious treatises attempting to pass off as Epistles. Because they are so short, we combined them in our study to get a better chance of an accurate stylometric read on them. We assume they are written by the same person, though based on these results, it's likely they were not written by the same person as 1 John or the Gospel of John.

In 3 John, we read of the author, supposedly the leader of a Christian community, and his associates getting rejected when visiting the nearby churches. Somewhere along the way, members of this group of churches started falling into some form of heresy. This heresy could have been Gnosticism, Marcionism, or something along these lines.

When this is revealed, the author writes 2 John to various *true* churches telling them not to allow the heretics into their communities if they preach such things (verses 7-11). 2 John ends with the hope to meet and talk in person, as the author says he does not want to write. This is another reason to think that this person was likely not the same author as the other works attributed to John.

We have one other reference point we can consider for these texts based on what we know of the church in its early years. Polycarp, who likely had a hand in writing the Pastoral Letters attributed to Paul, claimed to be a student of John. Traditionally, the John attributed to writing much of the Johannine (of or from John) content had his base and location in Ephesus, not too far from Smyrna. If there is any truth to these traditions, this would put Polycarp in the same religious community as this "elder" writing 2 and 3 John, and explain how these otherwise unimportant letters were collected and added into the Bible.

Eusebius considered 2 and 3 John to be disputed texts in his time, possibly attributed to another John. Irenaeus writes about 2 John in the 180s, but 3 John doesn't get attested to until the third century. The Muratorian Canon only lists two letters of John, and we only hear of Origen knowing it through Eusebius. Dionysius of Alexandria, a student of Origen who held the title of Pope from 248 to 264, seems to have read it or at least known of it. However, given their size and lack of theological content, it's unsurprising we don't have much use of them in early Christianity. Our guess is that these letters were falsely attributed to John sometime around the lives of Polycarp or Irenaeus, and originated from the John community in modern-day Turkey. This would put the letters anywhere from the 140s-170s.

Finishing Paul

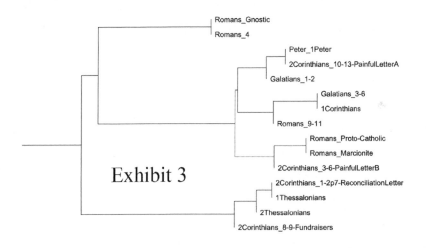

In Exhibit 3, we see the remainder of the Pauline letters. This branch contains 1 Corinthians, 2 Corinthians, Romans, 1 Thessalonians, 2 Thessalonians, Galatians, and, perhaps surprisingly,

1 Peter. We will return to 1 Peter later, but for now let's get started on the letters in this group attributed to Paul.

The Thessalonian Letters and 2 Corinthians

Because they are off on their own branch, we are going to start with 1 and 2 Thessalonians and then return to the remaining letters afterwards. While 1 Thessalonians is considered authentic by most mainstream scholarship and 2 Thessalonians inauthentic, our stylometric investigation indicates that the two letters are both from the same authorship community along with a portion of 2 Corinthians.

The understanding of the Thessalonian letters varies from scholar to scholar. Some believe the letters to be complete and whole letters with only minor interpolations, some believe them to have significant additions from later dates with only a portion of the letters being the "originals," and others believe that they are both composite letters. We did attempt the run splitting the texts, but the results were not significantly different and some of the resulting letters were too small to work with. As such, we left them as they are found in the canonical versions.

While it might be tempting to say that these are from the same author as Romans, 1 Corinthians, and Galatians since they come up broadly together, the stylometric distance between the Thessalonian letters and these other texts is greater than we see between Paul's Prison Letters and Ignatius' letters and almost as distant as the Prison Letters are from the Pastoral Letters. What we are likely seeing here are different authors with a common editor. In short, there is a different author or authorship community responsible for the Thessalonian letters.

If both Thessalonian letters are inauthentic, as the results show, it opens their date ranges up to 144 CE when they are both published by Marcion. Do we have anything that might suggest dates for these texts? We might.

2 Thessalonians 2 contains an extended passage on "the man of lawlessness" or "man of sin." This section is written as a prophecy, but as with other prophecies such as this, they are actually descriptions of current or recent events. We see similar prophecies used as literary devices in Revelation, Mark, and elsewhere. Likewise, the author of 2 Thessalonians is describing a person active around the time the letter is being written.

The person described in 2 Thessalonians 2 is said to be performing false signs and wonders, takes or sits in the Temple, exalts himself above all others including God, will be revealed after an *apostosia* (the root of the modern word for apostasy but literal meaning falling away or defection from something), leads people to believe the wrong things, and will be destroyed by the breath of the mouth of Jesus.

In particular, the line about the Temple stands out as a potential marker in time. Was there anyone who sat in or otherwise tried to indicate the Temple was theirs or otherwise treated it as their own? There are three possible answers to this question. The first is Caligula, the Roman Emperor from 37 to 41 CE who, according to Josephus and Philo, shipped a statue of himself to be put in the Temple. However, the statue was never put up due to Caligula's death taking place before its arrival. Furthermore, this is too early even for the traditional dating of either of the Thessalonian letters, which tradition dates to around 48-51 CE.

The second option is Hadrian, the Roman Emperor from 117 to 138. According to later sources and other references in the Bible, Hadrian had a statue of himself and Jupiter placed on the Temple (multiple authors attest to this, including Cassius Dio and Jerome).

Hadrian also worked toward a revitalization of Roman culture, which included pushing Roman religion and the imperial cult, which fits the description of leading followers to believe false things from the perspective of the 2 Thessalonians author. Hadrian, being a Roman Emperor, was also effectively a god in Roman culture, and given his statue was alongside that of Jupiter, the description of being exalted above others also fits. And, as with any figure of this stature also had miracles or "signs" attributed to them as well.

Finally, the last possibility is Simon bar Kokhba. Bar Kokhba led a rebellion against Rome from 132 to 136 until he was defeated by Hadrian at great cost. Prior to his defeat, coins were issued with his symbol - a star - above the Jewish Temple, which at that time had been destroyed. Some believe that once he took Jerusalem that he had a makeshift temple built, but it's uncertain whether this was done. The Bar Kokhba symbol over the Temple on the coin might have also appeared on any makeshift temple, and such a move might be seen as claiming the temple for himself. While it seems unlikely that Bar Kokhba's forces ever took back Jerusalem temporarily - only some Bar Kokhba coins out of our large total volume of them have been found inside Jerusalem itself - even the image could be enough to offend. We do, however, know from later Christian authors that Bar Kokhba persecuted Christians as they would not fight for him, meaning Christian authors of the time would likely have an unfavorable opinion of him. He was also known for supposedly breathing fire, making Jesus defeating him with his own breath a possible reference and form of retribution. The breathing of fire was also interpreted by many as a sign.

Some translations also interpret *apostosia* as rebellion or defection from Rome, which would also be another possible indicator that either Bar Kokhba or Hadrian was the subject of this section.

Some also point to 1 Thessalonians 2:14-16 as discussing the same subject in which the author of the letter discusses how the "wrath of God" has come upon the Jews at last. Such a phrase would really only be reasonable after the destruction of the Temple in 70 or the defeat and razing of the region in 136 after the Bar Kokhba Revolt. The destruction of the Temple in 70 wouldn't fit given the traditional dates of Paul's life even if we could posit a figure the section was about, meaning the Bar Kokhba Revolt is the subject just as it is in the Little Apocalypse in the Synoptic Gospels.

Given Caligula is out as a possibility and there are no other figures that come close to fitting the description in 2 Thessalonians, it must be talking about either Hadrian or Bar Kokhba. Fortunately, this matters very little, given the figures were active at the same time. The return of Jesus and his destroying of the person by his breath was the one part of the passage the author had actually made a prediction of happening rather than describing current events, and he was wrong. As such, it was written sometime shortly before the death of the person in question. Bar Kokhba died in 135 and Hadrian died in 138, meaning 2 Thessalonians was written somewhere in the 130s. 1 Thessalonians, given its stylometric similarities and passages containing references to related events happening, would seem to indicate a similar date range as well.

2 Corinthians

Now that we've addressed the Thessalonian letters, we should address the fact that parts of 2 Corinthians show up in this section as well as in the section with Romans, 1 Corinthians, and Galatians. Mainstream scholars have suspected for quite some time that 2 Corinthians is a composite letter of up to five smaller letters. We split the letter along the lines of what many scholars suspect as independent letters and we found that it's not the work of a single author, but at least two authors. It would appear that parts of 2 Corinthians actually contain work from the Thessalonian author as well as others. As we've just dated the Thessalonian letters, this means we can also date the compilation of 2 Corinthians to around the 130s-140s as well. This leads us into the biggest and most important section of Paul: Romans, 1 Corinthians, and Galatians.

Core Letters

We've now addressed all but three letters attributed to Paul. If there were any hope left for an authentic Christian Paul who actually existed at any point in time, it would be here. We aren't the first to assert that the entirety of Paul's existence depended on these texts. 19th century German scholar Ferdinand Christian Baur considered only four letters attributed to Paul as authentic: Romans, 1 Corinthians, 2 Corinthians, and Galatians. Other scholars following up from F.C. Baur fell into two camps: those who considered these four and usually three more (1 Thessalonians, Philippians, and Philemon) to be authentic or those such as Allard Pierson, Bruno Bauer, Arthur Drews, and others who considered all of Paul to be forgeries and Paul a fictional character used as a literary device and theological mouthpiece.

We know that even if parts of 2 Corinthians were written by the same author as Romans, 1 Corinthians, and Galatians that not all of it was, meaning the letter as we have it today is not authentic. As we see in our stylometric results, however, these three letters also do not have a single, consistent author throughout. Let's talk about the divisions we used for our study before addressing the results directly.

1 Corinthians

While all Pauline letters have inserted words and lines from one degree to another or otherwise show signs of multiple authors involved in their writing, 1 Corinthians takes this to a new level. The author(s) can't agree on a number of things, including important Christian ethics. For example, 1 Corinthians 8:4-8 and 1 Corinthians 10:27 seem to say that eating food sacrificed to other gods is fine, but then 1 Corinthians 10:20-21 and 1 Corinthians 10:28 seem to say no and then provide what seems to be a compromise, respectively. Speaking in tongues? 1 Corinthians 14:2-5, 14:39, and 14:18 say it's good, but 1 Corinthians 14:8-9 seems to say it is pointless. There are similar passages at odds within this one text itself.

Furthermore, there seems to be rather extensive evidence of some form of Gnosticism both directly in the writings of Paul but also being combatted or argued against in the letters, 1 Corinthians included. If not Gnosticism, then certainly what became Marcionism - though we can arguably see both in the texts. The thing is, Gnosticism and Marcionism are widely considered to be second-century phenomena by mainstream scholars. These writings were significantly impacted by Gnosticism and Marcionism, leading to an ongoing debate between the Christians as to who would go on to become the mainstream church, and who would be branded a heretic.

Much of the religious content in 1 Corinthians tends to be an attempt at unifying the church and attempting to get the readers to conform to a single set of beliefs. At times it seems to directly combat Gnosticism, where at other times it seems to promote Gnostic positions and figures, while at others it is directly appealing to readers to avoid factionalism. 1 Corinthians 1:11-12 is an interesting example, where Paul uses his authority to tell readers not to follow factions based on the authority of the faction leaders and includes himself as an example. This self-defeating statement is likely a later addition by someone pretending to be Paul using his voice to get this message across, because if Paul had written it, he would've realized the hypocrisy in the statement. Verses like this are peppered throughout the text in which they are either anachronistic, contradictory, or otherwise out of place. Another good example is verse 7:1, in which Paul brings up the issue of married couples abstaining from sex for religious reasons. It's unlikely this was written in the traditional era of Paul unless Christians up through the third century ignored the passage. We see the subject is still being debated as late as John Chrysostom in his Homilies on the Pauline Epistles in the late 300s. It also seems to have been a major issue for Marcion's churches that caused disagreement with the church in Rome.

Verses 9:20-22 capture an interesting development in Pauline mythology, in which he claims to be a Jew to Jews, a Greek to Greeks, and so on. According to church historian Epiphanius, sometime in the middle or late 2nd century CE, a Jewish Christian group known as the Ebionites said that Paul was a pagan who went to Jerusalem and wanted to marry a priest's daughter. He was circumcised and became a proselyte but failed to win over the girl (or her father) and then "in his anger wrote against circumcision, the Sabbath, and the law."[2]

This passage attempting to blend or explain the various interpretations of Paul makes more sense when we understand Paul shows up for the first time in the 2nd century as opposed to a more traditional date for Paul. It's the same reason we get works like the Acts of Paul and Thecla and other apocryphal works regarding Paul in the second century (and later) as well. He was not a real person documented by his letters, oral tradition via Acts, or his deeds across the Roman Empire, but rather a late creation with a story in need of elaboration.

Throughout the rest of the Pauline texts there are contradictions and other pieces of evidence of various authors writing under the name of Paul, and while we can't address them all we should stop to briefly discuss chapter 15, particularly the first quarter or so of it. While this creed documenting the appearances of Christ has long been considered a partial or even whole interpolation by many scholars, it is considered by those from a more apologetic bent to be one of the earliest traditions or references to a historical Jesus. What it actually reveals is an encapsulation of 1 Corinthians as a whole - competing traditions attempting to cram their group or beliefs into the letter. For example, we get Cephas "and then the Twelve," which is an odd wording given Cephas (or Peter, supposedly) was one of the Twelve. Then, we get the claim that 500 followers saw him, which the later text Acts of Pilate explains as 500 guards assigned by Pilate at the tomb of Jesus. Then, we get James "and then to all the apostles," again as if James were somehow separate from the apostles, and the apostles were somehow separate from the Twelve. Then, of course, he appeared to Paul as almost an afterthought. This seems more like different sects trying to claim appearances to their leaders or groups, which later all get merged into a more coherent unit in the gospels and Acts.

Back to the stylometric analysis, because of the difficulty separating the authorship of 1 Corinthians, we let it act as a "canonical Paul" anchor. In other words, if Paul were truly a single author as tradition holds, and 1 Corinthians were largely authentic, we would be able to see the texts most closely related to it. Our results showed that 1 Corinthians and Romans were almost always together, with Galatians and parts of 2 Corinthians nearby, if not floating a bit further away. 2 Corinthians has work from multiple authors in it, making the reading of it as a singular text misleading. We will soon see that this type of writing - a composite work collected from multiple authors - isn't only found in 2 Corinthians, but other texts as well.

Romans

When we looked at Romans, it was easier to separate out the authors than with 1 Corinthians. We first did a chapter-by-chapter analysis, and then applied the divisions found in Robert M. Price's *The Amazing Colossal Apostle*,[3] in which he identifies several author styles based on theological principles and other means. While we don't use theological principles as dividing lines for our texts, we were willing to test the results, and you see them here.

Price correctly identified that what he considered a Gnostic author was an entirely different authorship community from the rest of Romans. He incorrectly identifies Chapter 4, which he does not call Gnostic, but shows up with the Gnostic writings consistently. We see, on the other hand, that his Marcionite and proto-Catholic (those that opposed Marcion and would become today's Catholics, Protestants, and Orthodox churches) authors are actually a single authorship community. Likewise, Romans 9-11, which he considers an interpolation, actually seems to be a single authorship community as well, though possibly different from the Marcionite and proto-Catholic one.

Then, there is one other segment that is so far away from the rest of Romans that it didn't even show up on this graph that we called the Stolen Sermon: Romans 1:18-2:29. Scholar L. Gordon Rylands believed this section to be Gnostic, but as we see, it does not share stylometric qualities with the Gnostic sections identified elsewhere in Romans. John Cochrane O'Neill, another New Testament researcher, identified it as a Jewish sermon or text instead. This might be possible, and would fit with what our results showed regarding this segment.

This portion of the text was clearly written by someone completely different and incorporated into Romans, but the text flows pretty well. It's almost as if the letter were written with this piece of text in there originally, fitting well with our theory of a collaborative effort in creating Paul. It also seems to be in the earliest version we have of Romans, that of Marcion from his publication in 144, another sign that this was possibly in the original version.

Galatians

Finally, we get to Galatians. Some argue Galatians is a composite letter, and the stylometric analysis seems to indicate that this is very possible. Galatians is a heavily interpolated text, making a clearer stylometric read difficult. The first two chapters of Galatians seem to be a mishmash of writers attempting to explain Paul's backstory, including striking parallels to Marcion's personal story. Throughout the second half of the 2nd century and into the 3rd century there are varying accounts of what the letter said at the time, so we know it was still going through edits quite late. On the other hand, in line with what Tertullian says about Marcion "discovering" the letter, the content in chapters 3-6 tends to align more with Marcionite theology aside from verses scattered here and there which seem to contradict the bulk of the content. Such verses are likely from a later early church editor sometime in the process of the creation of our canonical version of the letter.

What seems most likely is that Galatians 3-6 represents the original content of the letter as drafted by someone in Marcion's church. This was written prior to the falling out with the Roman church, so likely the late 130s or early 140s. Then, after Marcion is excommunicated, more biographical information is added into Paul primarily in chapters 1 and 2. Significant portions of the content in these chapters seem to reflect Marcion's experiences, and they are likely projections of Marcion's biographical information back onto Paul. This would explain why the authors look slightly different but still within the larger branch. It could be the same author at a different time or someone else writing a bit later. Eventually, other church leaders affiliated with the Roman church would add verses throughout the text to try to make Paul more acceptable to their theology.

Regardless, both sections of the text come up in the same general group as 1 Corinthians and the majority of the Romans segments. This indicates that no matter how many hands were initially involved in writing the letter, it was written around the same time and by the general same group as the other two letters. These three letters, along with parts of 2 Corinthians makeup whatever the core Paul character might have been.

1 Peter

Now we've addressed the bigger part of Paul. But why is 1 Peter here? 1 Peter is actually a Pauline letter written by the same people pretending to be Paul. The vocabulary is similar, the structure is similar, and we don't hear about it until after the letters of Paul. 1 Peter was one of the most consistent texts in our study, always showing up in the Pauline tree. We're not the only ones to find this, either. Numerous other studies on the subject have found that this letter overlaps with Pauline writings, though they are often perplexed as to why, as they hold many of the letters to be authentic.

1 Peter was likely added after the Pauline letters had begun to circulate, but perhaps before they were put together in a consistent canon accepted by what would become the early Christian church. We suggest a date range of 130-160 for the letter, as it reflects the more orthodox content in Paul that goes against Marcion as well as a number

of references to Ephesians. This means the author was writing after the publication of Marcion's canon. It's possible the letter was written by someone who left Marcion's church or school after the falling out with Rome, or perhaps someone who was trying to "Paulinize" the character of Peter.

Peter the disciple was said to be illiterate in Acts, and others have noted that the author of 1 Peter seems to be well-trained in writing as well as have a background in rhetoric. Furthermore, Peter would be a native speaker of Aramaic, not Greek, and the text shows no signs of being from a non-native Greek speaker, which it would have if Peter were able to write.

Another issue is the description of Jesus' Passion and death in 1 Peter. Peter was supposedly there, but the description seems to be directly derived from other texts like Isaiah and shows no sign of first-hand knowledge. This use of Old Testament Scripture was frequently used by early Christian authors starting in the middle of the second century onward. And as with additions to Paul's letters, we see in chapters 2 and 3 a reinforcement of social hierarchies the Roman church considered important during that same era. Finally, we get no references to Peter anywhere outside the Bible until 1 Clement, which is also in the middle of the second century. If 1 Peter had been around earlier, and especially if it were truly from a direct disciple of Jesus, we would have heard about it from other authors.

Summary of the Core Letters of Paul

What does this all mean? Romans, just as with 1 Corinthians and 2 Corinthians, had multiple authors. The same seems to be the case for Galatians. We don't just mean a few phrases here and there were added, but rather there are enough significant portions of text that the computer can tell there are different people writing different segments once they are separated out. Really, there are only two ways this could have happened: either they were edited over time with each author or author group adding portions and somehow passing it off as the original each time they shared it, or these texts were created as a joint effort by multiple authors in the second century.

Many scholars who consider the possibility that Paul was a made-up character or even just had his letters heavily edited over time usually tend toward the first option, that there were some kind of core texts for each of these letters that got expanded over time. Some make the case that 1 Clement seems to know 1 Corinthians and possibly Romans, indicating these were the earliest letters. However, as we will discuss later and have touched on in Chapter 5, 1 Clement is not written by a single author either and is a second-century text. We also don't have any earlier versions of the letters without a particular authorship group or section that is clearly not by the same author as the rest of the text, and the texts all come to us around the same time in 144 when the texts first appear in the historical record.

The strongest argument for this process would seem to be in Romans. Romans has conclusions at 11:36, 15:32, and 16:27, with some arguing that there are even more. There is also indirect evidence of a 14-chapter version of the letter circulating for centuries in the Roman Empire, and Papyrus 46 seems to potentially indicate that there was another version that had only 15 chapters. Chapter 16 itself seems to be a letter on behalf of Phoebe added to the end of the rest. However, none of these omissions particularly stand out in our Stylo results, meaning it could just be multiple authors signing off on a letter that is crafted collaboratively over time as our theory presents.

And, as with just about all canonical New Testament texts, we have manuscripts that, while otherwise complete, will omit whole verses or passages, likely either for theological reasons of the scribe making the copy. Codex Boernerianus, for example, lacks the references to the Roman churches as the audience of the letter in Romans 1. As mentioned earlier in the book, textual variants outnumber the total word count of the New Testament itself, so it's likely that many of these don't amount to much in regard to the historical record of the text.

We present the possibility that these letters were written as a collaborative project shortly before this publication. We know Marcion came to Rome in the late 130s, likely after the Bar Kokhba Revolt, and tried to join the church there. We're told that around 144 he was excommunicated and published his collection of 10 letters from Paul, his gospel Evangelion, and a text he wrote called *Antitheses*. As mentioned earlier, Tertullian even tells us that Marcion "discovered" Galatians. We have no mention of Paul or a gospel before this date, and right after they are published we start to see a boom in gospels as well as numerous other fake Paul letters show up. All signs point to a fabricated character.

What we suggest is that during the time he was in Rome or perhaps sometime before, Marcion worked with a number of other Christians there on creating a canon. This would be something like a literary school, common in the Roman era. Scholars such as Thomas L. Brodie, Robin Faith Walsh, and others document the writing process and presence of such schools in detail in their works. Some of these schools might be local, focused around a single teacher, while larger ones might span across multiple cities throughout the empire.

Marcion had traveled across the Mediterranean Sea and was from modern-day Turkey and close to where many of Paul's letters were addressed. With him, he brought a number of religious writings from these regions, such as the Thessalonian letters. Perhaps these letters were already written under another name, or perhaps they were written as part of a larger production process in the Marcionite school. Once in Rome, given the various factions fighting, Marcion attempts to unite the church. Sometime around this time, a significant portion of the work attributed to Paul is written. Marcion also has a copy of Proto-Mark which is used to write Evangelion and includes a "prophecy" about the end of the Bar Kokhba Revolt in 136 that is known today as the Little Apocalypse. Another round of edits are made to the Pauline texts at this time, as well.

1 Corinthians, Romans, Galatians, and parts of 2 Corinthians are also written around this time, probably using some kind of core text or story Marcion picked up in modern-day Turkey or Greece. We mention BCE Paul as a possibility of this earlier in the book, and this is one possibility of what this core text might have looked like. These letters then had biographical content added paralleling Marcion's experience - this was likely done near the end, around the time of his excommunication. We read about Paul taking money to the Jewish Christians in Jerusalem just as Marcion does the church in Rome, we know of both their journeys to Rome being significant, and a number of other suspicious parallels given that he is the one to publish these texts.

By 144, there are 10 letters with Paul's name on them as an apostle who was too late to hear the earthly teachings of Jesus who descended from the sky in Evangelion, but was given a separate revelation after his earthly followers such as Peter failed to properly deliver the good news. After the Church split with Marcion, one of the collaborators likely went on to write 1 Peter in order to build him up or perhaps intentionally make Peter look Pauline, too. Given this person was responsible for some of the Pauline content, it explains why the style, theology, and vocabulary match Paul exactly.

This doesn't exclude the possibility of slightly different versions of all of these letters having existed. There would certainly have been drafts and given the extra endings tend to be at the end of sections within letters, it would have been relatively easy to add the content after these endings, which largely consists of greetings and names of fellow Christians. Marcion took his version and spread it across the Roman Empire, and the opposing early Christians in Rome and elsewhere were left to react and attempt to counter the spread. We know Tertullian, writing in the third century, attempted to pass an even more anti-Marcionite version off in his writings as the authentic version - his deception was revealed, however, by our discovery of earlier manuscripts that included some of his deletions such as in Galatians 1:19 where he attempts to make Paul pro-circumcision. Eventually, this opposing group added a few of their own "Pauline" letters and "found" letters from Peter, James, Jude, and John to reinforce their idea of Jesus as well. They even went as far to write their own versions of Evangelion and edit what would become Mark.

While the idea of Paul's writings being a collaborative effort, perhaps within a literary school, that effectively resulted in a compromise text might seem outlandish to some, it actually fits perfectly into how Christianity developed throughout history. Theology was often effectively voted upon, with the "true" doctrine being what received the most support at what were called councils. The most famous of these is the first ecumenical council known as the First Council of Nicea in 325, but church tradition places them going back all the time to the first century with the Council of Jerusalem. While we discuss why this one likely never happened earlier in the book, the next earliest council took place in 155 in Rome - around when we would expect if Christianity started the way the evidence in this book shows. Did nothing happen worthy of discussing in this 100-year period? It's more likely that the council in Rome was the first and regarded how to react to Marcion.

The creation of the Pauline letter collection being a compromise, a consensus work rather than that of a single author, would be in line with how Christians would develop the religion for centuries to come. It would almost be an exception to the rule if it weren't created this way.

Matthew Britt

John Documents

Now we move into the works attributed to John. First, we will look at the Gospel of John at a chapter-by-chapter level.

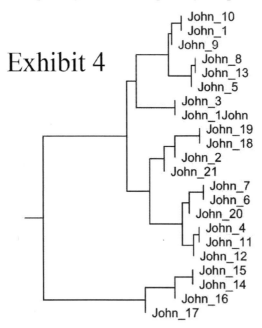

Exhibit 4

As you can see in Exhibit 4, it shows up by itself (with the exception of 1 John). We saw earlier 2 and 3 John come up closer to the Pastoral Letters attributed to Paul, so these are clearly not by the same author as the other texts attributed to John. This makes sense reading these texts, too. The author of 2 and 3 John states he does not like writing long letters, and neither of these are very long. On the other hand, 1 John is quite long for an ancient letter and the Gospel of John is also a long text. This author seemed to have no problem writing lengthy documents.

There are numerous theories about the structure and development of the Gospel of John, but one thing we can see for certain is that the only part that is somewhat different from the rest is what is known as the Farewell Discourse, found in John 14-17. Some use it to attempt to say that an original version of John was written earlier, ending at or near the Farewell Discourse and later chapters were added. This looks unlikely to be the case for several reasons. First, the Farewell Discourse seems to be a separate author from the rest. If it were the ending of the original text, it should come up with other chapters. Second, if this were the case, then we would see all the remaining chapters by themselves and removed from the rest of the text as far away as the Farewell Discourse is. Instead, while we do see 3 of the later chapters in a subgroup, they are with an earlier chapter, and chapter 20 is with a number of other texts. What it looks like we see is that while John was a group effort, it was done by a single authorship community and no particular part stands out as distinctly different enough to date as far as a century before the rest of the text.

The text admits as much. In John 21:24-25, the compiler or compilers of the final version of the gospel effectively tell us that they have put together stories they received from someone else. They don't claim that any part of the text was even written by the "beloved disciple," but only that he passed these things down to them to write down. In verse 25, there's even the implication that a lot was left (or cut) out, and could also be a reference to other the other gospels given John was one of the latest to be written.

Revelation

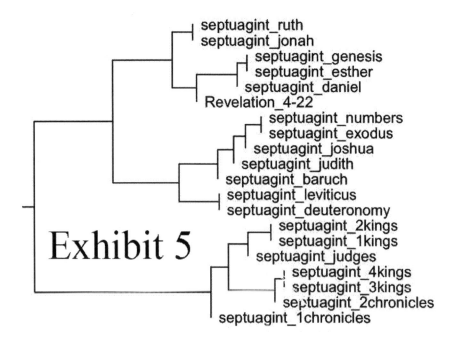

septuagint_ruth
septuagint_jonah
septuagint_genesis
septuagint_esther
septuagint_daniel
Revelation_4-22
septuagint_numbers
septuagint_exodus
septuagint_joshua
septuagint_judith
septuagint_baruch
septuagint_leviticus
septuagint_deuteronomy
septuagint_2kings
septuagint_1kings
septuagint_judges
septuagint_4kings
septuagint_3kings
septuagint_2chronicles
septuagint_1chronicles

Exhibit 5

This leads us to Revelation, as seen in Exhibit 5. No part of Revelation came up with any other John text, but we did notice something interesting. Revelation was not written by one author, and the bulk of it was likely not originally a Christian text. In fact, the vast majority of Revelation was a Jewish text, written in Hebrew and slightly edited later to add references to Jesus in the Christian's Greek version. What we saw were three distinct authors, and this lines up well with the text as well. Revelation 1 is written by a second-century compiler, the person who put the final letter together. The letters in Revelation 2-3 are written by another author, this one a Christian from the second century as well. Finally, Revelation 4-22 was written by a Jewish author at an unknown period of time, but possibly as far back as the translation of the Septuagint. How can we tell?

Our runs of Stylo included every Jewish text written in Greek we could find up to the third century CE. Revelation 4-22 consistently showed up with the Septuagint, specifically Daniel as well as Ruth, Jonah, Genesis, and others. While some will say that the themes in these texts are similar, thus they showed up together, we would remind them that Stylo doesn't look at theology or theme, but word and character frequency. The majority of words in a given text tend to be function words such as articles, pronouns, and the like, not theological words.

Aspects of the original Hebrew being translated come through, indicating that Revelation was originally written in Hebrew just as the Septuagint was. The fact that it didn't come up with later Jewish Greek texts means that it was definitely a translation. The mainstream consensus is that the Pentateuch, the five books attributed to Moses, were translated first back in the third century BCE and translation of the Minor Prophets and Writings was completed sometime around or before 130 BCE.[4] Given we know Revelation isn't mentioned until the 150s-160s CE, the date range for the original Hebrew text could be anywhere from the second century BCE to the second century CE. Of course, the original did not mention Christ as this was added by one of the second-century authors that would adapt the book for their purposes, so the date ultimately has little impact on the rest of the New Testament.

The Finale

To demonstrate where Revelation 1-3 shows up, we now look at the section containing a number of authors from the second century. This section will contain some of our most revealing finds and help us date a number of early Christian texts.

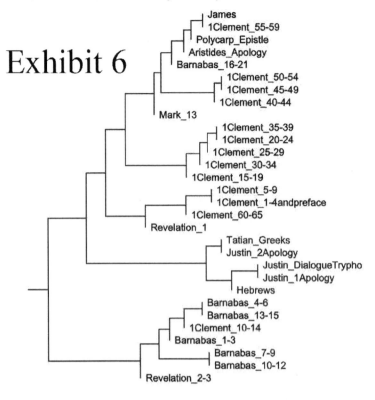

Exhibit 6

First, let's revisit our dates from Chapter 5. Justin Martyr, whose three extant texts are found here, dates to the 150s-160s. Tatian, his student, was working up through the 170s. Given their texts show up together, this lends credence to the authorship community idea. Even when one author might not be responsible for all the texts in a branch, at the most distant relation, their students or others in their community played a part. For example, Tatian studied under Justin Martyr and this is likely why their texts show up close to one another. Next, we get Aristides, whose *Apology* is usually dated to the 130s, but more recent scholars push potentially as late as the 160s. Next comes Polycarp. While Polycarp's letter is possibly a forgery, Polycarp himself was active in the middle of the second century as well, and no one could have written the letter in his name until after he had an established reputation in the second half of the second century. Mark 13, containing the Little Apocalypse, is dated to sometime after 136 due to its references to the Bar Kokhba Revolt and having not been added to Mark until the other two Synoptics were written or being written. Mainstream scholars date the Epistle of Barnabas up to the 130s, and we give it a range of the 130s-160s.

The only non-canonical text in this group attributed to before the middle of the second century is 1 Clement, the anonymous letter that knows 1 Corinthians and possibly some of Paul's other writings. Clement of Rome, the person the letter gets attributed to by Irenaeus around 180, is said to have written it in the 90s. As we discuss in Chapter 5, however, and as we see here, there were multiple authors involved in writing this text. Every text it shows up with seems to date to the second century, and as such, it is almost certainly a second-century text as well.

To sum up, the dates for these texts seem to range from the 130s to the 180s and seem to have a connection to Rome. Justin wrote in Rome, Tatian was in Rome for some time, 1 Clement was supposedly written in Rome by the bishop of Rome, Aristides supposedly gives his Apology to the Emperor (possibly in Rome), Mark goes to Rome, and in the *Clementine Recognitions* Barnabas also goes to Rome. What we see here appears to be the church in Rome in the middle of the second century, writing and consolidating its theology.

That then means when we see Revelation 1 and 2-3 here, both by different authors, the entirety of Revelation starts to make sense. One earlier author in Rome or otherwise affiliated with it wrote the letters, another Roman Christian took these letters and added an intro, and then the translated text of Revelation 4-22 was edited and added at the end. Unsurprisingly, Justin Martyr, writing in Rome in the 150s-160s, is the first reference to Revelation we get. He likely had access to it soon after its creation because it came from the broader community he was part of.

1 Clement

Some scholars have pointed out that 1 Clement seems to actually have been more of a work continuously added to rather than a single, whole letter (and given its length it is arguably more of a treatise or even book-sized for its time period). Our stylometric analysis proves this to be the case.

Individual chapters in 1 Clement are too small to run on their own, so we grouped 5 or more chapters together at a time, depending on their length. While there was no logic aside from ensuring adequate size for analysis, it still allowed us to break the text into parts and look at each a little more closely. What we see is that 1 Clement is indeed a composite text.

1 Clement 1-9, 60-65, and the prologue are written by someone entirely different from the rest of the text, but the same person. It's possible some portion of chapters 10-14 are written by this author as well, as these chapters show up far away from the rest of the text too, but are usually somewhat disconnected from chapters 1-9. 1 Clement 15-39 seems to be another author, and 40-59 seem to possibly be another, though in this case might be in the same community rather than being significantly distant from each other. As mentioned above, the borders of these are a bit fuzzy given our divisions are based on size of text and not pericope or theme in the text, but they give clear results nonetheless and open the doors for further research into the document.

There are also a number of other works attributed to Clement, but none of them come up with 1 Clement meaning different authors used the name in other fake letters. It seems that Clement is a figure like Paul - made up as a mouthpiece placed back in time in order to push a theological agenda. Later authors picked up his name, as they did with Paul and others, and wrote their own views in an attempt to add credibility to them. Some of these forgeries go as late as the 9th century CE in the collection of false texts known as Pseudo-Isidore or the False Decretals. Pseudo-Isidore is the name given to the author(s) responsible for over 100 forged documents pretending to be various figures across multiple centuries. The fake texts shaped the understanding of church history and the implementation of church policy for centuries before they were proven to be fakes in the 1600s.

The implications of 1 Clement being a composite text are quite significant. 1 Clement is usually considered the first reference to Paul outside of the New Testament. However, if the letter was actually pieced together over time, this means that it's possible the parts that mention Peter and Paul were added later. It seems they certainly were written by another author than the bulk of the letter. This means our first reference to Paul outside the Bible is now into the 130s at the earliest, possibly as late as Marcion's introduction of him in 144 when publishing Paul's letters alongside Evangelion.

Epistle of Barnabas

The Epistle of Barnabas is also a composite text, as seen above. In this case, rather than being pieced together over time like 1 Clement, the author of the Epistle of Barnabas has lifted from another author and incorporated it into his own work. Like with 1 Clement, we made divisions based on chapter size, and we found that Barnabas chapters 16-21, the ending portion of the text, were largely written by another author. In our discussion on Barnabas in Chapter 5, you may remember that the name Jesus is never mentioned after chapter 15.

Given the results of our stylometric analysis, this further confirms that the author took from another source and added it into his text.

Hebrews

We also see Hebrews here, and this is unsurprising. Hebrews is an anonymous letter written in the style of Paul. Even in the time of Eusebius, there were doubts about whether Paul wrote it. We see here that these doubts were vindicated, and it is actually associated with the church in Rome around the time of Justin Martyr and Tatian. While these two figures may not be the author, it's possible. Hebrews has extensive references to the Hebrew Bible, and both Justin and Tatian were adept at doing the same.

Mark 13 and the Little Apocalypse

Mark 13, as we have discussed multiple times, is known as the Little Apocalypse and written on the subject of the end of the Bar Kokhba Revolt. While the case for this is written extensively by scholar Hermann Detering in his article *The Synoptic Apocalypse: A Document from the Time of Bar Kokhba* and we've discussed it briefly elsewhere, we will revisit it here for a moment. It's clear that the Little Apocalypse found in Matthew 24, Mark 13, and Luke 21 is discussing some disaster, usually considered to be the destruction of the Temple in 70 CE. However, the text actually fits better with descriptions of the events of the 130s (our stylometric evidence which shows the same put aside for the moment).

First and foremost is Mark 13:14, which mentions the "abomination that causes desolation standing where it does not belong." In 70, this makes no sense, but if we consider that Hadrian put a statue of himself and Jupiter on the Temple Mount, the line makes more sense. What makes it even clearer is that the only other time this line "abomination of desolation" is used in Daniel 9:27. It's used in reference to when Antiochus Epiphanes did something similar in 165 BCE to the Temple with an image of Zeus. This is an intentional, direct parallel between the two historical incidents.

Mark 13 tells readers to hope that the time to flee "will not take place in winter." While this is meaningless in regard to the events in 70, in the Bar Kokhba Revolt, the winter is when the Roman troops partially withdrew to regroup. Likewise, the warning in the verse to those in Judaea would also be more apt in the 130s as the destruction and slaughter was more extensive across the region than in 70. The warnings of false prophets and messiahs could easily apply to either time, but given the entire movement behind the Bar Kokhba Revolt was led by a messiah figure and his religious teacher Rabbi Akiva, this seems much more likely to be describing the events of 130s in these sections of the Little Apocalypse, as well. There are other aspects of the Little Apocalypse that fit the 130s, as well.

While we show Mark 13 above, Matthew 24 and Luke 21 also show up removed from the rest of their texts. When we ran New Testament scholar Matthias Klinghardt's reconstruction of Marcion's Evangelion,[5] seen below, the equivalent chapter came up with the rest of the body of the text. Notice how, unlike canonical Luke, Acts and Evangelion come up as completely distinct authors with no overlap. Evangelion's Little Apocalypse also shows up with the rest of the text rather than being removed.

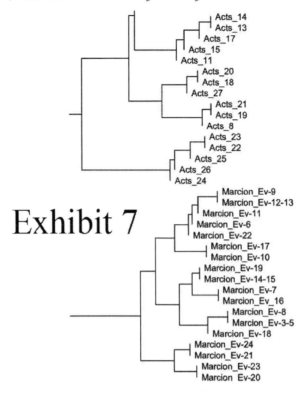

Exhibit 7

While results from any reconstruction should be taken with a grain of salt, this and the fact that Matthew and Luke have material that come with their respective versions of the Little Apocalypse indicate that the section was first added with Marcion's Evangelion and thus not in the original version of Mark. Mark's Little Apocalypse actually seems to be an abbreviated version of Matthew's, and it is likely the author of Matthew that inserted it into the text of Mark.

James

And now we get to James. We discussed James the figure quite extensively earlier in the book, and now we can address the letter attributed to him. As with the rest of the texts in the above image, James is a second-century creation. This is unsurprising, as even in the fourth century CE we have references of people questioning the authorship of the letter of James, such as Eusebius. In fact, we seem to have no references to James at all until the third century. Origen of Alexandria has the first explicit reference to James in his works, written between the 230s-250s, and accepts it as authentic with some hesitation. Some claim Irenaeus might have referenced a line of the text, but it's unclear and even if he did, that only pushes the earliest reference date to the 180s.

This shouldn't be surprising if we take into consideration the theological debates going on at the time. The explosion of New Testament texts comes about after Marcion's canon is published in 144. In response, a number of other letters and texts are written attributed to various supposed followers of Jesus. Just as this happened with Peter, it happened with James as well. The text of James seems to be an attempt to be a direct counter to some aspects of Pauline beliefs, and as such shows awareness of the Pauline letters. However, the author of James seems to misunderstand parts of Pauline theology - dismissing the needs of works of the Law, interpreting them as general moral behavior or deeds instead, for example. This would suggest that the author of James is removed from the original publication of Marcion's canon by quite some time or, alternatively, had an incredibly poor grasp on the situation - also not befitting for the supposed "brother of the Lord."

Summarizing Our New Testament Findings

Here is a brief list of our findings regarding New Testament texts and the documents that show up the closest to them:

1. Marcion's Evangelion came before canonical Luke. The content missing from Evangelion matches Acts more closely than the content found in Evangelion, indicating that it was written

by the author of Acts and not Evangelion. As Evangelion was published around 144, this puts our canonical version of Luke and Acts after this date, as well as the rest of the canonical gospels.

2. The Long Ending of Mark found in chapter 16 is not authentic and was added around the same time canonical Luke and Acts were sent to Theophilus of Antioch - around or after 160.

3. Paul was not one person and likely did not exist at all. A community of Marcionite authors in the second century wrote the majority of what is attributed to Paul, along with the possibility of some letters or parts of letters having been lifted from other authors and then attributed to Paul. The Pastoral Epistles are an exception, having been written even later in the second century by a group or author opposed to Marcion's movement.

4. The close relation between the letters of Ignatius of Antioch and Paul's so-called Prison letters seems to indicate a relationship or even common authorship or shared authorship circles. This is further evidence that Paul's work was not written until the second century. We believe that the author of some of the Prison Letters went on to either become Ignatius of Antioch or otherwise be responsible for his letters, such as Onesimus, a figure who appears in both sets of letters.

5. The "Little Apocalypse" in the Synoptic Gospels where Jesus predicts the destruction of the Temple was not written by the same author as any of the gospels. It was added into Mark at some point likely around or after 136 CE.

6. 2 John and 3 John were written by the same person or group of people that wrote the Pastoral Epistles, but not 1 John, Revelation, or the Gospel of John. We believe this was Polycarp of Smyrna, and that Irenaeus, student of Polycarp, put them under John's name as an attempt to increase the Johannine content in the New Testament.

7. 1 Peter was a Pauline letter, written by someone responsible for some of the content found in Paul's letters. Either the author was from the same community of authors as Paul's letters and it was written around the 140s or it is someone very intentionally and closely imitating the works attributed to Paul, placing it slightly later.

8. 2 Peter is also a very late text, chronologically closer to the Pastoral Epistles. The same goes for the Epistle attributed to Jude.

9. 1 John is associated with the Gospel of John, likely a member of the same community if not a contributor to the gospel itself. We can confirm that there was a Discourse Source for John 14-17 that was a single author within the Johannine community in the second century. The Gospel of John itself likely dates to around 160, with 1 John dating to around that time as well.

10. Revelation had at least three authors and was originally a Jewish text, likely originally written in Hebrew. When the Septuagint (the translation of the Jewish scriptures in Greek) is added into the equation, Revelation 4-22 acts more like the Septuagint than any Christian material. The letters in chapters 2-3 were from a Christian author in the second century, as was chapter 1, though it likely came from a third author.

11. 1 Clement is a composite second-century piece of literature. This undermines the belief that Paul was mentioned in the first century, and also throws into question other aspects of church history regarding the early development of the church.

12. The Epistle of Barnabas is also a second-century composite work. The end of the text was likely taken from another text and added on by the author of the earlier parts of the letter.

13. Hebrews was not written by Paul and tends to show up closer to mid-second-century documents from the church in Rome.

14. James is a second-century text likely produced by the Roman church, as well.

15. Mark was stitched together over time. With Mark 13 dating to 136 CE at the earliest (and likely not added until quite some time after that) and Mark 16's longer ending dating to at least the 150s-160s, it looks as though it went through numerous edits throughout the century.

"What other results were found?"

We made a number of other findings in our stylometric analysis that fall outside of the New Testament canon. Below, we'll briefly address them and their implications.

Reconstructing Proto-Mark

While Proto-Mark, the precursor to our current canonical version of the Gospel of Mark, technically appears in some form in the version we have today, we include it here because it does not technically exist in the New Testament as we have it. Proto-Mark would have likely been the first Christian document to have been written down. We know canonical Mark went through a number of edits with various sources, as shown in the above results. This drove us to want to reconstruct what this text might have looked like prior to the various additions it received.

To reconstruct Proto-Mark, we only had to go a step beyond reconstructing Evangelion, which BeDuhn, Klinghardt, and others had already done an excellent job of doing. As Evangelion is a later expansion on Proto-Mark, it would have kept the majority of the text in it and only added to it. Thus, if something is in Evangelion and canonical Mark, it was likely in Proto-Mark. The Gospel of Matthew was not around yet, so any material exclusively shared between it and Mark is likely a later addition. Likewise, if a verse is shared between Luke and Mark but not also with Evangelion, it's likely that verse came from later additions because we know the content in Luke was written significantly later than Evangelion.

This leaves overlap with Mark and Evangelion, as well as content unique to Mark. Content unique to Mark is likely later as well, given it would defeat the purpose of creating an expanded version by removing existing material. It's possible something might have been left out for theological or other reasons, but we try not to assume more than we have to. We know Marcion or whoever wrote Evangelion was writing a longer version of the Christ story, and that motivation is evident. Beyond that, we do not know the motives of the author. Likewise, there is an equal risk that the editor of canonical Mark took content found in Proto-Mark and Evangelion out, which we would have no evidence of. As such, in our reconstruction of Proto-Mark, we removed content unique to Mark and did not add anything from Evangelion without a parallel in canonical Mark.

Then, we cross-referenced our stylometric analysis to see what content of canonical Mark does not show up as the same author as the rest of the text. We know this is chapter 13 and chapter 16, or at least the bulk of these. The Little Apocalypse in chapter 13 and the longer ending of Mark were not in Proto-Mark, so these were removed. The results from our analysis also confirm the chronological priority of Evangelion over canonical Luke, meaning that using a reconstruction of Evangelion would provide more accurate results than using our modern version of Luke.

Less Than Full Marks

What we found is that Proto-Mark was roughly one third of the length of canonical Mark. It's roughly the size of 1 Corinthians or Hebrews and lacks a significant portion of the miracles and teachings of Jesus found in canonical Mark. The travels and historical details are much more scarce, as well. In fact, the entire story seems to potentially take place over a period of just a few weeks. Despite having significant portions of the canonical version cut, though, the text still flows well.

We believe it is likely, given Jesus descends to Earth in Evangelion, that this is how he first appears in Proto-Mark. In canonical Mark, a dove descends on Jesus and God declares him his son. The original was likely Jesus himself descending, with God declaring him his son. Jesus does not get baptized by John the Baptist, but immediately begins his teaching after descending. Likewise, the scriptural passage referencing Elijah (John the Baptist) coming before Jesus is usually cited at the beginning of canonical Mark, but it seems to be absent in Proto-Mark. Rather than first getting disciples, the disciples join after Jesus has already built up a reputation. They miss the early days of his ministry, and this was likely flipped in the canonical version to add credibility to the disciples which various members of the second-century Christian movement liked to claim authority from.

Jesus has almost no moral teachings, and his miracles seem to scare people as much as impress them. A consistent theme that stays in Proto-Mark is that people don't seem to like him. Roughly halfway through the text, Jesus declares that in order to live, one must lose their life, and that the Son of Man (apparently referring to himself) must also die so that later he can rise.

After a few more miracles, Passover comes and Judas betrays him. From the Passover scene through to his crucifixion, the text is very brief. Jesus is not accused of threatening to destroy the Temple, as is the case in canonical Mark. In fact, Jesus never mentions the Temple in Proto-Mark. This is likely because when it was written, the Temple had been gone for so long that it was irrelevant to the conversation. It only became a theme in Christianity again with Evangelion, in which the destruction of the Temple is used as a metaphor for the Bar Kokhba Revolt, which took place in the 130s.

Jesus' crime in Proto-Mark seems to be claiming to be the Christ. However, as we know from the earliest manuscript evidence, it was likely written in nomina sacra as XS. This could be Christ, meaning Messiah or Anointed One, or it could mean Chrest, the Good. While canonical Mark makes Christ seem more likely, many of the scriptural references and political themes in canonical Mark which lend credence to the Christ interpretation do not appear in Proto-Mark.

The Chrest interpretation is stronger in Proto-Mark than in any other Christian documents. As we discussed earlier, Chrest means "good," "useful," "kind," or "virtuous." While scholars still do not know what the phrase "the Son of Man" meant, it makes its first appearance with the definite article "the" in Proto-Mark. If, as many suspect, it is an adaptation from the concept "son of Adam" from Hebrew, then it might be a general "person" or "human being." In relation to a Chrest interpretation, this would then make Jesus a metaphor for those who wish to live a good or virtuous life. The story can then be understood as an account of more worldly people reacting negatively to those who live by a different moral standard which was promoted by the early Christian movement, and this is exactly what we see in Pliny's letter and in various other early references and descriptions of Christians by outsiders.

We also know that, as many others have pointed out before us, Buddhism was present in the Roman Empire at the time Christianity was forming. While it has been known that Christians such as Clement of Alexandria interacted with Buddhists in the late second century, the 2022 discovery of the Berenike Buddha statue pushes the dates back even earlier. This Buddha statue dating to around 90-140 CE was found in Berenike, an Egyptian town which was one of the Roman Empire's biggest trade ports that had interaction with India. We also know that Caesar Augustus received an Indian embassy sometime between the years 22 BCE and 13 CE. Greek and Indian records indicate that Indian missionaries and convoys were being sent into Greece and the surrounding area as far back as the 200s BCE. In fact, multiple Indian texts record a monk known as Mahadhammarakkhita living in cities under Greek control with a large number of Greek Buddhists during the reign of Menander I. This is just one example of the Greco-Buddhist movement influencing both the Indian and Greek worlds of the time centuries before the rise of Christianity.

These Buddhist groups, along with the Therapeutae, various Greek philosophical movements such as the Stoics, Pythagoreans, the Middle Platonism movement, and others likely all contributed to the creation of Christianity either through philosophical influence or perhaps direct membership in what would become Christian churches. It's possible that some of these not only influenced the teachings found in Evangelion, but also the writing of Proto-Mark. The theology in it is much different than what would become Christianity even just a few decades later, when the text would make its way to Rome. Without earlier manuscripts or writings we can't be sure about the exact beliefs that created Proto-Mark, but we can clearly see the Jesus of Proto-Mark is far less a Messiah figure here than elsewhere in Christian writings.

Proto-Mark's lack of more standard Christology found in the rest of the New Testament also makes the letters of Paul even less likely to have been the earliest documents. Many argue for Mark having been a Pauline text, and that might be true with the canonical version, but Proto-Mark is less theologically aligned with Paul than Evangelion and canonical Mark. This further supports our position that the writings of Paul are actually second-century documents meant to elaborate upon the theology of Marcion's version of Christianity and were first published alongside Evangelion in 144.

There are a number of other things of note found (and not found) in Proto-Mark. There is not a single mention of anyone named Mary (the mother of Jesus or otherwise). After denying Jesus, Peter never appears again. There is also no stone in front of the tomb Jesus is laid in. There is nothing apocalyptic in Jesus' sayings. There are far fewer references to the Hebrew Bible, though some remain. There is no reference to Nazareth - Capernaum is clearly his "hometown" to the extent he has one. Key things that remain include the Transfiguration, Jesus' death, and his body's disappearance shortly afterwards.

Marking the Timeline

There are a number of internal references we can use to help identify a rough date range for Proto-Mark. The story still retains a number of references to and echoes of Josephus. This would indicate that the date of Proto-Mark cannot be earlier than the start of the second century. The lack of Temple references would seem to indicate it did not play a role in the religion or in the setting of the story, meaning it would have to be gone at that point. Furthermore, the lack of references also seem to indicate it had been gone long enough that it was not fresh on the mind of the author. Again, the early second century would seem fitting here.

Also potentially important for the dating of Proto-Mark is the fact that John the Baptist himself does not seem to appear. We see multiple places where his followers are referenced and a reference about how Jesus might be John the Baptist risen from the dead, but no actual John. Though the story seems to be set in the 30s with Pilate and Herod, this seems to be a slip up. John the Baptist was clearly dead at the time of writing and only his followers were around.

We also have the fact that this text is not quoted and does not appear or seem to be used until Evangelion uses it. That is the latest possible date that Proto-Mark could appear - around Evangelion's publication in 144. Mainstream scholarship insists that the Synoptic Gospels must have come in succession of one another within one to two decades after when they believe Mark was written. While this is ultimately arbitrary, using their reasoning would put Proto-Mark in the 120s-130s given Evangelion makes its appearance around 144. This reasonably fits the internal references, as well.

Proto-Mark likely came into something closer to its canonical form sometime between 135 and the early 150s. The primary shift that this text would have gone through would be adopting structural additions from Evangelion or at least an attempt to respond to it, particularly relating to the theme of the destruction of the Temple, which was a metaphor for the Bar Kokhba Revolt. After this, there is a close development between this pre-canonical version of Mark and with the Gospel of Matthew. Matthew uses this pre-canonical version of Mark more closely than canonical Luke, and we know Matthew was a response to Evangelion. Our stylometric results showed that Matthew was never originally a Hebrew text as some claim and comes up with later second-century texts.

Mark reaches its short ending version some time between the 160s to 170s. Someone using the Gospel of Matthew goes in and reinserts certain content, which can be seen in places like Mark 14 when Jesus is in front of the Sanhedrin where verses effectively repeat themselves unnecessarily. The long ending of Mark was then added around the time of Irenaeus, and was drawn from canonical Luke and Acts. In fact, the stylometric evidence directly shows that these texts and the longer ending of Mark are tied together by a similar author.

Our canonical version of Mark became, in a way, its own harmony gospel. Its core is rooted in Proto-Mark, but after each new Synoptic gospel came out, content was added to it. Ironically, versions of Mark were the source for the Synoptics, but this is likely what made it ideal for adding in content from the other gospels. It was clear the outline was there, but editors just felt that certain things were missing.

Reconstructing Proto-Mark might be the closest we get to seeing the "original" form of Christianity that we can access with the resources available today. Though it involves a small degree of speculation (given it is a reconstruction and also relies on a reconstruction), the flow of the text and consistent themes and narrative indicate that there is some form of a Proto-Mark found within our canonical version.

Papias, Dionysius of Corinth, and Polycrates

As discussed earlier in the book, a number of early Christian authors we only have fragments of through later authors such as Eusebius, and these tend to be unreliable sources. We had hoped that there was enough material pieced together from multiple sources to determine whether these quotes from Church Fathers whose work was lost were authentic or not. If they were authentic, they would show up far away from their source, which was often Eusebius. If they were inauthentic or there wasn't enough data, they would likely show up alongside the person that provided the quotes.

In many cases, there simply weren't enough direct quotations to make it worth testing. In others, they were near or below our cutoff line in terms of length even when combined together. Two authors who neared our cutoff were Papias and Dionysius of Corinth, both second-century Christian authors. We clipped the quotes out of the Eusebius text in order to prevent overlap and ran these fragments to test for authenticity.

When we ran the fragments of their writings, unfortunately they came up alongside Eusebius, the source for the majority of the fragments. While this doesn't mean they didn't exist or that the quotes are entirely fake, it does give us inconclusive results regarding the authenticity of the quotes we have. As mentioned, they are quite short, and it's possible there simply isn't enough material for the computer to analyze when it comes to these authors. Also, given their length, if Eusebius had reworded any of it or added only a small bit of content, this also could have thrown the results off.

However, there was one author whose content we were able to verify as independent of the person reporting it (Eusebius, in this case): Polycrates of Ephesus. Up to this point, we hadn't mentioned Polycrates as the only remaining work we have from him is a letter inside of Eusebius' *Church History*. He lived from around 130-196 CE and the one letter we have from him is regarding the Easter Controversy when early Christians were trying to determine when to celebrate Easter. While Polycrates' position was not adopted and Easter was instead celebrated on a Sunday going forward, being able to authenticate this letter is exciting. It not only verifies the letter is at least not written by Eusebius, but (supposing the correct attribution to Polycrates) also helps verify Polycarp, who is mentioned in the letter.

Josephus

We also ran the works of Josephus. We are able to confirm that Josephus did not write any of the New Testament, despite a small minority claiming this to be a possibility. The majority of the works of Josephus come up together, as expected for an author, but there was one small oddity. *Antiquities of the Jews* Books 17-19 came up noticeably more distant from the rest of *Antiquities* and the rest of the works of Josephus. While it doesn't seem to be enough to indicate an entirely different author, we suspect that these chapters were either heavily edited by someone (Eusebius) or Josephus sourced significant portions of these chapters from somewhere else. Given that Josephus had written texts in Hebrew or Aramaic before having written in Greek, it's also possible he was using either a translation or other draft of his own work from another language, too. Regardless, this too is an interesting find given that Book 18, one of the chapters that stood out, contains the Testimonium Flavianum, the later interpolation regarding Jesus.

Pseudo-Ignatius

Another minor finding we had in the course of our study was that the letters of Pseudo-Ignatius, the six extra forgeries in the Long

Recension attributed to Ignatius of Antioch, likely were not written by the same author. Though it's agreed upon by almost all scholars that these letters are not authentic, which our analysis confirmed, it seems that multiple authors were involved in writing these letters rather than a single one. While we did not extensively look into these letters or try to date them (usually they're dated after Eusebius given he does not reference them), the stylometric differences were significant enough that the letters did not appear as one author but rather as at least two or three authors.

Various Greek-Language Jewish Texts

Some might be wondering where books such as 3 Baruch, 4 Baruch, the Testament of Abraham, the Testament of Job, and other Jewish texts written in Greek from roughly the same time as Christian texts show up. These texts never really showed up very close to New Testament or apocryphal Christian texts - they were off on their own branch in many cases. If they weren't off in the branch primarily containing such texts, they would show up alongside the Septuagint, which is also not surprising. The same goes for a number of Christian texts we ran but that do not appear here - they were just too far away to say much beyond, "These texts were not written by the same people." Stylo does not look at themes, theology, or genre - only at writing style, which is particular to authors and authorship communities.

Hebrew Bible

While beyond the scope of this book, we also ran the Hebrew Bible, or Old Testament, in its original Hebrew language independent of our study of Greek texts. We do, however, want to mention a few findings given the heavy use of the Hebrew Bible in the creation of the New Testament and later Christian theology.

We did not make any divisions in the Hebrew text, but many scholars consider a number of the books of the Hebrew Bible to be the creation of multiple authors or the results of layers of edits over time. This includes the popular Documentary Hypothesis. We also looked for signs that would indicate the possibility of other theories such as those that posit the texts were largely written in the Persian era (538-332 BCE) or the Hellenistic era (332-167 BCE).

While these might seem like late dates, our oldest physical copies of Hebrew Old Testament documents are the Dead Sea Scrolls, potentially as old as 250 BCE. While some claim the Ketef Hinnom discovery of silver scrolls or amulets dating to around 586 BCE, documents actual biblical verses, it is a fragment of a variant of the Priestly Blessing which likely predates the writing of the Hebrew Bible itself. In other words, oral tradition that had its final version codified once the texts were written.

In fact, the Elephantine Papyri dating to the fifth and fourth centuries BCE show that Jews there around the year 400 BCE did not have the Torah Law, were polytheistic, had a temple of their own (which was forbidden - Jerusalem was supposed to have the only one according to the Bible), were asking the high priest in Jerusalem for help rebuilding their temple (meaning Jerusalem also did not have this law yet either), and had a number of other practices that show there was no written Hebrew Bible in that time.

Intertestamental texts such as 1 and 2 Maccabees suggest a canon was collected around 167 BCE. 2 Maccabees also records the tradition of a collection being made around the year 400 BCE by Nehemiah, but it's unlikely this was something like our current collection nor is the story found in Nehemiah necessarily historically reliable. Sirach, living in the 180s BCE, and his grandson, living around 132 BCE, seem not to have all the names or texts of our current collection in the Hebrew

Bible. Given we know Daniel was likely written in the 160s BCE, this is not surprising. Josephus, writing at the end of the first century CE, only mentions a smaller number of books in his collection than what became canon later. We don't get a reference to the full collection of texts until 2 Esdras, which was written anywhere from the end of the first century to the beginning of the third century CE. There are some that believe there was an event known as the Council of Jamnia, which debated and established the Hebrew canon sometime late in the first century as well. Regardless of the exact date, though, the process of inaccurate authorship attribution, a deliberative process to determine scriptural status, and later authorship dates than tradition holds, appears not only in Christianity but in Judaism as well.

Our brief analysis seems to suggest that the theory of a Hellenistic era origin of the majority of the Old Testament texts is most likely the case. Every larger group of text - the five books attributed to Moses, the various histories, the major prophets, and so on - came up with texts we know to be later such as Daniel, dated to around 164 BCE, 1 Chronicles and Ezra-Nehemiah which is dated to around the early Hellenistic era in the 300s BCE even by mainstream scholars, and so on.

If there are texts dating to before the 300s BCE, it would be a few of the Minor Prophets such as Haggai and Obadiah, which were outliers in our stylometric analysis and fell on the edges of communities that appeared to be from the Hellenistic era. This could also be due to their small size - Obadiah, for example, only has 440 words, which might be too small for an analysis in Hebrew. This would make sense with a Hellenistic origin, though, as Obadiah does not seem to know or reference the Law (found in Exodus, Leviticus, Numbers, and Deuteronomy) and Haggai, which seems to preserve Persian-era writings (though was likely edited later along with most of the other texts - the Old Testament texts were edited as heavily as New Testament texts in most cases). It's possible that there are some portions of other texts, such as some Psalms or segments of other prophets, that date before the 300s BCE but we did not separate the texts out nor would many of these fragments be long enough to test by themselves.

We can say with certainty that Mosaic authorship is out of the question, as Genesis consistently showed up with later texts such as Judges and 1 and 2 Samuel. Likewise, the other four books attributed to Moses show up with Joshua, and consistently clustered slightly further away from all of these are 2 Chronicles, 1 Kings, and 2 Kings. Given that 1 Chronicles seems to be by the same author as Ezra and Nehemiah as our stylometric analysis showed, the idea of a Deuteronomistic history written prior to the 400s-300s BCE also seems highly unlikely.

What would be the context that spurred on the writing of these books in the Hellenistic period? Exposure to Greek literature, such as Hecataeus of Abdera's highly idealized and nationalistic presentation of Egyptian history written around 320 BCE. Likewise, a number of authors such as Phillipe Wajdenbaum, Russell Gmirkin, Thomas L. Thompson, and others suggest that the similarities throughout the Old Testament to Greek literature and philosophy such as Plato, the Odyssey and Iliad, and other texts indicate a literary dependence. Early Christian writers actually made the argument that Plato was dependent on Moses due to some of their similarities, though we now know it likely went the other direction.

The Hebrew Bible, like the New Testament, seems to have not quite been written in the fashion that many religious figures and early compilers of the canon would have us believe. With later dates than often believed, heavy layers of redaction, and later authors attempting to justify the falsified earlier dates, it seems to have been a trend in ancient religious communities.

Chapter Notes:

1. Hansen, Chris M. *THE EMPTY PRISON CELL: The Authenticity of Philemon Reconsidered*. Wipf and Stock, Forthcoming.

Hansen's work on Philemon is one of the deepest dives into the letter that we've ever seen. The points she makes on the connections between Philemon and Colossians, as well as the logical issues she identifies for Paul's authorship, are quite damning for the traditional attribution. Despite slightly differing paths on how we got to the result, our theory seems to be very compatible with her findings on the "Pauline" text.

2. Epiphanius, and Frank Williams. *The Panarion of Epiphanius of Salamis, Book I (Sects 1-46)*. Brill, 2009. 30.16

3. Price, Robert M. *The Amazing Colossal Apostle: The Search for the Historical Paul*. Signature Books, 2012.

Price has some odd positions on a number of things, but his work on Paul is nonetheless valuable. As a former Baptist preacher with two PhDs in the field and a member of the Jesus Seminar, Price is intimately familiar with the New Testament. While we don't agree with him on a number of topics, and clearly his divisions of some of the texts don't match up with the stylometric results, *The Amazing Colossal Apostle* is one of the few books that takes the kind of critical approach on Paul that should be considered.

4. Gentry, Peter J. "The Septuagint and the Text of the Old Testament." *Bulletin for Biblical Research*, vol. 16, no. 2, 1 Jan. 2006, pp. 193, https://doi.org/10.2307/26424076. Accessed 17 Dec. 2023.

5. Klinghardt, Matthias. *The Oldest Gospel and the Formation of the Canonical Gospels*. Peeters, 2021; Bilby, Mark, 2021, "Normalized Datasets of Klinghardt's Reconstruction of Marcion's Gospel", https://doi.org/10.7910/DVN/BVEOEX, Harvard Dataverse, V1

Jason BeDuhn's reconstruction is another great resource, which we also highly recommend.

Further Reading:

1. Adler, Yonatan. *Origins of Judaism: An Archaeological-Historical Reappraisal.* Yale University Press, 2022.

   Yonatan Adler, associate professor in the department of Land of Israel Studies and Archaeology at Ariel University in Israel, makes a compelling case based on the archaeological evidence that the Hebrew Bible was likely written later than many assume. Instead of using traditional biblical studies methods and standards, which likely wouldn't hold up in other fields, he uses the methods and standards used in the field of archaeology.

2. BeDuhn, Jason. *The First New Testament Marcion's Scriptural Canon.* Polebridge Press, 2013.

   Jason BeDuhn's book was the first book regarding Marcion's works that we read. It has an English reconstruction along with extensive notes and documentation as to how was able to reconstruct the text. Other authors, such as Matthias Klinghardt, have also done similar reconstructions.

3. Brodie, Thomas L. *Beyond the Quest for the Historical Jesus: Memoir of a Discovery.* Sheffield Phoenix Press, 2012.

Thomas Brodie, the Dominican priest and biblical scholar, documents his journey to his conclusion of a mythical Jesus in this book. While it doesn't present all of his more extensive arguments, it covers many basic versions of his ideas in an easy-to-read format. Many of his conclusions parallel ours found here in our Stylo results.

4. Detering, Hermann, and Darrell Doughty. *The Fabricated Paul.* 2018.

Hermann Detering, preacher and biblical scholar, published a number of works that indicate the texts of the New Testament come from the second century. While we don't agree with all his conclusions regarding Simon Magus, the bulk of his work is very insightful.

5. Gmirkin, Russell E. *Plato and the Creation of the Hebrew Bible.* Routledge, 2019.

Gmirkin makes the case in this book and his others that Greek works from Plato inspired numerous concepts in the Hebrew Bible and that the Hebrew Bible itself is a Hellenistic era creation (with fragments of older texts having made their way into the books). Similar authors we would like to recommend regarding this topic include Philippe Wajdenbaum, author of *Argonauts of the Desert*, and Thomas L. Thompson, author of *The Mythic Past*.

6. Humphreys, Kenneth. *Jesus Never Existed: An Introduction to the Ultimate Heresy.* Nine-Banded Books, 2014.

Kenneth Humphreys works are arguably the closest to what we present here in the book.

7. Walsh, Robyn Faith. *The Origins of Early Christian Literature.* Cambridge University Press, 2023.

Dr. Robyn Faith Walsh's book *The Origins of Early Christian Literature* was informative in regard to our conceptualization of how authorship took place in the second century CE. While the book is a bit heavier of a read, the information presented is very useful if you want to understand how books were written, published, and spread during the time of early Christianity.

Chapter 8 | *Further Reading:*

CHAPTER 9

The Timeline of Christianity

Occam's Razor postulates that the simplest explanation is usually the best one. Historicists are quick to point out that mythicism doesn't give too many "simple" answers. They beg the mythicist authors for an explanation that would compete with the simplest solution: Jesus existed and people wrote about him later.

What we have done in this book is show you that even the natural stories of Jesus are soaked in supernatural and lifted from other sources, the miracles and teachings are virtually all stolen from previous messiahs and gods, and the creation of the stories didn't happen until roughly 90 years after the supposed death of the main character. But the most important portion of all of this is the level of editing, adding, and whitewashing done by the Christian church for centuries after the formation of the religion. We cannot overstate the role that the constant historical revisionism played in creating a religion that has lasted this long. It is with the knowledge of this revisionism that we simply state, "it just isn't that simple."

Throughout this book, we have presented our mythicist theory. We have shown, in portions, just how well our theory lines up with historical reality. Questions from historians and scholars are answered with our theory. Problems found within texts and debates are solved. One could argue that the puzzle piece we have suggested may be the wrong one, but it is absolutely fitting into the puzzle correctly, and as a result, we demand an explanation.

Just as advancements in DNA evidence have helped solve cold murder cases from decades prior, advancements in stylometry, computer software and ancient text reconstructions have allowed for us to uncover the truth of the evolution of early Christianity. Using our analysis and the work of other scholars, we're able to determine which mythicist claims hold merit and piece together the puzzle of a timeline. We present before the jury this timeline of events, restored after years of deterioration, destruction, and alteration:

Before the First Century CE

Well before the start of the first century CE, the building blocks of Christianity were forming. Centuries removed from the writing of the Torah, the genre of apocalyptic Jewish writings continued to grow. Hopes for the Messiah swirled through the minds of the Judaean populace, thanks to priestly interpretations of the Old Testament "prophets."

The rise of the Roman Empire only added fuel to the fire. Despite being able to govern themselves to a small extent, the Jews were not free. Due to the ever-looming presence of an Emperor and the many levels of government officials below him, a return to a theocracy as portrayed in the Torah was seeming further every day.

Mystery cults and new faiths were springing up as ideas were shared throughout the Empire. Many people worshiped the Greek or Roman gods, with some regions adopting a local god for their own pride and peace of mind. Gods like Asclepius for healing, Dionysus for wine and merriment, and Mars for military success were worshiped and had their own priests.

The Jewish scriptures were translated into Greek, and for the first time, tens of thousands of people could read the books that compose today's Old Testament. These texts, along with the epics, plays, books, and memoirs written during this period, would all help sculpt the New Testament.

Near the turn of the century, it is possible that some short letters/teachings which would eventually become part of the Pauline texts were written. If these documents were religious in nature, they would have used the Nomina Sacra (abbreviations for religious words found in early Christian writings) when discussing whatever god the author worshiped. Obviously, this god would not have been Jesus, and likely would have been either the Roman gods, the Emperor, or possibly a variation of the Jewish god.

The Therapeutae, a peaceful commune of Jews who were living in Northern Egypt by the early first century CE, would have likely started around this time. Christian authors hundreds of years later would claim these serene Jews were the first Christian monks, despite being around at the time of Jesus' supposed death.

Early to Mid-First Century

Not a lot happened during this time. There were multiple censuses that were held at different times decreed by different leaders, but there is no proof that any of them required someone to go to the land of their ancestors, as the goal of a census is to count how many people there are in a specific place. Even if the census told you to go where you came from, it wouldn't require you to pick your 12th great grandfather's hometown. Rome wasn't even established that far back, and some people would have to leave the Empire to complete the census if that were the case.

No large-scale murder of small children around Bethlehem was recorded by any historians (critics of Herod or otherwise) during this time. No star that would have been shining over a particular city was mentioned by any astronomers. Nazareth wasn't a town either. Sepphoris, a small city a few miles from where Nazareth supposedly was located, was alive and well during the first century, but wasn't mentioned at all in the gospels.

As for the darkness during the crucifixion, there was a solar eclipse in 29 CE, but it was only partially visible from Jerusalem anywhere from about 8 a.m. until about 1 p.m. This means there was no real darkness in Jerusalem stemming from the eclipse. On top of that, the Bible claims the darkness started at 3 p.m. The eclipse was also on Thursday, November 24 - not a Wednesday or Friday in April like the gospels claim.

The total eclipse *was* visible in part of modern-day Turkey, where many of the founders of Christianity were from, but for less than 50 seconds - not for three hours like the Bible claims. Though Christian authors stretching from Origen in 248 CE to the many historicists writing articles today claim the eclipse was the reason for the crucifixion darkness, the only source they have was an Ancient Roman writer named Phlegon. But all Phlegon said was there was an eclipse during the reign of Emperor Tiberius (14-37 CE). He was correct, but thanks to research and further understanding of eclipses, we know both when and where he needed to be to observe the darkness for no more than 50 seconds.

Synagogues and Pharisees were both uncommon in Galilee during this period, so there was no real reason to come into frequent contact with either of them - despite the constant mentions of them in the gospel stories.

The wine god Dionysus was worshiped in Galilee, known for its wine production. It's no surprise mentions of wine flowed throughout the gospels. The healing god Asclepius was worshiped long before and after this period as well. The Pool of Bethesda, used as a backdrop in John 5:1-15, was an ancient holy site known as an Asclepion made for sick and injured people to use for healing. Not only does the pool itself get mentioned in the Gospel of John, but the supernatural healing abilities of the pool get brought up as if they were legitimate and are not once dismissed by Jesus as phony.

John the Baptist is the only gospel character of note in the early first century. A popular preacher who was likely heralded as the Messiah during a time of many messiah claimants, John was put to death after speaking ill of Herod Antipas' love life. He was not a cousin of Jesus, as the gospels don't all claim him to be, he doesn't consistently act like someone who was completely familiar with Jesus' divine mission, and he doesn't get talked about in relation to Jesus or Christianity in the historian Josephus' take on him.

Late First Century to Mid-Second Century

Finishing his monumental religious and historical commentaries (along with his autobiography) by 99 CE, famed Roman historian Josephus fails to mention Jesus or Christianity once. That doesn't stop later Christians from adding to his work and trying to, as proven liar and admittedly biased Christian author Eusebius put it, "make use of Josephus the Jew."

Josephus' *Antiquities of the Jews* and *The Life of Flavius Josephus* both have stories borrowed to tell the story of the character of Jesus, who would make his first appearance somewhere around 120 CE.

Prior to this, there is no evidence that the name Jesus was used by the Christians. Even when threatened with violence for more information about their cult, the only term they use is Christ, and no identifying details such as Jesus' family, hometown, or even the disciples are mentioned.

The Bar Kokhba Revolt takes place between 132 and 136, with its messianic leader Simon Bar Kokhba dying in 135. Bar Kokhba caused Rome heavy losses, resulting in the total destruction of all of Judaea. This event was the spark for much of Christian literature. Multiple apocalyptic writings such as those found in Mark 13 and 2 Thessalonians 2 are written about the events in these years, and the turmoil sends numerous people toward Rome. One of these figures was Marcion of Sinope.

Marcion, a wealthy shipowner, arrives in Rome after leaving his home region in modern-day northern Turkey sometime in the late 130s. Marcion believed that while the Old Testament god was real, he was simply a malevolent, cruel creator god and one of possibly many. The only way to be free of this malevolent creator, he claimed, was to follow the god and father of Christ, who we see called God the Father throughout Christian literature. With him, he brought a number of letters and a gospel, an early form of what would become Mark. He made a generous donation to the church in Rome and started teaching there after likely already having established churches across modern-day Turkey.

Though he found an audience in Rome, he also found enemies. A number of Christians there were insistent that Marcion's creator god and the father of Christ were the same deity. It's likely Marcion tried to compromise, and in doing so expanded the gospel he brought with him into what would become Evangelion, likely with the help of other Christians. This is why there are parts of Evangelion that don't seem to line up completely with Marcion's theology. Through this somewhat "group effort," the creation of Evangelion commenced. Likewise, the creation of Paul began around the same time as a project of the Marcionite school of thought. Various literate Marcionite authors created the works of the figure we now know as the apostle Paul, leaving behind hints that these works were actually not that of a single first-century figure.

By this time, the Christ figure had morphed into an actual historical figure for a number of Christians, and this historical figure was given disciples. By claiming a direct line to these disciples, early church leaders attempted to claim a more reliable authority than Marcion. In response, Paul, who - in "his own" words - received the gospel from no man but from a direct revelation from Christ, was born. Marcion now had a claim to authority directly tracing to Christ.

How did the idea of a historical Jesus come about? Misinterpretation. Mark is clearly allegorical, using content and tropes from the Old Testament, Josephus, and Greek literature of the time. The authors using Paul's name (aside from the Pastoral Epistles) all understood Christ to be a divine figure as well, not having an actual physical form.

Evangelion's embellishment of Proto-Mark added more detail to the historical setting, as well as more allegory and references to other texts, and this is likely where the misunderstanding happened. Some read it as history, and the Gospel of Matthew is the first text to present a fully human Jesus likely sometime around the 150s-160s built upon a literal reading of Evangelion before it. In fact, we see proof of Matthew's application of literal readings of the Hebrew Bible as well, such as Matthew 21's instance of Jesus riding two donkeys. The appeal of a story being literally true is strong, and it's also often the default interpretation if one isn't anticipating something being allegory or is otherwise unable to tell the difference.

The theological disagreements between Marcion and other church leaders came to a head around the year 144, and Marcion was excommunicated, kicked out of the Roman church, and his donation returned to him. In response, he published his 10 letters of Paul now with added biographical experience paralleling Marcion's own experiences with the Roman church, Evangelion, and a document called *Antitheses* which he wrote to point out the differences between the god of the Old Testament and the god of what he was the first to call the New Testament. This was the first Christian canon to be published.

Late Second Century and Beyond

After Marcion publishes his canon, we see our second boom of Christian literature in response. Dozens of gospels arrive on the scene, including our canonical gospels. New forged letters are added in Paul's name, as well as the names of other figures such as John, James, Peter, and Jude. At this time, the majority of Church Fathers and other Christians we hear about are still converts, showing us this religion is still quite new.

Justin Martyr and Tatian, who wrote between the 150s and 170s, are our first Christian authors who appear to be familiar with at least three of the canonical gospels we have today. While these texts would still be edited and go through minor changes, the bulk of the texts are as we see them today at this point. Matthew had been written in the 150s-160s as a response to Evangelion, and the author also made extensive edits to Mark around the same time. Luke is a direct adaptation of Evangelion, coming some time shortly after Matthew and adding a number of chapters. These added chapters, written by the author of Acts (almost certainly Irenaeus or Polycarp), would be the tell from what otherwise would have been a perfect crime. Church Fathers coming after its authorship would claim that Marcion stole from Luke rather than the other way around, but our stylometric analysis and textual evidence show that Evangelion came first. Finally, John shows up before 170, completely rewriting the Synoptic story.

In the late 170s and early 180s, Irenaeus writes the earliest surviving book against the so-called heresies of his time. In it, we get significant pieces of information that would later become church doctrine, such as the attribution of the four canonical gospels to Matthew, Mark, Luke, and John. We also get attestation to 21 of the 27 books that would make up the New Testament, and for many of these books, this was their first reference. Irenaeus also gives us crucial background information, accurate or not, regarding various sects, beliefs, and traditions of Christians around his time.

By the start of the third century, the foundations of Christianity were mostly laid. Within a couple decades of the start of this century, we get attestation to the few remaining canonical books of the New Testament that we don't hear about in the second century. We also get crucial information from writers early in this century that helps tell us more of what happened in the second century, but even at this point historical revisionism is the default position. The 90+ year gap between the supposed death of Jesus and the beginning of Christianity as we know it needed to be filled, and name after name was added into that void by Christian writers in the third century.

At times, laws were enacted against Christianity, but none were in time to stop the spread of the cult. Eventually, Christianity was accepted as a religion that was in the Roman Empire to stay, and it grew to become the official religion of the Empire in 380 CE.

The Christians wasted no time in destroying temples, statues, and art work they found to be satanic or evil. Christian authors wrote about how cults that ate bread and drank wine during their rituals before Christianity did the same were actually influenced by Satan to take the Lord's Supper in advance of Jesus. The Christians even subsumed holidays and festivals into their own (a la Christmas and Easter).

Through revisionism, the cult grew into the religion we see today, and centuries of restricting books and the Bible to just the leaders of the church led to countless edits, cover-ups, and disinformation campaigns. The Bible was translated from Greek into Latin, and then from Latin into English. Original words and meanings get lost during this process, with problematic words that would point to a second-century origin of Christianity becoming words that try to keep it all in the first century.

It is here where we leave you, esteemed members of the jury, with all this evidence forming our theory. We believe this theory to not only fit like the missing puzzle piece, but also answer questions that have plagued scholars for years. The story of the natural life of Jesus was stolen from previous works, saturated with outlandish supernatural claims, and in certain parts, historically impossible. The subsequent supporting works of the New Testament were nothing more than historical fantasy filled with revisionism written for the purpose of filling timeline gaps and maintaining power during political infighting. The second-century church leaders knew what they were doing, but were so convinced they were doing the right thing they ostracized even those who were different but willing to help them. The religion evolved out of multiple cults in times of war and crisis. But before there was a gospel story, the concept of a Christ figure had been around for centuries.

As a title for kings and a potential messiah to free the people of Judaea from their perceived persecution, the word Christ was swirling around the area well before the Gospel of Mark was written. But Jesus was the name the Christians gave their Christ. Yeshua in Hebrew, the name Jesus was a derivative of Joshua, the Old Testament figure who led the Jews into the Promised Land. The Christians' mythical founder may have had a well-chosen name, but seeing as the stories about him never happened, we can confidently say there was a Christ Before Jesus.

The prosecution rests.

TL;DR

We know some people may not have time to read a full book and want to make our work accessible to everyone. Here are some quick chapter summaries and pieces of evidence for our theory that we believe are some of the strongest. While we encourage our readers to consider all the evidence, these are the anchors that we can hold on to, allowing for us to step off of the potential carousel of circular reasoning.

- ○ In Chapter 1, we explained what exactly our theory is, and why we have no concerns about going against mainstream scholarship.

- ○ Chapter 2 had us showing smoking-gun evidence that the Gospel of Luke used Marcion's gospel, Evangelion, as a source. The fact that Luke has Jesus talking about being in Capernaum before he ever went there, but Evangelion has Jesus in Capernaum at the beginning, shows that Luke stole from Marcion, added a birth story, and forgot to cover his tracks. Evangelion came out in 144 CE, so Luke was written after that. We also reveal how Matthew was a response to Evangelion, and John was written to an audience who had already read the other gospels. This places

Luke, Matthew and John no earlier than about 150 CE, so no less than 120 years after the supposed death of Jesus.

○ With this new dating, Theophilus (for whom Luke and Acts were written) is found to be none other than Theophilus of Antioch, a bishop from 169 to 182 who was a prior convert.

○ We also show that the Gospel of Mark used the stories of Josephus and other sources to create the narrative of Jesus' ministry, Nazareth wasn't a town in the early first century, and Mark 13 (which is often used to date the gospel to 70 CE) wasn't added until after the Bar Kokhba Revolt in 136 CE.

○ If you're wondering about what the ancient historians have to say about Jesus, in Chapter 3 we went into detail about how Christians aren't mentioned until the early *second* century, and even then Jesus isn't named at all. The Christians in the early second century had some beliefs in a spiritual Christ, but that's not the same as having a gospel about a man named Jesus.

○ Paul and the New Testament Epistles are discussed in Chapter 4, and we explain that no one even knew who Paul was until his letters (which are too long to be real letters) were published by Marcion in 144 CE. There are anachronisms and plagiarized stories all throughout the Epistles and Acts, and both Peter and John were said to be illiterate, yet we have letters written under their names. The Epistle of James was not written by the brother of Jesus, and when Josephus spoke about a James, he did not mention Jesus Christ.

○ Another strong piece of evidence is given in Chapter 4: the converts. Nearly all the early church leaders in the second century were converts. While this wouldn't be surprising at all if the religion had just started, it's shocking that so many people in high religious positions wouldn't have grown up in said religion if it had been around for 100 years or more.

O In Chapter 5, we describe the level of deceitfulness the early church leaders displayed in order to fill the gaps between the supposed death of Jesus in roughly 30 CE and the early second century.

O A few more smoking guns are presented in this chapter, as we explain that none of the New Testament books get mentioned outside the Bible until the second century, Marcion's book *Antitheses* gets mentioned in 1 Timothy, two second-century figures get mentioned in 2 Timothy, and Justin Martyr is the first one to quote or mention anything like a gospel (and he does so after Marcion writes).

O As the final strong piece of evidence in Chapter 5, we reveal that none of the actual pieces of books or copies that historians and archaeologists have found date earlier than the late second century. The fact that we have manuscripts going back roughly 1850 years, but absolutely nothing for those extra 100 to fill in the gaps is damning. With the dating method used changing over time and showing that the estimated dates for these early manuscripts might actually be later, we don't recommend holding your breath for any first-century copies.

O Chapter 6 goes into further detail about how different cults and beliefs (some Jewish, some not) evolved over time and merged to create Christianity. It also details why the early Christians would have lied despite possible repercussions. We also discuss how Christians destroyed numerous works of art, statues, and literature from other cultures and religions once they came to power in the fourth century.

○ We explain what stylometric analysis is in Chapter 7, and show you how to run Stylo for yourself. As a reminder, we have resources online with links and downloadables.

○ Our biggest contribution to mythicism is presented in Chapter 8 and our findings are laid out in chronological order in Chapter 9. The stylometric results show that our theory and other evidence lines up with what can be mathematically and linguistically proven using modern technology. We explain that the analysis identifies Irenaeus as the author of the Gospel of Luke and Acts, supported by the dates and dedication of the texts.

○ Thanks to the stylometric results and where the New Testament books are shown to be in relation to the writings of second-century Christian writers, we can see what parts were added later and what books were forged by certain groups and authors. This allows us to piece together when these books were actually written.

○ Stylometric analysis clearly and confidently confirms the author of the Gospel of Luke stole from Marcion, and not the other way around. This puts every New Testament book, from the gospels to Paul, into question.

Matthew and Jaaron would like to thank:

Kenneth Humphreys for the kind words and encouragement from across the pond; the online community of Vridar and Early Writings for all their discussions and deep dives into the New Testament; our absolutely amazing families who were there during each and every discovery and put up with our childlike excitement; Chrissy Hansen for your incredibly valuable feedback and questions; J. Joiner for bringing us together and teaching us so much that we have already forgotten; Ulises, Lindsey and Tyler for your support even when we're not "on", and for giving us an excuse to meet up for book discussions; Barthel and Moses for all the conversations that kick-started our passions; Jonathan G. for your incredible insight and patience with us (we love you!); Lou with LouDesigns for the outstanding artwork you created and your professionalism; Claire Handerson for her diligence and expert help with formatting; the Iron Chariots of Texas team for your ideas, entertainment, and help alpha reading (sorry about the toner, Austin).

Lastly, thank you to the great minds behind Stylo and to Jason Beduhn for all your hard work that makes research and books like this even possible.

For any further resources, check us out on Youtube, Tiktok, or
christbeforejesus.com.
Email us at christbeforejesus@gmail.com with questions, feedback, or
media requests.
Thank you!

Printed in Great Britain
by Amazon

55848095R00183